ISBN 978-1-331-23738-9
PIBN 10162592

1 MONTH OF
FREE
READING

at
www.ForgottenBooks.com

By purchasing this book you are eligible for one month membership to ForgottenBooks.com, giving you unlimited access to our entire collection of over 1,000,000 titles via our web site and mobile apps.

To claim your free month visit:
www.forgottenbooks.com/free162592

English
Français
Deutsche
Italiano
Español
Português

www.forgottenbooks.com

Mythology Photography **Fiction**
Fishing Christianity **Art** Cooking
Essays Buddhism Freemasonry
Medicine **Biology** Music **Ancient
Egypt** Evolution Carpentry Physics
Dance Geology **Mathematics** Fitness
Shakespeare **Folklore** Yoga Marketing
Confidence Immortality Biographies
Poetry **Psychology** Witchcraft
Electronics Chemistry History **Law**
Accounting **Philosophy** Anthropology
Alchemy Drama Quantum Mechanics
Atheism Sexual Health **Ancient History**
Entrepreneurship Languages Sport
Paleontology Needlework Islam
Metaphysics Investment Archaeology
Parenting Statistics Criminology
Motivational

POPULAR COUNTY HISTORIES.

A

HISTORY OF LANCASHIRE.

BY

LIEUT.-COLONEL HENRY FISHWICK, F.S.A.,

Author of

" *The Lancashire Library*," " *The History of Kirkham*,"
" *The History of Rochdale*," *etc.*

LONDON:
ELLIOT STOCK, 62, PATERNOSTER ROW, E.C.
1894.

PREFACE.

THE enormous amount of material, printed and in manuscript, which is available for a History of Lancashire, makes the writing of a popular work on that subject by no means an easy task; indeed, when first mentioned to me, I thought it was almost impossible, by any process of selection, to produce within the compass of an ordinary octavo volume such a book as would be a popular history, and yet not fail to present a faithful picture of the county.

However, I have made the attempt, and in accomplishing the task I must have necessarily left out much which many readers would prefer should have been inserted; but I trust that I have not inserted what some would wish I had omitted. I have endeavoured to confine myself as far as possible to the history of the county as a whole, and have not allowed myself to go into personal or local details except when such were required to illustrate the subject in hand. Of the large army of Lancashire authors and celebrities I have said nothing, as strictly speaking personal notices belong rather to biography than history; and if it were not so, I may, I think, stand excused, as to have merely given their names would have well-nigh filled the volume.

In making my selection of materials from the almost inexhaustible stores at my disposal, I have rejected everything which in my opinion is not capable of being well authenticated. In a work of this character it is not desirable to encumber the text with the very large number of references to authorities which otherwise might be required. The reader, however, may rest assured that I have in no case drawn on my imagination for my facts, neither have I accepted the statements of others without first satisfying myself that those statements are trustworthy and reliable.

HENRY FISHWICK.

THE HEIGHTS,
ROCHDALE.

CONTENTS.

HISTORY OF LANCASHIRE.

CHAPTER I.

INTRODUCTORY

LANCASHIRE, on its south and south-east, is bounded by the county of Chester, the division for about 50 miles, *i.e.*, from Stockport to Liverpool, being the river Mersey; on the west is the Irish Sea; on the east, up to Graygarth Fell, in the parish of Tunstall, lies Yorkshire; from thence to the waters of Morecambe Bay the boundary is formed by Yorkshire and Westmorland; across the bay is a portion of Lonsdale hundred (north of the Sands), which is almost surrounded by the counties of Westmorland and Cumberland, the extreme eastern boundary being formed by a portion of Windermere Lake. Lancashire from north-west to south-east measures 86 miles, and it is 45 miles across at its widest part; it contains 1,219,221 acres. It has within it 69 parishes (exclusive of 9 extra-parochial districts), 446 townships, and 16 Parliamentary cities and boroughs, which return 35 members, the county divisions adding 23 to this number.

The great divisions of the county are the six hundreds of Lonsdale (north and south of the Sands),

Amounderness, Leyland, Blackburn, Salford, and West Derby.

Lonsdale north of the Sands is situate in the extreme north of Lancashire, and is the most picturesque portion of the county, as it embraces a portion of the well-known Lake District; its highest mountain is the Old Man, near Coniston Water, which is 2,577 feet above the sea-level.

The two subdivisions of Lonsdale north of the Sands are Furness and Cartmel. The former is the larger district: its chief towns are Barrow, Ulverston, and Dalton; in the latter there is not a single town of any considerable size or importance. Barrow-in-Furness is one of those towns which the enterprise of the latter half of the present century has suddenly created. A few years ago it was scarcely a village; it is now an incorporated borough, and not only does a large business in iron, but is a port of some importance. With this exception, and a few iron mines, almost the whole district is agricultural in its character.

Furness Abbey, Coniston Priory, and Cartmel Priory were all located in the southern end of this part of the county.

Lonsdale south of the Sands is also chiefly an agricultural district, and is, compared with some other parts of the county, but thinly populated; here and there tall factory chimneys may be seen, but, except in the neighbourhood of Lancaster, they are few and far between.

Time-honoured Lancaster, with its castle and priory, form the central historic point of interest in this part of the hundred; here also were five of the largest forests in Lancashire—Wyersdale, Quernmoor, Bleasdale, Myerscough, and Fulwood. Coming south of Lonsdale, the county is much wider, and is divided longitudinally; the western portion, as far as the river Ribble, forming the hundred of Amounderness, which, like the more northern parts, is inhabited by people engaged in the cultivation of the soil, except in and immediately around the town of Preston, which is now one of the great centres of the cotton trade. The parishes of Kirkham, Garstang, St. Michael's-on-Wyre, Lytham, Bispham and Poulton are all in a district long known as the Fylde, and their respective churches are all of antiquarian interest. Preston is now by far the largest town in the division; the manufacture of cotton was introduced here in 1777, and the trade has since developed to very large proportions. Here were two religious houses, one a convent of Grey Friars, and the other a hospital for lepers. The Ribble, in its course from Mitton to Preston, intersects the county. To the east of Amounderness is the hundred of Blackburn, which, although it is twenty-four miles in length, only contains five parishes; its north-western extremity is more or less agricultural, but the rest of it is densely populated, and has become a great manufacturing district.

Blackburn, Burnley, Accrington, and several other towns in the district, are all engaged in the staple trade of the county. Clitheroe Castle, Whalley Abbey, and Ribchester are in this hundred.

The south bank of the Ribble forms the western boundary of the hundred of Leyland. The only market-town in the division is Chorley, which until 1793 formed a part of the parish of Croston; like so many other towns of Lancashire, it rose out of obscurity through the introduction of spinning mills towards the end of the last century, and it is now a town of considerable size and importance; in addition to its cotton-mills, coal, stone, and iron are found and worked in the neighbourhood. At Penwortham, on the bank of the Ribble, was a priory dedicated to St. Mary.

The ancient parish churches of Croston, Leyland, Eccleston, and Standish are all of historic interest.

The hundred of Salford has now an enormous population, and the very names of its principal towns call up a vision of tall factory chimneys, dense smoke, and the noise of machinery; manufactories of every kind abound, and it is not saying too much to add that few industries are unrepresented, coal, stone, iron, cotton and woollens, however, constituting the chief trade.

The city of Manchester and the boroughs of Salford, Oldham, Bolton, Rochdale, and Bury are all well-known names in the textile or mechanical world.

West Derby hundred completes the county. This was in Saxon times called Derbei, and was a recognised division; the river Mersey on the one side, and the Irish Sea on the other, have not a little contributed to render this one of the most important districts in England. Liverpool, with its miles of docks and its connection with every part of the world, has become the recognised second port in the country. In the north-east corner of West Derby are the extensive coalfields of Wigan.

A considerable portion of the hundred is as yet untainted with the smoke of the manufactory. Many of the parish churches are of great antiquity; amongst them may be named Ormskirk, Leigh, Wigan, Winwick, Warrington, Childwall, Walton-on-the-Hill, Prescot, Sephton and Huyton. Burscough Priory was in the parish of Ormskirk, and Liverpool had its ancient castle.

Having thus briefly (but at as great a length and in as much detail as the nature and scope of the series of County Histories will allow) described the County Palatine, we may at once proceed to deal with its history as a not unimportant section of the United Kingdom.

CHAPTER II.

PRE-ROMAN LANCASHIRE.

NOTWITHSTANDING what has been written upon the so-called "glacial nightmare," it still remains an undisputed fact that at some far-distant period the whole of Lancashire was sunk beneath a sea, the waters of which carried along with them huge masses of ice, which, in their passage southward, deposited boulders which they had borne in their chill embrace for hundreds of miles. The hills which rose above the sea were covered with perpetual snow, and the valleys between them were filled with glaciers, which in many instances left a terminal moraine.

The direction which these icebergs took was invariably from north-west to south-east, or north-north-west to south-south-east, that being sufficiently indicated by the polished and striated rocks frequently discovered in all parts of the county. A careful investigation of the erratic blocks which have been discovered in one small district alone[1] shows nearly 400 of these rocks, some of which have travelled from Scotland, but by far the larger number have come from the Lake District; these are occasionally found in the valleys, but are generally located

---

[1] "Recent Results of the Investigation into Local [Rochdale] Erratic Blocks," by S. S. Platt.

on the sides and tops of hills at an elevation of from 600 to 1,200 feet above the sea-level. Geology furnishes abundant proofs that at this period the level of the land in what is now known as Lancashire was fifty or sixty feet higher than it is at the present day; this is very apparent along the coast-line, where the remains of submarine forests are frequently met with. It is more than probable that, from the mouth of the Mersey to the estuary of the Dudden, what are now sand banks were in prehistoric times dry land on which grew forests of the oak, the birch, the ash, the yew, and Scotch firs.

All along the coast-line from Liverpool to Preston have been found at low water the roots and trunks of trees.

Near Fleetwood and Blackpool frequent traces of these forests have been met with below the high-tide level, the trunks of the trees all pointing eastward, with their torn-up roots to the west; stumps of Scotch firs were found near Rossall, and near to them the cones which had fallen from their branches; trunks of oak and yew trees were also discovered at Martin Mere (in Poulton).

In these forests the brown bear, the wild boar, roes and stags, the wolf and the reindeer, and a host of other wild animals, would all be discovered by the neolithic man when he first made his appearance in the district.

Whence came this earlier settler? and at what exact period did he come? are questions which modern scientific research has failed to satisfactorily answer.

It has been suggested—and with some show of reason—that the early neolithic man in Lancashire had been driven from the Yorkshire coast by the victorious invader, who came armed with a war-spear and polished stone axe.[1] Be this as it may, the evidence of such a race of men having for some time lived in parts of the county is of the most conclusive character. Although odd

[1] H. Colley March, F.S.A., "The Early Neolithic Floor of East Lancashire," p. 7.

specimens of flint instruments have been unearthed, in various districts, it is only in the eastern portion of the county that distinct traces of a neolithic floor have been discovered—that is to say that, on removing the top soil, beneath it has been found a surface so profusely sprinkled with flint chippings and implements as to leave no room for doubt but that at some very early period there was settled upon it a race of men whose weapons of offence and defence, as well as the few instruments required for their simple personal wants, were made out of the flints collected from this drift.

This neolithic floor is found on both sides of Blackstone edge, and is generally at least 1,300 feet above the sea-level, but on the Lancashire side its area is not very large, as it does not reach Burnley on the north, nor Bolton on the west. The depth of the soil or peat above this floor varies from one to ten feet. The flints consist of knives, scrapers, arrow-heads, spear-tips, and minute instruments, probably used to bore holes in bone needles; they are none of them polished or ornamented.

In the parish of Rochdale alone there are twenty-five places where these implements have been found; in fact, there is scarcely a hill-top in the district where traces of them have not been unearthed. The great number of chippings met with in small areas of these high lands indicate that these are the sites of the primitive man's workshop—here he sat and laboriously fashioned the weapon or the instrument which he required. Barbed arrow-heads are extremely rare, but a beautiful specimen was lately found on Trough Edge, a hill near Rochdale.[1]

These men have left no traces of their dwelling-place, and they do not appear to have made pottery; probably they lived in earth dwellings or caves in the hillsides. The single fact of their inhabiting only the high ground indicates that the fear of an enemy was ever before them,

[1] Engraved, with other flints, in "History of Rochdale," p. 4.

and it may well be that the foe which drove them from Yorkshire may have ultimately expelled them from their hillside settlements.

At some later period the district became inhabited, though probably only sparsely, by Celtic races and people of Celtic extraction ; of the latter were the numerous tribes of the Brigantes, one of which was the Setanii or Segantii (the dwellers in the water country), which is said to have been chiefly located between Morecambe Bay and the ridge of hills which divide Lancashire from Yorkshire. Another tribe also located here was the Voluntii.

At this date Lancashire contained many extensive forests, and in every direction were trackless morasses. As these almost savage tribes lived in tents or huts, and spent their time in hunting or fighting, it is not surprising that the traces of their existence are faint and unsatisfactory, and that it is often impossible to decide whether particular remains belong to the early Celtic or the late British. The geographical nomenclature of the county furnishes some examples of Celtic origin, but for the most part it clearly points to a later period. That these Celtic settlers were well spread over the entire district is certain, as traces of them have been discovered in almost every parish.

Stone hammers, stone axes, spear-heads, socketed celts, cinerary urns, and remains of that class, have been unearthed in many places, amongst which are Aldringham, Cartmel, Tatham, Penwortham, Garstang, Preston, Pilling Moss, Silverdale, Kirkham, Bolton, Cuerden, Flixton, Liverpool, Winwick, Lancaster, Manchester, Royton, Rochdale, and Burnley ; this list is alone sufficient to demonstrate that the early settlers had penetrated into all parts of the county.[1]

[1] A complete list, up to date, will be found in Rev. William Harrison's "Archæological Survey of Lancashire," which will appear in the next volume of the Lancashire and Cheshire Antiquarian Society.

In the Furness district remains of entrenchments, ramparts, stone rings, and other evidences of these early settlers are abundant; they have been unearthed at Hawkshead, Hall Park, Bleaberry Haws Torver, Holme Bank, Urswick, Heathwaite Fell, Coniston, and other places in the neighbourhood, proving beyond a doubt that here was an extensive British settlement. Beside these there are several cairns, and portions of stone wall attributable to the same period.

One of the most extensive of the latter group is the one at Heathwaite Fell, where on the top of an elevated piece of moorland is a site near half a mile long by 700 yards wide, which has been encompassed by a stone wall originally 2 feet thick. This enclosed space has been subdivided into five or more smaller enclosures by cross walls, and each of these divisions had its own water-supply. The apex of the ground has been cut by a wall, and this encloses the north elevation of the site. About midway along the west side another wall leaves the outer one and crosses the summit, and cuts off the west angle. On the centre of this wall are situated the "homesteads" or head-quarters of the settlement. The homesteads are situated upon the south-east slope of the hill, and upon the cross wall dividing off the western ward. They consist of seven walled courts or yards, three smaller chambers, and two very small mural huts and chambers. The walls of these are usually of dry-built masonry, and are in some places 3 feet thick and in others from 6 to 7 feet.

The main entrance to these enclosures is on the south. The mural huts are placed at the north-west angle of the west court and the south-west angle of the south court. The first is the most interesting; it is contained in a small rectangular block of masonry filling up the angle, and the plan of the chamber itself is that of a joiner's square. There is no trace left of any covering to these huts, but they were probably covered with stone flags or branches of trees. Within and without the enclosures are cairns of all sizes, one of which is known as The Giant's Grave. It is remarkable that all the settlements in the Furness district are found on the fells, and never in the dales, some of them being 300 feet above the sea-level. Of any actual defensive structure there is no trace. The settlers here evidently buried their dead close to their homes, and from the calcined bones found it is clear that the bodies were burnt.

These earthen burial-mounds are, however, very scarce in the district; rude-stone cists have been unearthed, but no trace of metals or ornamental workmanship except a few pieces of rude pottery.

At Holme Bank, Urswick, the rampart of earthed stones encloses a five-sided figure, within which are traces of cross walls, the general plan of which points to the site of an early settlement. The rampart or entrenchment discovered at Hawkeshead Park is of a similar character. At Scrow Moss, near the foot of Coniston Old Man, is another of these enclosures, a drawing of which is given in *Archæologia* (vol. liii., part 2). At Dunnerdale Fell is an enclosure very similar to that found at Heathwaite, though much smaller, the central homestead being formed by a single wall, near to which are several cairns and remains of walls. On Birkrigg Common, at a place called Appleby Slack, is another of these small enclosures, consisting of a single rampart or vallum of earth, enclosing a pear-shaped area, not far from which is a tumulus, and about half a mile to the south-east is a double concentric stone circle. Concerning these various remains in the Furness district, the writer of the exhaustive article in *Archæologia*[1] just referred to is of opinion that their elevated position is due to the fact that the lower ground was at that period such a dense mass of scrub and jungle that it was utterly

[1] H. Swainson Cowper, Esq., F.S.A.

untenable for residential purposes. These various en-closures do not appear to have been forts, as the home-steads themselves were all on the sloping sides of the hills, but were rather the dwelling-places of a very early tribe of settlers, who were living at peace with their neighbours, and had, therefore, no need of a system of defence, such as we find traces of in other parts of the county. The plan of these settlements was simple —the smaller courts were the living apartments, and were no doubt covered with some kind of roof; the larger enclosures were for the cattle, or possibly for the lower orders of the tribes who held the place.

Many tumuli belonging to the early British settlers have been opened, as at Briercliffe, near Burnley, where the covering of earth had been partly wasted away, leaving a rudely-marked circle of stone, near to which in 1885 was found a sun-baked hand-made urn of pre-Roman origin, containing the remains of an adult and a child. At Wavertree, near Liverpool, in 1867, a large tumulus, since called Urn Mound, was opened, and six urns con-taining partly-calcined human bones were discovered, all of which were early British. Near to these were found a flint arrow-point and several "scrapers."[1]

Canoes assigned to this period have not infrequently been dug out of peat which once formed the bottom of lakes, such as Marton Mere, in Poulton-le-Fylde, and at the estuary of the Ribble, near Penwortham. A very remarkable bronze beaded torque of the late Celtic period was found by some workmen in 1832 at Mowroad, in the parish of Rochdale. This ornament had probably been worn round the neck of some person of rank; it weighed one pound five ounces, was made of bronze, and was of superior workmanship and ornamentation.[2] The British tribes did not congregate in such numbers as to establish

[1] *Hist. Soc. of Lanc. and Ches.,* xx. 131.
[2] Engraved in "History of Rochdale," p. 5. See also *Archæologia,* xxv. 595.

anything like a town, or even a large village, in these Northern parts; but no doubt when the Romans took possession they found here and there clusters of hut dwellings, which the geographer Ptolemy afterwards described as British settlements. One of these was Regodunum, which was somewhere near the mouth of the Ribble, perhaps at Walton-le-Dale. The author just referred to (who lived about A.D. 140) mentions the estuaries on the west coast, three of which, from the latitude and longitude given, clearly refer to Lancashire rivers; they are named as the Estuary Moricambe, the Haven of the Setantii, and the Estuary Belisama. Belisama was the old name for the Mersey; the Haven of the Setantii was at or near the mouth of the Ribble; and the other estuary was at the conflux of the Kent with the waters of Morecambe Bay.[1]

At Walton-le-Dale and at Lancaster the Romans are believed to have founded their stations on the sites of British settlements, as in both these places have been found celts, arrow-heads, cinerary urns, and other signs of the earlier race.

[1] See *Transactions of Hist. Soc. of Lanc. and Ches.*, xxx. 81.

CHAPTER III.

THE ROMANS AS CONQUERORS AND RULERS.

THE coming of Julius Cæsar in August, B.C. 55, with his legions of Roman soldiers to punish the men of Kent for having sent assistance to one of the Gallic tribes, the *Veneti*, then at war with Rome, was what led on to the subsequent subjugation of the whole of Britain. This did not, however, take place for nearly a century afterwards, as, on the Britons undertaking to pay tribute, the invaders withdrew. In A.D. 43 the Emperor Claudius appears to have looked at this country with an envious eye, and finally decided to annex it to Rome; and with this view he sent his General, Aulus Plautius, with an army of some 48,000 men, to subdue the natives, who were, however, found to be a race not easily conquered. After severe fighting, he entrenched himself on the bank of the Thames, where he was joined by the Emperor himself in the following year. Step by step, slowly but steadily, the invaders made their way northwards.

The building of a line of forts by the Imperial Legate from the Severn to the Nene, thus dividing the country, led to a rebellion of the tribe of Cenimagni (or Iceni), the dwellers in what is now Norfolk or Cambridgeshire. In this case the natives were again unsuccessful; and in recording their defeat Tacitus[1] first mentions the Brigantes

[1] "Annals," xii. 31.

in terms which clearly indicate that even before this time
they had given the Romans some trouble.   The passage
runs: " He (Ostorius Scapula) now approached the sea
which washes the coast of Ireland, when commotions,
begun amongst the Brigantes, obliged the General to
return thither, as he had formed a settled determination
not to prosecute any new enterprise till his former were
completed and secure.   The Brigantes, indeed, soon
returned to their homes, a few who raised the revolt having
been slain and the rest pardoned."

The *Silures*, inhabiting the western part of Wales, under
their King Caractacus, maintained a fierce resistance to
Ostorius, but were ultimately compelled to bear the
Roman yoke.   At this period the Queen of the Brigantes
was Cartismandua, whose betrayal of Caractacus has preserved her name from oblivion.   She afterwards married
a leader of the Silures named Venusius, who, according
to Tacitus, was for some time under the protection of the
Romans; but having been divorced from Cartismandua,
she again took up arms against the invaders.

In A.D. 58 in the eastern district of Britain reigned
Queen Boadicea, who, taking advantage of the Roman
Governor, with many of his soldiers, being engaged in the
country of the Brigantes, attacked the towns of St. Albans,
Colchester and London, with victorious results, the legion
being destroyed and many thousand settlers slain.   This
probably led to a withdrawal of the Romans for a time
from the north-west, and thus left Lancashire in peace.
The whole of South Britain in A.D. 62 was finally conquered by the Romans; but it was left to the Roman
Governor, Petilius Cerealis, to fight out the battle with
the Brigantes, who were reputed to be the most populous
state in the whole province.   Many engagements took
place, attended with much bloodshed, and the greater
part of the tribe were either subjugated or slain.[1]

[1] Tacitus, " Hist.," book iii., ch. lix.

Although there is no positive evidence that any of the men of Lancashire were engaged in these struggles, it seems scarcely possible that it could have been otherwise. Cerealis was Governor from A.D. 71 to 75, and during that time he was constantly fighting battles with these hardy North-country men; but neither he nor his successor, Julius Frontinus, could effectually subdue them, and it was not until A.D. 79 that the final conquest was made by Julius Agricola, the father-in-law of Tacitus, who relates that in the spring of that year Agricola reassembled his army, and having personally carefully examined "the estuaries and woods," he allowed the enemy no respite, but harassed them with sudden incursions and ravages, the result being that several communities, which had not before yielded their independence, submitted to the foe, gave hostages, and allowed fortresses to be erected.[1] There are many reasons which make it almost a certainty that these estuaries include those of the Dee, the Mersey, the Ribble, the Wyre, the Lune and Morecambe (the Kent). Very difficult indeed must have been the task of overcoming the fierce and determined resistance offered by the natives. Much of the country was covered with timber, particularly to the west, and on every side were large tracts of moss and fen, the pathways through which were treacherous, and known only to those who used them; and Agricola was acting like a wise and ex- perienced general when he directed his first attention to the mouths of the rivers and to the almost pathless forests.

Agricola is allowed by all historians to have been a judicious governor, and to have made efforts to accustom the conquered race to the comforts and luxuries of Roman citizens. He also taught them to build temples, houses and baths; to many of them the Roman language was taught, and they were encouraged to live together in towns and villages. Probably in his time arose the forts

---

[1] Tacitus, "Vita Agricolæ," cap. xx.

at Mancunium (Manchester), Bremetonacæ (Ribchester), and Galacum (Overborough).

After the middle of the second century, the Brigantes as a tribe disappear from the page of history; henceforth they are Britons.

The Hadrian Wall, which stretches for seventy miles from the Solway Firth to the Tyne, nowhere touches Lancashire, but the frequent battles which raged in its vicinity were near enough to have an effect upon the district, and no doubt occasionally the invading forces from the North penetrated into the county. The Caledonians, in A.D. 180, broke through the wall, and for some time remained masters of a considerable portion of the North of England.[1] In A.D. 208 the Emperor Severus, with his sons Caracalla and Geta, visited Britain, and sent some of his soldiers to the North, as he found that the inhabitants of what is now Lancashire, Yorkshire and Cumberland had not yet become reconciled to the Roman government, and, to add to the difficulty, the people on the other side of the Hadrian Wall—the Picts and Scots —required repression.

Severus died at York in 211, and for the next fifty years little is known of the Roman rule in Britain beyond the fact that the names of several legates, who acted as its governors, are on record. Between A.D. 258 and 282 the historians are also silent about this district, yet coins of Posthumus, Victorinus and Tetricus (three of the usurpers known as the "Thirty Tyrants") have been found in various parts of Northumbria which are now known as Lancashire. In A.D. 282 the Emperor Carus gave the island of Britain to his son Carinus, who was murdered in the year following. Passing over the next two Emperors, we find Carausius has the govern-

---

[1] Xiphiline's abridgment of Dion Cassius. It may be well here to state my general indebtedness to the late W. Thompson Watkin's "Roman Lancashire"; Liverpool, 1883.

ment of Britain ceded to him, and whilst on a visit to the
Brigantes' district he was assassinated at York, A.D. 293,
by his minister, Allectus, who at once usurped the purple
in Britain; but not being acknowledged, a powerful force
was sent against him from Rome, which met him not far
from London, and in the engagement which followed he
was slain and his army defeated. In the beginning of
the next century, the Emperor Constantius Chlorus
undertook an expedition against the Scots, and for that
purpose appears to have made York his headquarters;
he died in that city on July 25, A.D. 306, and his son
Constantine was at once proclaimed Emperor by the
garrison there stationed. The exact date of the introduction of the Christian religion into Lancashire is
unknown, but we know that in 303 the Emperor
Diocletian persecuted the followers of the new religion
in Britain, and that the first recorded British martyr,
St. Alban, died in 304 near the city which bears his
name. Great must have been the change in the aspect
of religious thought which, in 311, led to the conversion
of Constantine the Great. This illustrious Emperor had
no doubt a powerful influence over spiritual affairs in
Lancashire, although the latter part of his life was not
spent in Britain; he died in A.D. 337. The latter half
of the century witnessed the beginning of the decline of
the Roman power; the supposed unpassable Hadrian
Wall was not enough to keep back the Northern warlike
tribes, who, making their way through it, soon became
masters of the district near its southern side, and by
A.D. 368 the invaders had even reached the metropolis.

At this time was sent to Britain a great general,
Theodosius, who, with a large army, drove back the
Picts and Scots to the north of the Clyde; he also
restored and rebuilt many of the towns and fortresses,
and to him is attributed the naming of the province of
Valentia, which is comprised between Solway Firth and

the Tyne, and the Clyde and the Firth of Forth. All this, however, did not prevent the Picts, Scots, and Saxon pirates from re-entering the country as soon as the Roman legions were withdrawn, their services being required elsewhere. Rome, in fact, at this time was fast declining in power, and by the year 410 she had been obliged to call all her troops away from Britain, and Honorius had proclaimed Britain to be an independent state—in other words, the Romans left the country either because they could not any longer retain it, or they did not consider it worth the great drain upon their resources which it must have been.

The so-called independence which followed was so disastrous that the Britons found the last state worse than the first, and entreated their former rulers to assist them in repelling the foes they themselves were unable to overcome. They wrote: "The barbarians chase us into the sea, the sea flings us back on the barbarians; the only choice left us is to die by the sword or by the waves."

The appeal was in vain, and the wretched Britons were left to their own resources. That they were disorganized and without leaders will easily be understood, and to this must be added that for years the best of the youths had been trained as recruits and drafted off to the Continent, from whence very few returned; and then, again, the inhabitants, especially in the North (including Lancashire), must have been dreadfully reduced by the ravages continually made by the Picts and Scots. Thus it was that Lancashire, with the rest of the country, became an easy prey, first to the marauding foes from the North, and afterwards to those races which ultimately became the makers of England.

It is curious to notice the Roman influence on traditions still common in modern Lancashire—the beating of parish bounds` recalls the Roman *Terminalia* in honour of the god of limits and boundaries; May Day is the festival of Flora; the marriage-ring, the veil, the wedding gifts, and even the cake, are all Roman. Our funeral customs are also Roman—the cypress and the yew, the sprinkling of dust on the coffin, the flowers on the grave, and the black clothes.[1]

[1] E. Sanderson, "Hist. of England," p. 19.

CHAPTER IV.

ROMAN REMAINS.

THE history of Roman Lancashire has so recently been published[1] that, even if our space would allow (which it will not), it would be unnecessary, in a work of this description, either to furnish too much detail, or to dwell too long on the vexed questions of the subject which have not even yet been settled.

When the Romans invaded Lancashire, one of their chief difficulties was the want of roads, which rendered many parts of the district almost untenable, and to remedy this state of things, one of their first acts after conquest must have been to construct a way by which access could easily be gained to the newly-acquired territory. As everyone knows, the Romans were skilful in all kinds of engineering work, and as road-makers they have never been excelled; so durable were their pavements that we find remains of them still in all parts of the country. Up hill and down dale they went, from point to point, nearly always in a straight line—if a bog was in the way it was filled up; if a mountain, it was crossed. Taking these roads as they are now acknowledged by antiquaries to have run, and following alone their route, we shall come across the chief remains which time has left of our conquerors and rulers.

[1] "Roman Lancashire," W. Thompson Watkin; Liverpool, 1883.

The main Roman roads in Lancashire are all believed to have been constructed during the Higher Empire; that is, at or before the time of Hadrian (A.D. 117-128). The minor roads are of later and uncertain date.

Of the nine towns which became Roman *coloniæ*, the nearest to Lancashire were Eboracum (*York*), and Deva (*Chester*), but Mancunium (*Manchester*) was also a great military centre, and from it there were five Roman roads.[1] Two of these came from the Cheshire side of the Mersey, one passing through Stretford, and the other through Stockport to Buxton.

All trace of the road from Manchester to Stretford has disappeared, but its course ran through Cornbrook (near which it was cut through by the Bridgewater Canal) and by the botanical gardens to Crossford Bridge, on the Mersey. A few small remains have from time to time been found at Stretford, but scarcely sufficient to justify the idea that here was a Roman camp.[2] On the Stockport side of the Mersey we have traces of the road to Buxton, but on the Lancashire side its site is covered by the modern highway, part of which is still known as High Street.

Another of the approaches to Manchester was from the east. This also only for a short distance was on Lancashire soil. It came from Yorkshire, and, passing through Glodwick and Hollinwood, in the parish of Oldham, skirts the township of Failsworth, where at the end of the last century it was visible for upwards of a mile, and was commonly known as the "Street," or "Street Lane."[3] At Newton Heath traces of it were seen in 1857, and Whitaker saw remains of it in Ancoats and Ardwick.

In making the Oldham Park, a number of copper coins from the period of Antoninus Pius (A.D. 135) to Victorinus

---

[1] There are also traces of two other supposed Roman roads.
[2] *Lanc. and Ches. Ant. Soc.*, iii. 262.
[3] Whitaker's " History of Manchester," 1771.

(A.D. 218) were found, and in 1887, during the excavations made for Chamber Mill, near the site of the road, a box was unearthed which contained 300 bronze and brass coins. The following were verified: Antoninus Pius (A.D. 135-161), Marcus Aurelius (A.D. 161-180); Commodus (A.D. 180-193), Septimius Severus (A.D. 193-211), Caracalla (A.D. 211-217), Julia Mamica (A.D. 222-235).[1]

Before referring to the other roads from Manchester to the North and to the West, it will be well to glance at the Mancunium of the Romans, and it is needless, perhaps, here to remark that the building of the modern Manchester and Salford must of necessity have almost obliterated every material trace of this ancient stronghold.

Somewhere about the time of Agricola (A.D. 78-85), or possibly a little earlier, the Romans erected a *castrum* on a tongue of land made by a bend of the river Medlock. Whitaker, the Manchester historian,[2] thus describes what remained of this in 1773 :

The eastern side, like the western, is an hundred and forty [yards] in length, and for eighty yards from the northern termination the nearly perpendicular rampart carries a crest of more than two [yards] in height. It is then lowered to form the great entrance, the *porta prætoria*, of the camp : the earth there running in a ridge, and mounting up to the top of the bank, about ten in breadth. Then, rising gradually as the wall falls away, it carries an height of more than three for as many at the south-eastern angle. And the whole of this wall bears a broken line of thorns above, shews the mortar peeping here and there under the coat of turf, and near the south-eastern corner has a large buttress of earth continued for several yards along it. The southern side, like the northern, is an hundred and seventy-five [yards] in length ; and the rampart, sinking immediately from its elevation at the eastern end, successively declines, till, about fifty yards off, it is reduced to the inconsiderable height of less than one [yard]. And about seven-

---

[1] *Lanc. and Ches. Ant. Soc.*, viii. 156.

[2] Whitaker as an authority is good where he is describing things which he saw himself, but otherwise many of his theories border upon romance. (Vol. i., p. 49, 1773 edition.)

teen [yards] further there appears to have been a second gateway, the
ground rising up to the crest of the bank for four or five at the
point. . . .

One on the south side was particularly requisite . . . in order to
afford a passage to the river ; but about fifty-three yards beyond the
gate, the ground betwixt both falling away briskly to the west, the
rampart, which continues in a right line along the ridge, necessarily
rises till it has a sharp slope of twenty [yards] in length at the south-
western angle. And all this side of the wall, which was from the
beginning probably not much higher than it is at present, as it was
sufficiently secured by the river and its banks before it, appears crested
at first with an hedge of thorns, a young oak rising from the ridge and
rearing its head considerably over the rest, and runs afterwards in a
smooth line nearly level for several yards with the ground about it,
and just perceptible to the eye, in a rounded eminence of turf.

As to the south-western point of the camp, the ground slopes away
on the west towards the south, as well as on the south towards the
west. On the third side still runs from it nearly as at first, having an
even crest about seven feet in height, an even slope of turf for its
whole extent, and the wall in all its original condition below. About
an hundred yards beyond the angle was the *Porta Decumana* of the
station, the ground visibly rising up the ascent of the bank in a large
shelve of gravel, and running in a slight but perceivable ridge from it.
And beyond a level of forty-five yards, that still stretches on for the
whole length of the side, it was bounded by the western boundary of
the British city, the sharp slope of fifty to the morass below it. On
the northern and the remaining side are several chasms in the original
course of the ramparts. And in one of them, about an hundred and
twenty-seven yards from its commencement, was another gateway,
opening into the station directly from the road to Ribchester. The
rest of the wall still rises about five and four feet in height, planted all
the way with thorns above, and exhibiting a curious view of the
rampart below. Various parts of it have been fleeced of their facing
of turf and stone, and now show the inner structure of the whole,
presenting to the eye the undressed stone of the quarry, the angular
pieces of rock, and the round boulders of the river, all bedded in the
mortar, and compacted by it into one. And the white and brown
patches of mortar and stone on a general view of the wall stand
strikingly contrasted with the green turf that entirely conceals the
level line, and with the green moss that half reveals the projecting
points of the rampart. The great foss of the British city, the Romans
preserved along their northern side for more than thirty yards beyond
the eastern end of it, and for the whole beyond the western. And as

the present appearances of the ground intimate, they closed the eastern point of it with a high bank, which was raised upon one part of the ditch, and sloped away into the other.

Many inscribed stones have been found on the site of this *castrum*, which originally were built into the wall; one is noticed by Camden, which read :

> Ↄ. CANDIDI
> PEDES XX
> IIII

i.e., Centuria Candidi, Pedes xxiiii.

Another bore the inscription :

> COHO. I. FRISIN.[1]
> Ↄ. MASAVONIS.
> P.XXIII.

—which may be translated into, " The century of Masavo of the first cohort of the Frisians [built] 23 feet."

The Frisii were inhabitants of Gaul, who were frequently at war with the Romans, but towards the end of the first century, though they were not actually under Roman rule, they had agreed to contribute men for the imperial army; hence their presence in Lancashire.

There have been other centurial stones found near the Manchester settlement which are of considerable interest. One was discovered in 1760 on the south side of the Medlock, near Knott Mill; all that remains of the inscription is :

> . . . . ** QPOB
> XVAR ** CHOR. I.
> RIS. P. *****

The other centurial stone was found in 1796. It measures 15 inches by 11. It had inscribed upon it :

> COHR. I.
> FRISIAVO
> ↄ QVINTIANI
> Є P. XXIII.

---

[1] The late Mr. Thompson Watkin maintains that the N at end of the first line should be AV.

The translation would be, " The century of Quintianus, of the first cohort of the Frisians, [built] 24 feet." This stone was found near to one of the gateways to the *castrum.* A tile inscribed to " The twentieth legion, valiant and victorious," was found in 1829, and two others, bearing the words (when extended) *Cohortis III. Bracarum.* A small portion of the wall of a building within the *castrum* is still preserved ; a great portion of it consists of fragments of unhewn red sandstone.

In 1612, under the roots of an oak-tree, near to the Roman side, was found part of an inscribed altar. It was much mutilated, and had probably been built into a wall after the departure of the Romans. It is $27\frac{1}{2}$ inches in height, $15\frac{1}{2}$ inches in breadth, and nearly 11 inches thick. This altar passed through many hands, and its whereabouts is now unknown, but a copy of the inscription on its face has been preserved. It was dedicated to " Fortune the preserver, Lucius Senecianius Martius, a centurion of the Sixth Legion, (surnamed) the Victorious." This legion was stationed at Eboracum (York), A.D. 120.

Another altar (or, rather, a part of one) was found in Castlefield. It was of red sandstone, and was 2 feet 5 inches high. It is now preserved at Worsley New Hall. Its inscription may be rendered as, " To the god . . . Præpositus of the Vexillation of Rhætii and Norici performs his vow cheerfully and willingly to a deserving object." This inscription therefore informs us that part of the garrison of Mancunium consisted of a body of soldiers belonging to the Rhætii and Norici ; the former came from Switzerland, and the latter were Tyrolese. This is remarkable as the only description yet discovered in Britain which thus refers to these troops. The amount of pottery discovered has not been large, but amongst it were some fragments of Samian ware, on one of which is a representation of a hunting scene. Samples from the

Roman potteries of Upchurch have also been dug up, but none of them bear the maker's name.

About two miles from the *castrum*, in the bed of the river Irwell, was found in 1772 a golden ornament for the neck (a bulla), which was richly ornamented; along its upper border was a hollow tube through which to pass the cord by which it was suspended round the neck of the wearer. Only one other specimen of this kind of ornament in gold has been found in England, and that also was in Lancashire (in Overborough). Within the area of the *castrum* various minor remains have from time to time been discovered, including a massive gold ring, coins, urns, tiles, spear-heads, household gods, and Roman pottery.[1]

Amongst the coins were many of the reigns of Trajanus (A.D. 53-117), Hadrianus, Antoninus Pius, and Marcus Aurelius;[2] they were all found in or near what is still known as Castlefield.

Around this Roman stronghold something approaching a town was no doubt built, if, indeed, the conquering forces did not find some such settlement existing on their arrival. From the evidence of the remains found, this suburban quarter was mostly on the north of the *castrum*. In Tonman Street, in 1839, was discovered a bronze statuette of Jupiter Stator. Remains of domestic building have frequently been met with, and the site of the cemetery lying on the south-east side of the station is indicated by the numerous sepulchral urns discovered there, as well as human bones and lachrymatory vessels of black glass. Judging solely from the remains which are known to have been found here, the conclusion we must arrive at is that, important as Mancunium was as a military centre, the village or town around its *castrum* was not as important as that of Ribchester.

---

[1] " Palatine Note-Book," iii. 67.
[2] For full details of these see Watkin's " Roman Lancashire."

The dates of the various coins recorded (many more have been found but not recorded) clearly show that the Romans were settled at Mancunium from about A.D. 80 to the time when they left the country.

Traces of a road have been found between Manchester and Wigan, and the latter place was certainly a Roman station, though it has not been satisfactorily proved to be identical with the *Coccium* named in the tenth Iter of Antoninus. In 1836 the ditch and agger by which the station was fortified were still visible near the crown of the hill on which part of Wigan now stands.[1] Many Roman coins and urns have been found near the station, and a stone built into the present parish church is considered to have been a portion of a Roman altar. From Wigan the road went north and south.

Returning to Manchester: from this centre issued another road going in a straight line to Ribchester; it passed across Campfield and the site of what is now the Victoria railway-station; it went on to Prestwick, Lower Darwen, Blackburn, and finally to the bank of the Ribble near Ribchester; the remains of the road have been seen nearly over the whole of its length. It is not thought to be quite so ancient as the other roads out of Mancunium ;[2] however this may be, at Bremetonacum (Ribchester) was erected the largest *castrum* in the whole county.

Roman Ribchester was probably founded by the Emperor Agricola or by Hadrian.

Like nearly all the large stations, it was placed near to a river, and in this case the Ribble served as the fosse on the south-eastern side; its other boundaries have been clearly defined, the outline of fosse and vallum being still quite apparent, and within its limits are included the parish yard and Vicarage garden: its total area covers about ten statute acres. Its dimensions are: from the

---

[1] *Archæological Journal*, xxviii., p. 114, and xxx., p. 153.

[2] Watkin's " Roman Lancashire," p. 55.

vallum on the north-west to the bed of the river 615 feet, and from the vallum on the south-east to that on the opposite side 611 feet. The corners on the north and north-east are rounded off, the southern ones being lost in the bed of the river, which has considerably altered its course.

At the angle pointing north, in 1888, a gateway was discovered.[1] It was 14 feet wide, the end of the wall at each side being carefully rounded.

The construction of the vallum was at the same time exposed, and showed that it was formed of boulder stones put together with cement. It lies 6 feet below the present surface, and is about 5 feet wide.

Upon this base was raised the rampart of earth well beaten down. Outside the vallum on the south-western side is a fosse (or dyke), of which the outer limit is about 43 feet from the vallum.

In 1888-89 this rampart was cut through in seven places. At one of these cuttings on the south-western side the vallum was found to be 4 feet 6 inches wide at the base, and inside it, at a distance of 4 feet, and level with the base, was found a layer of oak shingles—that is, pieces of split oak—each about 4 to 5 feet long, 2 or 3 inches thick, and 3 to 4 inches wide; these were placed at right angles to the vallum, and at about 7 inches apart, with their widest sides lying horizontally.

These shingles are pointed at the end next the vallum, and broader and squarer at the other end. In the second cutting near the western angle the vallum was found to be 6 feet wide, and below the base there was a layer of imported clay; below this was a layer of red sand 2 feet thick, and under that a quantity of gravel. Here again were found the shingles, of which there were three rows, all lying at right angles to the vallum.

[1] Through the influence of the Rev. J. Shortt, Vicar of Hoghton, whose description of the find is here followed.

The longest of these shingles were from 9 to 14 feet, and were those at the greatest distance from the vallum. Two other cuttings exposed two jambs of a gateway, and the layer of shingles was found to extend from the inside through the gateway to the length of 7 or 8 feet outside; they were larger and longer than any of the others. Under them was a layer of gravel 9 inches thick, and below this, again, a floor of oak planks, smooth and tightly jointed, and stretching across the gateway. Beneath this was another layer of gravel, under which were four large shingles about 14 feet long, 1 foot wide, and 6 inches thick, which were laid at right angles to the shingles above them. On the north - eastern side of the vallum was a strong oak post found standing upright, which appeared to have been a gate-post. In 1725 Dr. Stukeley, the antiquary, visited Ribchester at a time when a portion of the south-eastern boundary was exposed through the action of the river, and he mentions having seen "the floor along the whole bank," which was no doubt made up of similar shingles. The use to which these oak shingles were put has not yet been satisfactorily settled, but the most probable theory is that they were intended to make sure the foundation of the path behind the rampart. They have not been discovered at any other Roman station in Britain. Another peculiarity of the Ribchester camp is the gates being placed in an angle of the quadrilateral instead of in the centre of one of the sides.

Outside the camp at Ribchester there was a settlement of considerable size and importance. There were at least two temples, the largest of which was probably over 100 feet long; it had sixteen pillars in front, and others around it, forming a peristyle. The inscription over the entrance (which was found some years ago) shows that it was dedicated "To the Deity: for the safety of the Emperor . . . and of Julia . . . the mother of our Lord [the Emperor], and the camps under the care of Valerius Crescens Fulvianus, his Legate [and] Pro-Prætor. Titus Floridius Natalis, Legate, our Præpositus and Governor, from the reply [of the oracle] restored the temple from the ground, and inaugurated it at his own expense." The mention of the Empress Julia fixes the date to between A.D. 211 and A.D. 235. The four pillars forming the entrance to the Bull Inn at Ribchester were from the ruins of one of the two temples. The bases of some of the columns of the larger building are preserved at the Rectory; they are of rude workmanship, but appear to be in the Doric style.

This temple is believed to have been destroyed by fire. From the inscription just quoted it would appear that it was then rebuilt, and it is at least possible that the original building may have been destroyed by the Scots, who at this time waged fierce war with the Romans.

The evidence as to the existence of the smaller temple is not so conclusive, although several stone cylindrical columns, each with a foliated capital, said to have belonged to it, are still preserved.

Beside the " finds " of coins, rings, querns, amphoræ, etc., there have been from time to time sculptured stones brought to light which tell their own history. A few only of these can here be mentioned : a walling stone inscribed LEG[IO] VICESIMA V[ALARIA] V[ICTRIX] FECIT (The Twentieth Legion, Valiant and Victorious, made [it]) ; a large sculptured altar which bore an inscription " To the holy god Apollo Maponus for the welfare of our lord [the Emperor], and of the Numerus of Sarmatian horse Bremetennacum [styled] the Gordian, Antoninus of the Sixth Legion, [styled the] Victorious. [His] birthplace [was] Melitene." The date of this is believed to be between A.D. 238 and A.D. 244.[1] In 1603 Camden saw

---

[1] Watkin's " Roman Lancashire," p. 133.

at Ribchester an altar which he describes as the largest and fairest that he had ever seen; this is now at Stony-hurst College. It was dedicated "To the goddess mothers, Marcus Ingenuius Asiaticus, a decurion of the cavalry regiment of the Astures, performs his vow willingly [and] dutifully to a deserving object."

Altars dedicated to these Deæ Matres are not un-common in Britain; they are often represented by female figures each bearing a basket of fruit. Another altar was dug up in the churchyard; its inscription refers to Caracalla and his mother Julia Domna (the widow of Septimius).

In 1796 a boy playing near the road leading to the church accidentally discovered a helmet, which its subse-quent owner[1] thus described: "The superior style of workmanship of the mask to that of the headpiece is also remarkable. It measures ten inches and a half from its junction to the skull-piece at the top of the forehead to its bottom under the chin. A row of small detached locks of hair surrounds the forehead a little above the eyes, reaching to the ears, which are well delineated. Upon these locks of hair rests the bottom of a diadem, or *tutulus*, which at the centre in front is two inches and a quarter in height, diminishing at the extremities to one inch and an eighth of an inch, and it is divided hori-zontally into two parts, bearing the proportionate height just mentioned. The lower part projects before the higher, and represents a bastion wall, separated into seven divisions by projecting turrets, with pyramidal tops, exceeding a little the height of the wall. These apertures for missile weapons of defence are marked in each of the turrets. Two arched doors appear in the middle division of this wall, and one arched door in each of the extreme divisions. The upper part of the diadem, which recedes a little so as to clear the top of the wall and of the turrets,

[1] Mr. Townley. See "Vetusta Monumenta," iv. 5.

was ornamented with seven embossed figures placed
under the seven arches, the abutments of which are heads
of genii.   The central arch and the figure that was
within it are destroyed, but the other six arches are filled
with a repetition of the following three groups: a Venus
sitting upon a marine monster; before her a draped
figure with wings, bearing a wreath and palm-branch, and
behind her a triton, whose lower parts terminate in tails
of fish.   Two serpents are represented on each side of
the face near the ears, from whence the bodies of these
reptiles surround each cheek and are joined under the
chin.   From the general form of the diadem being usually
appropriated to female deities, and the circumstance of
the lower division being composed of a wall and turrets in
the same manner as the heads of Isis, Cybele, and the
Ephesian Diana are decorated, added to the effeminacy
and delicacy of the features of the mask, one may
conclude that it alludes to these goddesses; but the
manner in which the face is accompanied with serpents
strongly indicates that it also comprises the character of
Medusa. . . ." The head portion of the helmet is ornamented with soldiers on horse and on foot.   This is considered one of the finest specimens of a Roman helmet yet
discovered.   In 1875, in the bed of the Ribble, was found
a sepulchral slab representing a horse-soldier spearing
a fallen foe.   The stone is 5 feet long and 2½ feet
in breadth.[1]   Several other tombstones have been discovered here, the inscription on one of which, being
translated, records that " In this earth is held that which
was at one time Ælia Matrona; she lived twenty-eight
years, two months, and eight days: and Marcus Julius
Maximus her son; he lived six years, three months
and twenty days: and Campania Dubitata her mother; .
she lived fifty years.   Julius Maximus, a sigularis con-
sularis of the Polish cavalry, the husband of an incom-

[1] Abram's " History of Blackburn," p. 159.

parable wife, and to a son most dutiful to his father and to a mother-in-law of very dear memory, has placed this."

The number of miscellaneous Roman articles which have been found at Ribchester is considerable. In 1884, just outside one of the gateways leading to the camp, a massive gold brooch was found; its weight is 373 grains, and it is in the shape of a harp, measuring 2 inches in length. Roman brooches of gold are very rarely met with.

In making graves in the churchyard from time to time small articles have been found; and in the Vicarage garden, almost every time the soil is turned, fragments of Samian pottery, etc., are brought to light.

These various *finds* have, perhaps, given rise to the local tradition that:

> It is written upon a wall in Rome :
> Ribchester is as rich as any town in Christendom.

But much of old Ribchester is lost through the shifting of the bed of the river, which formed one side of the *castrum.*

From Ribchester issued five roads: (i.) To Yorkshire through Chadburn; (ii.) to Manchester; (iii.) to Morecambe Bay through the Fylde; (iv.) to Lancaster, joining the main road at Galgate; (v.) to Westmorland *viâ* Overborough.

The road to Yorkshire passed through Langho, crossed the Calder near a place called "Potter's Ford," and leaving Clitheroe on the east, went over the rising ground to Chadburn and over the Yorkshire border to Skipton. Roman coins have been found at Langho,[1] and also the remains of a rectangular building 70 feet square, which is believed to have been a small camp; its site is still known as "Castle Holme."[2] Between Chadburn and Worsthorne, in 1788, nearly 1,000 silver *denarii* of the Higher

---

[1] *Lanc. and Ches. Hist. Soc.,* xxv. 161.
[2] Whitaker's "History of Whalley," ii. 19.

Empire were found in an urn dug up by some workmen.[1]
The road through the Fylde district was no doubt made
to connect Ribchester with the Portus Sestantiorum (the
Haven of the Sestantii), the exact site of which has never
been satisfactorily proved, but it was probably near the
mouth of the Wyre. The agger is only traceable along bits
of the route from Ribchester, but it appears at "Stubbin
Nook," and, after passing Pedder House, becomes identical with what is still called Watling Street; it then
crosses Fulwood Moor near Preston, and goes on to
Kirkham, Marton Mere, and Poulton-le-Fylde. The late
John Just, in 1850, made a careful survey of that portion
of the road; he thus describes it : " Within a mile of the
town of Poulton are seen the first indications of a Roman
road. . . . But having got on to the high ground and to
a part of the flats of the Fylde district we meet with
striking remains of a road on the turfy ground where it
has been piled up in an immense agger. . . . Across
this the line is very distinct. . . . On the higher ground
the whole of the line has been obliterated . . . until we
again detect it in a low hollow towards Weeton Moss.
. . . Here is an immense embankment of several yards
in height, its base standing in the water. . . . The line
hence directs itself up the rising ground to Plumpton;
. . . from hence it directs its course to the windmill on
the high ground between Weeton Moss and Kirkham,
which there opens to the view. Near the windmill the
road forms an angle, and thence joins the public road in
a long-continuous straight line forwards towards Kirkham.
. . . About midway, within the long town of Kirkham,
the line of the Roman roads falls in with Main Street,
and continues up to the windmill at the top of the town.
Nearly the whole length of the long street of Kirkham is
upon the Roman road."[2]

[1] Baines' "History of Lancashire" (second edition), ii. 24.
[2] *Lanc. and Ches. Hist. Soc.,* iii. 3.

At Kirkham the Romans left many traces: amulets, axes, ivory needles, urns filled with calcined bones, lachrymatory urns, and coins, have all at various times been discovered, but the finest relic was the umbo of a shield found at Mill Hill; it is now in the British Museum. It is about 8 inches in diameter, and in its centre is a figure of a man seated, his limbs naked, but wearing on his head a crested helmet.[1]

In what was once the bed of Marton Mere, in 1850, the old road was clearly defined; its gravel was 12 yards wide and 2 yards thick; and at Fleetwood, in 1835, at some depth below the sand, a portion of the pavement was found intact. Between Fenny and Rossall Point, on the Wyre Estuary, upwards of four hundred Roman coins were found; their dates varied from A.D. 353 to A.D. 408. Many parts of the Roman road in this district were known as Danes' Pad.[2] The road from Ribchester to Galgate passed through places called Preston Wives, Writton Stone, Stoney Lane, Windy Arbour, Street Farm, and a little to the north-east of Shireshead joined the road from Walton to Lancaster. Westmorland was approached by a road which, after leaving Ribchester, has not been very clearly traced, but for a great portion of its route it ran through Yorkshire, passing through Slaidburn; it came into Lancashire a few miles south of Ivah, but soon again crossed the border line and re-entered Lancashire, and passed through Tatham to Overborough, the Roman *Galacum.* Of this place Camden (writing about 1580) says, "that it was formerly a great city upon a large plot of ground, between the Lac and the Lone, and being besieged, was forced to surrender by famine is what the inhabitants told me, who have it by tradition from their

[1] *Hist. Soc. of Lanc. and Ches.,* iii. 60; also Fishwick's " History of Kirkham," *Chetham Soc.,* xcii. 5.

[2] Fishwick's "History of Poulton-le-Fylde," *Chetham Soc.,* new series, viii. 4 ; also civ. 2.

ancestors; and certain it is that the place makes proof of its own antiquity by many ancient monuments, inscriptions, chequered pavements, and Roman coins, as also by this modern name, which signifies a burrow." Although nearly every trace of the Roman occupation has been cleared away, discoveries made since Camden's time abundantly prove that here was a Roman stronghold. Overborough is in the parish of Tunstall.

There now remains to describe the other Roman road, passing right through Lancashire, in almost a straight line for Warrington, passing Wigan, Preston, and Lancaster on its route to Natland in Westmorland.

This road began at Wilderspool, on the Cheshire side of the Mersey. The exact spot where it crossed the river is unknown, but traces of it are found near Warrington, at Winwick, Haydock, Ashton in Makerfield, and Wigan; from the latter place it continued to Standish, Whittle and Bamber Green, crossed the Ribble at Walton, then passed through some fields formerly known as Great Pathway Fields, Causeway Meadow and Pathway Meadow. From Walton the road went on to Lancaster, through Broughton, Barton Lodge, Brook, Claughton (where was formerly a road called Fleet Street) and Galgate; between Lancaster and Natland all trace of the road has disappeared, and its route is undefined. The remains found on the line of road from Warrington to Wigan are neither numerous nor of special interest.

At Standish many coins have been found, as well as gold rings, of undoubted Roman origin.

At Walton-le-Dale we find clear evidence of the existence of a minor station, between the bends of the Ribble and the Darwen. Here, in 1855, in excavating in a large mound called the Plump, were found the remains of a probably British foundation, upon which was a layer of large boulders, mixed with gravel a foot thick, near to which were lying coins of Antoninus Pius, Domitian, and

Vespasian, together with querns, fragments of Samian ware, bricks, tiles, fragments of amphoræ, etc.[1] In the immediate neighbourhood subsequent excavations brought to light other remains in large quantities, as well as portions of Roman masonry. All the coins found were of the Higher Empire.

At Lancaster was another station, and probably a very early one, as it is certain that in the time of Trajan (A.D. 98-117) there were Roman buildings of some kind here; the proof of this is the discovery, about twenty years ago, beneath the floor of the parish church, of a triangular-shaped stone upon which was inscribed in letters 2 inches high, IMP. NER. TRAIAN; AVG. C.; this being completed would read, " Imperatori Nervae Trajano Augusto cohors."[2]

On the site of, or within the area of the *castrum* have been erected the castle, the priory, and the church, so that it is not to be wondered at that its original boundaries are indefinable. Without placing too much reliance upon the statements of such writers as Leland and Camden, sufficient fragments of the Roman walls have from time to time been exhumed to afford ample proof that such a station existed; and from inscriptions found, together with the discovery of large quantities of horses' teeth, it may be assumed to have been occupied by cavalry troops only.

The remains found within the walls and in the immediate neighbourhood have been very numerous and varied. Amongst the altars was one dedicated " to the holy god Mars Cocidius," the latter word referring to a British god, which shows the accommodating spirit of " Vibinius Lucius," the pensioner of the Consul who thus "performed his vows." From the fact that over many parts of the station uncovered there was found to be a thick layer

---

[1] Watkin's " Roman Lancashire," p. 203.
[2] " The Palatine Note-book," iv. 201.

of ashes, it is conjectured that Roman Lancaster was destroyed by fire. Many milestones have also been found, and two burial-places. There was also a road from Lancaster to Overborough; its route was over Quernmore and through Caton, where a milestone of the time of Hadrian was discovered. In Lonsdale north of the Sands we have no distinct trace of Roman occupation.

There were, of course, several other Roman roads of later date and of minor importance; one only of these is it necessary to refer to, that is, the road which is supposed to have run from Manchester, through Chadderton, Royton, Rochdale, Littleborough, and over Blackstone Edge to Aldborough in Yorkshire. John Ogilby, the King's cosmographer in 1675, states that this road was 8 yards wide and paved with stone all the way. Warburton, the Somerset Herald, shows it as a Roman road in his map drawn in 1753; later writers, however, do not agree as to its exact course, and nearly all trace of it has long ago disappeared, except for a short distance on the steep side of Blackstone Edge, where its course can be fairly traced from Windy Bank, near Littleborough, to the division line between Lancashire and Yorkshire. The portion best preserved is that which ascends the hill in a perfectly straight line, commencing about 1,600 yards from the summit. The parts which have been recently cleared from the overgrowth of heath show a road 15 feet wide, exclusive of curbstone, paved with square blocks of stone, and slightly arched to throw the water into a trench which runs on either side. In the centre of this road, where it ascends the hill at a steep gradient (in some parts one in four and a third), is a course of hard millstone grit stones, which have been carefully tooled and set together so as to form a continuous line from the top to the bottom. These blocks are of stone, are 3 feet 8 inches wide, and in them has been cut (or as some think worn) a trough about

17 inches wide at the top, and a little over a foot at the bottom, and of a depth of some 4 inches. The bottom of this trough is found to be slightly curved. The question as to the use and age of these central stones has been the subject of much discussion. The author of Roman Lancashire gives them a Roman origin, and thinks the groove was to steady the central wheel of a three-wheeled vehicle. An easy explanation would be that the stones were worn hollow by the feet of packhorses, but the reply to this is, that on a well-paved road up a steep hill, a footway of smooth stones would not only be useless, but dangerous. Another theory is that the Romans placed them there to help the drivers of chariots to " skid " the wheels of their vehicles, whilst some have urged that the central trough is of much more recent date, and was used in working the quarries at the top of the hill.[1]

Roman coins and tiles have been found near Littleborough and at Underwood, near Rochdale; and at Tunshill in Butterworth, in the same parish, in 1793, was discovered the right arm of a silver statue of Victory, to which was attached an amulet with an inscription to the Sixth Legion.[2]

From this rapid survey of the Roman roads, stations, and settlements, with the evidence of the vestiges which time has preserved for our inspection, it must at once be seen that through the length and breadth of Lancashire (except, perhaps, Lonsdale north of the Sands) the all-conquering Roman was found, and that for nearly four centuries he held possession. That he did much to educate and civilize the conquered tribes cannot be doubted, and the Lancashire people at the close of the Roman occupation must have been a very different race to those half-naked barbarians who fought so desperately

---

[1] Fishwick's " History of Rochdale," p. 7 ; also *Lanc. and Ches. Arch. Soc.,* p. 73 *et seq.*

[2] *Ibid.,* p. 12.

to defend their soil against the invading legions. Although the ancient Briton was not quite an untutored savage, still, the influence of the higher cultured Romans had a very material effect upon his character and surroundings, and led to the acquirement of many arts and industries, which produced corresponding results of prosperity and comfort. The culture of the land was improved, the people were shown how to make roads and build houses of stone, mines were opened, iron was smelted, and ships were built.

CHAPTER V.

THE SAXON AND THE DANE.

I F it is true—as generally supposed—that the Britons, after being grievously oppressed by the Picts and Scots, called in the German tribes to assist them, then it naturally followed that, after driving back the Northern invaders, they themselves took possession of the land they had been fighting for.

In Lancashire, the desertion of the Romans probably led to a considerable part of the county being again laid waste, and the inhabitants scattered.

All authorities agree that for some forty years after the departure of the Romans the Britons were in continual strife, and that their independence brought to them only war and misery. The three Teutonic tribes known to the Romans as the Jutes, the Saxons and the Angles, in A.D. 449 appear to have called themselves Englishmen, and in that year they won their first battle against the Britons at Aylesford, in Kent. After this it took nearly 150 years to acquire the land from the South to the Forth. The Northern parts were for the most part taken possession of by the Angles, and divided into kingdoms, the boundaries of which are not known; some authorities place part of Lancashire in the kingdom of Deira, which had York for its centre, whilst others maintain that the kingdom of Strathclyde extended southward to the banks of the Dee; be this as it may, towards the close of the sixth century Lancashire formed part of the kingdom of Northumbria, which was held by the Angles. The inhabitants of these Northern parts, in their contests with the invaders, had the great advantage of having possession of the Roman strongholds, and no doubt offered a stubborn resistance. With the new rulers came new names, new language, and new customs, and many things that had been established by the former invaders were swept away.

We now come to the introduction of Christianity into Northumbria, which arose through the marriage of Æthelbert, King of Kent, at the close of the sixth century, with Bertha, daughter of King Charibert of Paris, who, being a convert to the Christian religion, made it a condition of her marriage that she should be allowed to worship in a small Roman-built church near Canterbury. Early in the next century Edwin, King of Northumbria, married Æthelburga, the daughter of Æthelbert, who, also being a Christian, took with her Paulinus, a follower of St. Augustine (see Chapter IX.).

It was not so easy, however, to make a convert of her husband, but after some delay he called together his Council, who declared themselves in favour of the new religion, and many of them were baptized at York, A.D. 627. This conversion led to a war between Edwin and the King of Mercia, who still held to his faith in Woden and Thor, when the King of Northumbria was killed at the battle of Hatfield in 633.

Shortly after this, Cædwallon, King of the Welsh, became ruler over Northumbria, but only for a short time, as he was defeated and slain in battle by Oswald, who, afterwards succeeding to the thrones of Bernicia and Deira, again united Northumbria, and re-established the Christian creed. But Penda was determined to maintain the pagan religion, and, defeating Oswald at the battle of Maserfeld in 642, again held Northumbria. Subsequently another division appears to have taken place, and Lancashire became part of the kingdom of Deira, its ruler being Oswine, and continued so for some six years, when Oswi, who reigned in Bernicia (the other portion of Northumbria), caused Oswine to be slain, and again united the two kingdoms. Alcfrid, the son of Oswi, having married Cyneburga, daughter of Penda, was about this time appointed Regent over Deira, and afterwards a further fusion of the two families was brought about by the marriage of Alcfrid's sister to Peada, son of Penda.

Oswi in 655 had a pitched battle with Penda at Winwæd in Yorkshire,[1] where the latter was defeated and slain. To celebrate this victory Oswi established twelve religious houses, six of which were in Deira (see Chapter IX.). Oswi died in 670, and his son Egfrid (or Ecgfrith) succeeded to the throne of Northumbria, which was now become a Christian and powerful kingdom. His short reign was marked by several military victories, the chief being his defeat of the King of Mercia, by which he gained the province of Lindiswards, or Lincolnshire; but in A.D. 685 Egfrid went across the Forth to repress a rising of the Picts, and in a great battle at Nectansmere in Yorkshire he and many of his nobles were slain, and with them fell the supremacy of ancient Northumbria From this date to the establishment of the Heptarchy, Northumbria, though allowed to elect tributary rulers, was, except for a very short period, under the overlords of first Mercia and then Wessex. Green, in his " History of the English People,"[2] says that Northumbria was " the literary centre of the Christian world in Western Europe. The whole learning of the age seemed to be summed up

---

[1] Authorities differ as to this locality : one writer places it on the Firth of Forth, another in Worcestershire.

[2] Pp. 36, 39.

in a Northumbrian scholar, Bæda—the Venerable Bede, later times styled him." The same writer adds: " From the death of Bæda the history of Northumbria is in fact only a wild story of lawlessness and bloodshed. King after king [tributary kings] was swept away by treason and revolt, the country fell into the hands of its turbulent nobles, the very fields lay waste, and the land was swept by famine and plague." In A.D. 827 Egbert found no difficulty, after subduing the rest of England, in coming to peaceful terms with the Northumbrian nobles, and reducing the whole country from the British Channel to the Forth into one kingdom. For some time before the close of the eighth century Northumbria had been subject to frequent attacks from the Northmen, or Danes, who mostly came from Denmark and Norway, who have been frequently described as sea-pirates, distinguished for courage and ferocity and a strong hatred to the Christian religion, they themselves being worshippers of Woden and the other pagan gods. Soon after the middle of the tenth century the Danes were no longer content to make marauding expeditions, but aspired to become owners of the soil, and in 867, after a great victory near the city of York, they practically took possession of Northumbria, and a few years later the whole of England north of the Thames was in their hands. The subsequent wars between Alfred the Great and the Danes belong more to the general history of England; it will suffice here to state that in 878 was concluded the treaty of peace known as " Alfred and Guthrum's Peace," whereby the Danish settlers were recognised and the land on the east and north of Watling Street given up to them, that is, nearly all the east side of England from the Thames to the Tweed, where they were to be independent dwellers, with their own laws and institutions.[1] Thus, almost the whole of Lancashire was left to the Danish invaders; but not,

[1] Sanderson's " History of England," p. 44.

however, for a long period, as Edward the Elder, the son and successor of Alfred, having wrested Mercia from the Danes, marched against Northumbria, where a contest was avoided by the submission of the inhabitants, and, according to the Saxon Chronicle,[1] having taken possession of Manchester, which he found almost in ruins, he refortified and garrisoned it in the year 923. Athelstan, the son of Edward the Elder, had frequent disturbances from the Northern Danes, who in 937, having united the Scots and the Welsh, met the King's forces at Bruanburgh (supposed to be in Northumberland), where they were defeated; only, however, for a time, as they were not finally suppressed until the year 954, when Northumbria was placed under a governor with the title of Earl.

The beginning of the next century found the country in a very unsettled state in consequence of fresh invasions by the King of Denmark and Norway, and on the death of Ethelred, in April, 1016, London proclaimed Edmund King, whilst a council at Southampton accepted Canute the Dane; ultimately the English nobles compelled a division, and Northumbria, Mercia, and East Anglia fell to Canute, who a month later, on the death of Edmund, became King of England. Canute (or Cnut) during his reign did much to remove the hatred felt towards the Danes, but the tyranny and oppression exercised by his two sons, who succeeded him,[2] revived the old feelings, and on the death of Harthacnut in 1043, after five-and-twenty years of Danish rule, the people elected one of the old English stock as the King, and Edward the Confessor ascended the throne.

During these six centuries Lancashire had many rulers,

[1] A.D. 923.

[2] After the death of Cnut, in 1035, the kingdom was again divided, and Mercia and Northumbria fell to Harold. Harthacnut was (in 1039), however, King of all England.

and must have been the scene of many a pitched battle. Its people were never long at peace, but rebellions, invasions, and wars of every kind fast followed each other. At one time they were governed by kings of Northumbria, at another by kings of England; at one time they were ruled by only tributary kings, or even only by tributary earls; sometimes the Christian religion was upheld, and sometimes they were referred back to Woden and Thor and Oden. Nevertheless, churches were built (see Chapter IX.), religious houses endowed, and castles erected. Many of its parishes were now formed, and its hundreds and tithings were meted out. Many of the parish and township names in Lancashire are suggestive of Saxon or Danish origin. Thus, Winwick, Elswick, Fishwick, Chadwick, Poulton, Walton, Sephton, Middleton, Eccleston, Broughton, Preston, Kirkham, Penwortham, Bispham, Cockerham, Oldham, Sowerby, Westby, Ribby, Formby, and a host of others, all point to their having once been held by the early settlers, as do also the terminative "rods" and "shaws" so common in the south of the county. In the old maps of the county a tract of land on the west side of the Wyre, between Shard and Fleetwood, is called Bergerode, which is a combination of the Anglo-Saxon words "Beor grade"—a shallow harbour. No doubt many of these places were held by Saxon Thanes, of which there were three classes; the highest of these held their lands and manors of the King, and probably had some kind of a castle or fortification erected on the manors, as well as in many cases a church, though probably only built of wood. To many places in the county have been assigned Saxon castles; Baines, in his "History of Lancashire,"[1] has enumerated no less than twelve of these south of the Ribble, but for only two of them is there any absolute authority for the assumption, viz., Penwortham and Rochdale. At Penwortham

[1] Vol. i., p. 12, 2nd edit.

William the Conqueror found a castle, and around it were six burgesses, three radmen (a class of freemen who served on horseback), only eight villeins (who were literally servants of the lords of the soil), and four neat-herds, or cattle-keepers; and amongst other possessions its owner had a moiety of the river-fishing, a wood, and aeries of hawks. The castle was occupied in the time of Henry III., when ´Randle de Blundeville, the Earl of Chester and Baron of Lancaster, held his court within its walls.[1] All trace of it has now disappeared, but Castle Hill is its traditional site.

In the time of Edward the Confessor (A.D. 1041-1066) most of the land in Rochdale was held of the King by Gamel the Thane; part of this land was free from all duties except danegeld.[2] There can be little doubt but that a Saxon Thane of this order had both his castle and its accompanying church. As to the existence of the former, it is placed beyond dispute by the name Castleton, which occurs in many very early deeds, and by the fact that in a charter, without date (but early in the thirteenth century), reference is made to "the land lying between" a field "and the ditch of the castle" (*fossatum castelli*), and the right of way is reserved for "ingoing and exit to the place of the castle" (*locus castelli*), and the right of foot-way to lands "in Castleton in the north part of Smythe-cumbesrode and an *assartum* called Sethe." The boundaries detailed in the charter show that this castle, probably then in ruins, stood on the elevated ground still known as Castle Hill.[3]

There is a local tradition that at Bury, on the site called Castle Croft, once stood a Saxon castle; but there is no evidence to support this, and from the character of

[1] Coucher Book, Duchy Office, No. 78.

[2] Originally a tax paid to the Danes, but afterwards appropriated to the King. It was always a very unpopular tax.

[3] Plan of this in Fishwick's "History of Rochdale," p. 66.

a portion of the foundations discovered in 1865, it seems more probable that the building which gave its name to the place was of much more recent date.

Winwick, near Warrington, has also its traditional Saxon castle, and also lays claim to having within its parish the site of the battle-field where Oswald, King of Northumbria, fell on August 5, A.D. 642. Bede[1] records that the Christian King was slain in a great battle against the pagan ruler over the Mercians at a place called Maserfield, and adds that such was his faith in God that ever since his death infirm men and cattle are healed by visiting the spot where he was killed; some, taking the dust from the soil and putting it in water, were able to heal their sick friends; by this means the earth had been by degrees carried away, so that a hole remained as deep as the height of a man.

This Maserfield, or Maserfeld, was by Camden and others supposed to be near Oswestry, in Shropshire, but there are many good reasons for assuming that the engagement took place in Makerfield, near Winwick; the very ancient parish church is dedicated to St. Oswald, and half a mile to the north of it is St. Oswald's Well, which is at the present day in a deep ditch, and until within quite recent times was in the charge of a paid custodian, whose duty it was to keep the water from contamination;[2] an ancient inscription on the wall of the south side of the church also appears to confirm the opinion.

In Aldingham Moat Hill (in Furness) we have an example of the moated mound or " burh " of a Saxon lord, which probably dates from the tenth century.[3] The earthwork consists of three divisions. The rectangular camp, is surrounded by a ditch nearly 40 feet wide,

---

[1] " Eccles. Hist.," lib. iii., cap. 8.

[2] Baines' " Hist. of Lanc.," ii. 205, 2nd edit.

[3] The following account of it is compiled from an article in *Archæologia*, vol. liii., part iii., by H. Swainson Cowper, Esq., F.S.A.

and 4 or 5 feet deep, the space thus enclosed being about
100 feet square. About 100 yards south of this there is a
straight piece of ditch which runs almost at right angles
to the sea-cliff for some 250 feet. South again of this
ditch, but separated from it by about 40 yards, stands the
moated "burh" itself, on the very edge of the cliff; the
ditch and part of the mound have been washed away by
the sea. The "burh" is about 30 feet high, and 96 feet
above the sea-level. The ditch is about 10 feet deep, and
between 15 and 20 feet broad at the bottom. This was
the fortified home of the Anglo-Saxon clan settled in this
place. The rectangular enclosure may have been the
meeting-place of the folk-moot of the settlement. Pennington Castle Hill is a somewhat similar mound, but
some of the characteristics of a "burh" are wanting;
nevertheless, it was doubtless the fortified *ton* of the
Pennings. Near to it is a place called Ellabarrow, which
takes its name from a large tumulus 400 feet in circum-
ference, known as Coninger or Coninsher.

The remains which from time to time have been discovered, and which can with certainty be classed as
Danish or Anglo-Saxon, are not nearly so numerous as
one would have expected. Saxon stone crosses (or
portions of them) have been found at Bolton, Whalley,
Burnley, Halton, Heysham, Lancaster, and Winwick,
and the ornamentation of several of them is beautiful
and interesting. The so called "hog-backed" stone in
Heysham churchyard has given rise to much controversy,
and is undoubtedly of very great antiquity.[1] Saxon
tumuli have been opened at Langho, Winwick, and some
few other places, and coins belonging to this period have
occasionally been exhumed; notably at Cuerdale, where
nearly · 2,000 coins were found which were believed
to have been struck by one of the Danish rulers of
Northumbria, and large numbers of very similar coins

---

[1] See *Lanc. and Ches. Arch. Soc.*, v. 1 *et seq.*

have been dug up at Harkirke, in the parish of Sefton. Some of these coins were of King Alfred's time, others were of Guthred, or Gulfrith (son of Ivan), who was King of Northumbria A.D. 883 to 894, who was supposed to have on embracing Christianity taken the name of *Cnvt*, which is engraved on the coins.[1]

It is believed that at Billington, near Whalley, in A.D. 798, King Ethelred met the conspirator Wada, and defeated him in a battle in which on both sides great numbers were slain.[2]   Near to this place is a large tumulus known as the " Lowe," which has never been properly explored; but at Brockhole Eses (which is quite near to Billington) a tumulus was found to contain human bones and iron spear-heads.

At Claughton, in the parish of Garstang, a tumulus of this period was opened in 1822, and found to contain, in addition to charred human bones, large convex brooches of white metal, beads of coloured paste, iron and stone axes, spear-heads and a sword ;[3] remains very similar in character to these were also dug up at Crossmoor, in Inskip, in 1889.[4]

In the time which immediately preceded the coming of the Norman Conqueror, Lancashire must have been very sparsely populated; in every part of it there were vast forests, and great stretches of moss and fern; agriculture was everywhere neglected; towns, in the modern sense, there were none ; but here and there, clustering as if for protection round some Saxon Thane's castle or fortified dwelling-place, were groups of wooden houses and rude huts, and scattered sparsely over the county were the

[1] See *Lanc. and Ches. Arch. Soc.*, v. 227.
[2] Saxon Chronicle and the Chronicle of Simon of Durham.
[3] *Arch. Journal*, vi. 74 ; and " History of Garstang," *Chetham Soc.*, civ. 5.
[4] Fishwick's " History of St. Michael's-on-Wyre," *Chetham Soc.*, xxv. (new series), p. 2.

clearings (*assarts* or *rods*) and the *tons* of the primitive settlers, with, in some districts, a wooden building doing duty as a church. Except where the old Roman roads were still in use, the means of passage from one place to another was difficult and dangerous; the people were of many tribes and nations—remnants of ancient British families, Angles, Saxons, Danes, Scandinavians, and even Normans contributed to the general stock—and as there were many tribes, so were there various religions, although Christianity had now become the general accepted faith. But for all this, much had been accomplished by time and experience to prepare the mind of the people to accept the tenet that union is strength, and that only by an undivided kingdom could come peace, wealth, and prosperity.

CHAPTER VI.

THE NORMANS AND THE PLANTAGENETS (A.D. 1066—1485).

THE stirring events which led up to the battle of Hastings, which took place on October 14, 1066, and the subsequent complete conquest of England by William of Normandy, did not perhaps immediately affect the Northern part of the kingdom so much as they did those counties lying nearer the scene of action.

We have now arrived at a period when we have more definite and reliable evidence as to the actual position of Lancashire.

At the end of the year 1084 the King summoned his Great Council to meet at Gloucester, with the object of devising means whereby a full account could be obtained as to the state of the country, especially as to the land—how much was cultivated, and by whom and on what authority it was held. This is not the place more fully to describe the *modus operandi* of preparing the Domesday Book, but it may be mentioned that by some singular arrangement Lancashire as a county is not named, the southern portion being included in Cheshire, the hundred of Amounderness in Yorkshire, and the two northern hundreds in Westmorland, Cumberland, and Yorkshire. The value of the information contained in the return is threefold, as it records the state of the country in Edward the Confessor's time, the way each manor, etc., was dealt with by William on his taking possession, and the rateable value on the taking of the Survey.

Unfortunately, we do not get from it anything like a census of the whole country, but it will be useful for comparison to note that Yorkshire had about 10,000 inhabitants, London some 30,000, and that of the other counties Lincoln and Norfolk had the largest population. The Survey was taken in A.D. 1085.

In West Derby Hundred the following places are named [1] as places where there was land under such cultivation or occupation as to render it rateable : Roby, Knowsley, Kirkby, Maghull, Aughton, Huyton, Torbock, Toxteth, Sefton, Kirkdale, Walton-on-the-Hill, Litherland, Ince Blundell, Thornton, Meols, Little Woolton, Smithdown (now Liverpool), Allerton, Speke, Childwall,[2] Windle, Much Woolton, Wavertree, Bootle, Formby, Ainsley, Down Hollard, Dalton, Skelmersdale, Raven's Meols, Orrell, Lathom, Hurleston (in Scarisbrick), Melling, Lydiate, Altcar,[3] Barton, Halsall. At this time Lancashire between the Ribble and the Mersey was divided into six hundreds, viz., West Derby, Newton, Walintone (*i.e.*, Warrington), Blackburn, Salford, and Leyland. The places just named, with the addition of Newton and Warrington, are all that were recognised in the Great Survey, and many of these were manors held in the time of Edward by Thanes whose names are not given ; others were doubtless in the hands of Saxons, Danes or Anglo-Saxons, who had stuck to their holdings through all changes. Some of the surnames at once suggest this ; for example, we find Godiva, the widow of

[1] In the original document the names are often very different to the ones now in use, but they have all been identified as referring to the localities above given.

[2] "There is a priest there having half a carucate of land in frank amoign."

[3] Said to be waste.

Leofric, Earl of Mercia, returned as having three carucates of land in Melling. Amongst the other tenants *in capite* are Dot, Uetred, Chetel, Wibert, etc. Edward the Confessor had in West Derby one manor and six berewicks (sub-manors), a forest 3 miles long and $1\frac{1}{2}$ miles wide,[1] and an aerie of hawks. The whole of the land between the Ribble and the Mersey had been given to Roger de Poictou as a reward for his services to the Conqueror, but was forfeited to the Crown shortly before this date. All the manors were rateable to the danegeld, but fifteen of them paid nothing to the royal exchequer except that geld. The customary tribute for the manors was two hora or ores of pennies for each carucate ot land ;[2] the owners of the manors had also to assist in making and keeping up the King's houses, fisheries, hays, and stations in the forest ; they were also to find mowers to reap the King's corn, to attend the hundred court, and do other small services, under certain fixed penalties for omission.

Roger de Poictou had granted land here to eight men, whose holding was twenty-four carucates, and they had forty-six villeins, one radman, and sixty-two *bordarii*, two serfs, and three maids. Their wood was $4\frac{1}{2}$ miles long. The *bordarii* at this time formed about thirty per cent. of the entire population ; their exact status has never been very clearly defined. They were probably identical with the *cotarii*, and were a class somewhat above the *villeins* and *servi*, and were allowed a *bord* or cottage, and rendered occasional service to the demesne lord.

In Newton fifteen berewicks were held by as many men, who were described as *drenchs* or *drings*, who were a kind of military vassals, holding allotments as minor or sub-

---

[1] Other forests are named at Latham, Aughton, Milling, Lydiate, and other places.

[2] The hora was not a coin, but an equivalent for about 1s. 6d. or 1s. 8d.

manors. The service they gave was known as *drengage*. The manor had a church (Wigan), and St. Oswald's (Winwick) had two carucates of land. Some of the manors had curious exemptions from penalties; for example, Orrel, Halsall, and Tarleton were not liable to forfeiture through their owners committing murder or rape. The Warrington manor had been held by King Edward, who had allotted land to thirty-four *drenchs*. St. Elfin (Warrington) was free from custom except geld. In the whole of this division of the county we have no towns, cities, or castles, and five churches are mentioned in Childwall, Walton-on-the-Hill, Winwick (Newton), Wigan, and St. Elfin (Warrington).

Concerning the hundred of Blackburn, the information given in the Domesday Book is comparatively meagre. This portion of Roger de Poictou's vast possession had, before he fell into royal disfavour, been given by him to Roger de Busli and Albert Greslet. Edward the Confessor held Blackburn, where there were two hides and two carucates[1] of land; there was a wood 1½ miles long, and the usual aerie of hawks. To this "hundred or manor" were attached twenty-eight freemen, who held land for twenty-eight manors, and there was a forest 9 miles long. In the same hundred King Edward held Huncote and Walton-le-Dale. The church of Blackburn and St. Mary's, Whalley, also held land. The whole manor with the hundred yielded the King a farm rent of £32 2s. Leyland Hundred Edward the Confessor found to consist of Leyland Manor, which contained a hide and two carucates of land, and a wood 3 miles long, 1½ miles broad, with the customary aerie of hawks; to it belonged twelve other manors, with woods 9 miles long and over 4 miles wide. The men of this manor were not bound to work at the King's manor-house, or to mow for him in

---

[1] In South Lancashire it is believed that six carucates made a hide. A carucate was about 100 acres, but was a variable term.

August. They only made hay in the wood.[1] The whole
manor paid to the King a farm rent of £19 18s. 2d. The
tenants named are Hirard, Robert, Radulph, Roger, and
Walter, and there were four radmen, a priest, fourteen
villeins, six *bordarii,* and two neat-herds. Part of the
hundred was waste. Edward also had in this hundred
Penwortham (*Peneverdant*), where for two carucates of
land 10d. was paid, and it is briefly recorded that there
was a castle there (see p. 47).

In Salford Hundred the manor of Salford belonged to
Edward, and in his time it consisted of three hides and
twelve carucates of waste land, a forest over 4 miles
long and the same breadth ; the Confessor also owned
at Radcliffe a manor containing one hide of land. To
Salford Hundred belonged twenty-one berewicks, which
were held as manors by as many Thanes, whose land was
put down as eleven and a half hides and ten and a half
carucates ; the woods were said to be over 12 miles in
length. The only thane named is Gamel, who held
Rochdale (see p. 47). Two churches are mentioned,
St. Mary's and St. Michael's, both as holding land in
Mamecestre, this being the only mention of this great
city of the North. The whole of the hundred paid
£37 4s.

Certain land of this hundred had been given by Roger
de Poictou to the following knights : Nigel, Warin, another
Warin, Goisfrid and Gamel.[2] Living on these lands were
three thanes, thirty villeins, nine *bordarii,* one priest, and
ten serfs.

In the six hundreds of Derby, Newton, Warrington,

---

[1] This will serve as a proof that *foresta* (= a wood or forest) was not
necessarily a dense mass of trees, but rather a place where game of
every kind abounded.

[2] Their individual holdings are 3 hides and half a carucate, 2 carucates, 1½ carucates, 1 carucate and 2 carucates = 3 hides and 7 carucates. Their united holding is put down as 22 carucates, so that a
hide in this case equals 5 carucates.

Blackburn, Salford, and Leyland there were 180 manors, in which were 79 hides rateable to the danegeld. In King Edward's time the whole was worth £145 2s. 2d. At the taking of the Survey it was held by William the Conqueror, and he appears to have granted certain lands in fee to nine knights.

Amounderness had also been part of the estate of Roger de Poictou, and had been held by Earl Tosti, who at Preston had six carucates of land rateable to the geld, along with which he had the following vills in the hundred: Ashton, Lea, Salwick, Clifton, Newton-with-Seales, Freckleton, Ribby-with-Wray, Kirkham, Treales, Westby, Little Plumpton, Weeton, Preise, Warton, Lytham, Marton (in Poulton), Layton-with-Warbrick, Staining, Carleton, Bispham, Rossall, Brining, Thornton, Poulton in the Fylde, Singleton, Greenhalgh, Eccleston, Eccleston (Great and Little), Elswick, Inskip, Sowerby, Nateby, St. Michael's-le-Wyre (*Michelscherche*), Catterall, Claughton, Newsham, Great Plumpton, Broughton, Whittingham, Barton (in Preston), Goosnargh, Haighton, Wheatley, Chipping, Alston, Fishwick, Grimsargh, Ribchester, Billsborough, Swainsett, Forton, Chrimbles, Garstang, Rawcliffe (Upper, Middle, and Out), Hambleton, Stalmine, Preesall, Mythorp or Mythop.

There were, then, in this hundred sixty-two vills or manors, in sixteen of which the Survey reports there were "but few inhabitants, but how many there are is unknown," and the rest were waste. There were three churches then in existence; the names of these are not given, but they undoubtedly were Preston, St. Michael's, and Kirkham. Other churches there probably had been, but they had shared in the general ruin (see Chapter V.).

The names of places thus supplied give some clue to the early history of the district. Out of sixty-two vills, over one-third are "tons"; there are also found the

Anglo-Saxon and the Danish equivalent in the "bys" and "hams." But the most significant fact recorded by the Survey is that out of sixty-two settlements all except sixteen were deserted and the land lying waste; this must be accounted for by the ravages of constant intestine wars and revolutions, which were accentuated by the downfall of Roger de Poictou.

The Lancashire part of Lonsdale is not in the Survey found alone, but is mixed up with portions of Westmorland, Cumberland, and Yorkshire; the same proprietors appear as in Amounderness, Roger de Poictou and the Earl Tosti. The places named are Halton, Aldcliff, Thornham, Millham, Lancaster, Church Lancaster (*Chercaloncastre*), Hutton, Newton, Overton, Middleton, Heaton, Heysham, Oxcliffe, Poulton-le-Sands, Torrisholme, Skerton, Bare, Slyne, Bolton, Kellet, Stapleton-Terne, Newsome, Carnforth—all these vills belonged to Halton; Whittington, Newton, Arkholme, Gressingham, Cantsfield, Ireby, Barrow Leck—these and several others not in Lancashire belonged to Whittington; Warton, Claughton, Wennington, Tatham, Farleton, and Tunstall,[1] Killerwick, Huncoat, Sowerby, Heaton, Dalton, Swarth, Newton, Walton, Leece, Santon, Roose, Hert, Glaston, Stainton, Cliverton, Orgreave,[2] Marton (or Martin), Pennington, Kirkby-Ireleth, Burrow, Bardsey, Willingham, Walney, Aldingham (in Furness), Ulverston, Ashton, and Urswick; Melling, Hornby, and Wennington, Cockerham, Ellet, Scotforth, Yealand-Conyers, and Berwick.

It would be interesting to know how much land in the entire county was at this time under some kind of cultivation, but owing to uncertainty as to the exact area included by several of the measurements given in the Survey, and the absence of details, any calculation based

[1] Bentham (in Yorkshire), Wennington, Tatham, and Tunstall are described as four manors, where there were three churches.
[2] Now Titeup.

upon them would at best be uncertain, and might be misleading. With some of the parishes, however, it is possible to come at something more reliable; in the parish of St. Michael's-on-Wyre, Domesday gives twenty carucates of land as rateable, the rest being waste; estimating a carucate[1] at 100 acres, we have 2,000 acres accounted for out of an area of 18,888 acres; upon the same basis, Kirkham, with 31,000 acres, had a little over 5,000 acres under culture; whilst Garstang, out of 28,881, has only 1,400 acres.[2]

The amount of land usually held with these vills varied from two or three hides to half a carucate, the general figure being one or two carucates, so that it is quite clear that all over the county the great bulk of the land was waste.

One of the immediate effects of the completion of the Conquest was the introduction into England of Norman feudalism. By this system the whole country (except what was given to the Church) was handed over to tenants in chief or great vassals, who held their lands in fee and in perpetuity direct from the Crown, in return rendering what was known as knight's service, every estate of £20 a year being considered a knight's fee, and liable to furnish for the King one mounted soldier; the vassals or under-tenants òf these barons, or *tenants in capite*, were bound by an oath of allegiance not only to the King, but also to the owner of the fee. These sub-tenants would in many cases consist of such of the Saxon settlers as had not been expelled by the Norman ruler; doubtless many of the great Saxon Thanes on losing their land were expelled from or of their own will left the country. A detailed account of the various changes in the ownership

---

[1] Authorities differ on the exact area, but probably the above is not far from the figure.

[2] Fishwick's " History of St. Michael's-on-Wyre," *Chetham Soc.*, xxv. 3 (new series).

of the soil would here be out of place, but it should be noticed that all the land in private holdings shortly after the Conquest passed into fresh hands—that is, as far as regards the tenure in fee direct from the Crown. After the final defection and consequent banishment of Roger de Poictou in 2 Henry I. (1101-2), West Derby Hundred went to the King, and remained in royal hands until Stephen granted it to Henry, Duke of Normandy; Leyland passed to King John (1199-1200); Blackburn had been bestowed by the Conqueror on Ilbert de Lacy, who came over with him from Normandy; Salford passed through several hands to the Earl of Chester; Amounderness went to the Crown, and was by Henry I. or Stephen presented to Theobald Walter, son of Herveus, another Norman chief, but in 17 John (1215-16) it again fell to the Crown, and was granted to Edmund Crouchback, Earl of Lancaster; and in Lonsdale we find that in 1126 Stephen, Earl of Bologne (before he became King), made over a large portion of the northern part to the monks of Furness, but the history of the early grantees of this district is not very clear. From these few chief lords were granted out various manors subject to rent, suit, and service, some portions in each district being retained in the King's possession.

In the case of the transfer of the honour of Lancaster to Edmund Crouchback, it appears that the King had previously granted the custody of the county of Lancaster to Roger de Lancaster, to whom, therefore, letters patent were addressed, promising to indemnify him.[1]

The close of the twelfth and the beginning of the thirteenth century witnessed a considerable increase in

---

[1] Honour of Lancaster granted to him June 30, 1267, and letters patent issued to the tenants of the honour to do their homage and be obedient to him as their lord, February 16, 1268. In 1269 a similar letter was sent to William le Boteler, and in 1270 to Henry de Lacy, Robert de Stockfort, and the Abbot of Furness.

the population of the county, and the consequent advance in the importance of its now growing towns. Lancaster in 1199 had become a borough, having granted to it the same liberties as the burgesses of Northampton. Preston, a little before this, had been by royal charter created a free borough, in which the burgesses were empowered to have a free guild merchant, and exemption from tolls, together with many other privileges that King John confirmed in 1199, and granting the additional right to hold a fair of eight days' duration. Cartmel is reputed to have had its market before the time of Richard I. (A.D. 1189-1199). King John in 1205 granted to Roger de Lacy the right to hold a fair at Clitheroe,[1] and also, in 1207, gave to the burgesses in the town of Liverpool all the liberties and customs usually enjoyed by free boroughs on the sea-coast. Henry III. granted further charters to both Preston and Liverpool in 1227.

In or about the year 1230, Randle de Blundeville, Earl of Chester and Lincoln, granted that the town of Salford should be a free borough, and that the burgesses, amongst other privileges, should each have an acre of land to his burgage, the rent for which was to be 3d. at Christmas, and a like sum at Mid-Lent, the Feast of St. John Baptist and the Feast of St. Michaels. The barony of Manchester was at this time in the hands of the Greslet family, one of whom, in 1301, gave a somewhat similar grant to Manchester, save that the clause providing the acre of land was omitted. From these two charters several items may be extracted, as showing the position of burgesses in those days, and their relation to the lord of the barony or manor. At Salford, no burgess was to bake bread for sale except at the oven provided by the lord, and a certain proportion of his corn was to be ground at the manorial mill. The burgesses were to have common

---

[1] Charters of duchy. See 31st Report of the Deputy-Keeper of the Public Records, p. 6.

free pasture in wood or plain, in all pasture belonging to the town of Salford, and not be liable to pay pannage;[1] they were also allowed to cut and use timber for building and burning.

A burgess dying was at liberty to leave his burgage and chattels to whomsoever he pleased, reserving to the lord the customary fee of 4d. On the death of a burgess, his heir was to find the lord a sword, or a bow, or a spear.

The burgesses of Manchester were to pay 12d. a year in lieu of all service. In both charters power is given to the burgesses to elect a reeve from amongst themselves. The social difference between the free burgess and the *villein* is pointedly referred to in a clause which provides that "if any villein shall make claim of anything belonging to a burgess, he ought not to make answer to him unless he shall have the suit from burgesses or other lawful [or law worthy?] men."

In Lonsdale, the monks of Furness obtained a charter dated July 20, 1246, authorizing the holding of an annual fair at Dalton, where a market had previously been established. Edmund de Lacy, in 25 Henry III. (A.D. 1240-41), obtained a royal charter for a market and fair at Rochdale, and a little later (in 1246) Wigan became a free borough, with right to hold a guild. Warrington,[2] Ormskirk, Bolton-le-Moors, and Burnley, had each its established market before the close of the century; whilst on the north of the Ribble we find that Kirkham, which had as early as 54 Henry III. (1269-70) obtained a royal charter for both a fair and a market, was in 1296 made into a free borough with a free guild, the burgesses having the right to elect bailiffs, who were to be presented and sworn: this right subsequently fell into disuse. At Garstang, very early in the next century, the abbots of

---

[1] Toll for swine feeding in the woods.
[2] A fair in 1255.

Cockersand were authorized to hold both a market and fair. Possibly some few other towns may have received similar privileges, and the record thereof been lòst; but we have clear evidence that before the end of the reign of Edward I. (A.D. 1307) there were not far short of a score of Lancashire market towns, each of which doubtless formed the centre of a not inconsiderable number of inhabitants, some of whom were free men, whilst others were little better than villeins or serfs, their condition varying somewhat in the different manorial holdings into which the district was divided.

Churches and monasteries had sprung up (see Chap. IX.), and a few castles probably kept watch over the insecure places. The houses, such as they were, timber being plentiful, were built of wood; the occupation of the people was chiefly agricultural, and in the forests were fed large herds of swine, the flesh of which formed a large portion of the food of the inhabitants; but in each of the towns there were small traders and artisans, among whom, in many cases, were formed trade or craft guilds. The power of the great barons appears now to have become somewhat less, and the land through various processes began to be more divided, and we find in the owners of the newly acquired tenures the ancestors of the gentry and yeomen of a later date.

The forests of Lancashire at this date were of immense extent; they may be enumerated as these: Lonsdale, Wyresdale, Quernmore, Amounderness, Bleasdale, Fullwood, Blackburnshire, Pendle, Trawden, Accrington, and Rossendale. The law respecting forests dates back to Saxon times; Canute, whilst he was King, issued a Charter and Constitution of Forests. By this charter verderers were to be appointed in every province in the kingdom, and under these were other officers known as regarders and foresters.

If any freeman offered violence to one of the verderers

he lost his freedom and all that he was possessed of, whilst for the same offence a villein had his right hand cut off, and for a second offence either a freeman or a villein was put to death. For chasing or killing any beast of the forest the penalties were at best very severe: the freeman for a first offence got off with a fine, but a bondsman was to lose his skin. Freemen were allowed to keep greyhounds, but unless they were kept at least ten miles from a royal forest their knees were to be cut.

King John, whilst Earl of Morton, held the prerogatives of the Lancashire forests, and he granted a charter (which, when he became King, he confirmed) to the knights and freeholders, whereby they were permitted to hunt and take foxes, hares and rabbits, and all kind of wild beasts except the stag, hind and roebuck, and wild hogs in all parts of his forests, beyond the demesne boundaries.

In the succeeding reign, however, the freemen were again troubled by the arbitrary and harsh treatment of the royal foresters, and in vain appealed to the King for relief. Edward I. to some extent relaxed the rigour of the laws, but still assizes of forests were regularly held at Lancaster, and presentments made for killing and taking deer, and the like offences, but the penalties were not nearly so severe as formerly.

Many cases might be quoted. At the forest assize at Lancaster on the Monday after Easter in 1286, Adam de Carlton, Roger the son of Roger of Midde Routhelyne, and Richard his brother, were charged with having killed three stags in the moss of Pelyn (Pilling in Garstang), which was part of the royal forest of Wyresdale.[1] About the same date, Nicholas de Werdhyll having slain a fat buck in the forest of Rochdale,[2] the keepers of the Earl of Lincoln's forest came by night, seized him, and dragged

---

[1] Carta de Foresta : Record Office.
[2] Rossendale Forest adjoins this parish.

him to Clitheroe Castle, where he was imprisoned until he paid a fine of four marks.[1]

Sometimes it was not the individual who was the offender, but the whole of the inhabitants. Thus, in 34 Edward III. (1360-61) a sum of 520 marks was levied upon the men and freeholders within the forest of Quernmore and the natives of Lonsdale, being their portion of a fine of £1,000 incurred for their trespass against the assize of the forest.[2] No doubt this was a convenient way of raising money.

The number of writs of pardon for trespasses against the forest laws, which are still preserved amongst the duchy records belonging to the thirteenth and fourteenth centuries, suggest that the offender had to purchase his pardon. The religious men, as they were called, and the clergy often had granted to them the right to hunt in the forests, as well as other privileges. As an example of the latter may be named the grant made in 1271 by Edmund Crouchback to the Prior and monks of St. Mary's of Lancaster, to the effect that they might for ever take from the forests in Lancaster,[3] except in Wyresdale, two cartloads of dead wood for their fuel every day in the year, and have free ingress and egress into the forest with one cart for two horses, or with two carts for four horses, to seek for and carry such wood away. Gradually, as the population increased, and as the personal interest of the Dukes of Lancaster in the forests themselves became less, many of these old forest laws fell gradually into disuse; but as late as 1697 a royal warrant was issued to the foresters and other officers of the forests, parks, and chases of Lancashire, calling upon them to give annually an account of all the King's deer within the same, and

[1] Plac. de Quo War., Edw. I. : Record Office.
[2] Duchy Chancery Rolls, chap. xxv., A 2^b.
[3] The honour of Lancaster.

also to report how many were slain, by whom, and by whose authority.

The regulations as to fishing in the rivers of the county were not so comprehensive as the forest laws; but the value of various fisheries was fully recognised, and they became a source of revenue. In 1359 Adam de Skyllicorne had a six years' lease of the fishing in the Ribble at Penwortham, with the demesne lands, for which he paid six marks a year, and in the succeeding year justices were assigned to inquire into the stoppages of the passages in the same river, by which the Duke's fishery of Penwortham was destroyed and ships impeded on their way to the port of Preston. Fishing in the sea as a trade also met with encouragement, for in A.D. 1382 a precept was issued to the Sheriff to publish the King's mandate, prohibiting any person in the duchy who held lands on the coast from preventing fishermen from setting their nets in the sea and catching fish for their livelihood; and in 13 Richard II. (1389-90) an Act was passed appointing a close time for salmon in the Lune, Wyre, Mersey and Ribble.

Notwithstanding that the fishing rights on both sides the Ribble had been leased or sold with the demesne lands, nearly 200 years later the King still claimed all manner of wrecks and fish royal which were cast upon the shore. On this point a suit in the duchy court appeared in 1536, in which the King's bailiff charged one Christopher Bone with having taken away sturgeon and porpoises which had been washed ashore at Warton, in the parish of Kirkham, whereas they of right belonged to his Majesty.[1] It may be noted that at this time the porpoise was considered " a dainty dish to set before the King."

The Normans did not, as has been frequently stated, introduce that dreadful disease, leprosy, into England, as there were hospitals set apart for leprosy at Ripon,

[1] See Fishwick's " History of Kirkham," *Chetham Soc.*, xcii.

Exeter, and Colchester some time before their advent. In the twelfth and thirteenth centuries leprosy was very prevalent in the northern parts of Lancashire; and to meet the requirements a hospital was founded at Preston in the time of Henry III. How the lepers who were not in the hospitals were dealt with we have no evidence to show, but that they were harshly, not to say cruelly, treated, and were in a measure outcasts, may be safely assumed.

Shortly before April 10, A.D. 1220, Henry III. addressed a letter to Hubert de Burgh, instructing him to order the Sheriff and forester of Lancaster to desist from annoying the lepers there;[1] and this not proving efficient, a royal writ was issued to the Sheriff (dated April 10) directing that officer to see that they were no longer molested by Roger Garnet and others, and that henceforth they were to have their beasts and herds in the forest without exaction of ox or cow, and also to be allowed to take wood for fuel and timber for building.

From this it appears clear that these lepers lived apart from the rest of the community, in houses or huts erected by themselves, and were not allowed to enter even a church; hence the use of what are known as leper windows, one of which still remains in the north chancel wall of Garstang Church. Leprosy continued with great severity for upwards of a couple of centuries, but towards the time of Henry VIII. it appears to have gradually decreased, and in the days of his immediate successor had almost died out.

The various Crusades of the twelfth century found many followers from Lancashire, and even when the Christians were fast losing their Asiatic possession it was thought worth while to appeal to this county for help, as we find, in June, 1291, the Archbishop of York instructing the Friars there to send three Friars to

[1] Royal Letters, Henry III., No. 185.

preach on behalf of the Crusades; one was to address
the people at or near Lancaster, another at some place
convenient for the Lonsdale inhabitants, and a third at
Preston, in such a locality as it was believed the greatest
congregation could be got together.[1]

The history of the wars between England and Scotland
is a page of the general history, but it will be necessary
here to state that in 1290 there were thirteen claimants
to the Scottish crown, and this led to the beginning of
the "Border warfare" between the people on the two
sides of the Solway Firth, the Cheviots and the Tweed.
Edward I., taking advantage of the position, put in a
claim to the Scottish throne, and afterwards took possession as suzerain of the disputed feudal holding.

In 1292 Baliol was appointed King of Scotland with
the consent of Edward I., to whom, however, homage
had to be done, and out of this right of appeal, thus
claimed by the King of England, arose that long series
of wars between the two kingdoms which began in the
early part of the year 1296, when Edward crossed the
Tweed with an army of 12,000 men.

These wars were a great tax upon Lancashire, as,
besides being subject to constant invasions, and bearing
its share of the subsidies, from it were drawn from time
to time large numbers of its bravest and best men. In
1297 Lancashire raised 3,000 men, and at the battle of
Falkirk, in the vanguard, led by Henry de Lacy, Earl of
Lincoln, there were 1,000 soldiers from this county.
Another 1,000 foot soldiers were raised in 1306, and this
constant drain continued for many years. After the
battle of Bannockburn in 1314, the victorious Bruce
besieged Carlisle, but after a long struggle he was obliged
to retire, the commander of the castle, Sir Andrew de
Harcla, as a recognition of his gallant services, receiving
from the King the custody of Cumberland, Westmorland

[1] "Letters from *Northern Register*," p. 97.

and Lancashire.[1] Within a very few years, on a charge
of treason, he was hung, drawn and quartered at Carlisle,
one of the pleas raised against him being that he had
allowed Bruce to pass into Cumberland and Lancashire,
where his army had plundered and marauded in every
direction; this was in July, 1322.

In the second half of this century we find several levies
made upon Lancashire for soldiers to march against the
Scots, but after this the county was not subjected to the
frequent invasions with which its inhabitants had been
too long familiar. The most serious of these invasions
was the one in July, 1322, and of the effects of this and
other raids we have an authentic record in the *Nonarum
Inquisitiones*, taken (for North Lancashire) in 15 Edward III.
(A.D. 1341). The commission appointed to levy this tax
on the corn, wool, lambs, and other tithable commodities
and glebe lands, were specially instructed to ascertain the
value in 1292 (Pope Nicholas' Taxation), and the then
value, and where there was a material difference between
the two, they were to ascertain the reason of such increase
or decrease. They reported that at Lancaster much of
the land was now sterile and uncultivated through the
invasions of the Scots, that Ribchester and Preston
had almost been destroyed by them, and that at the
following places the value of the tithes was very seriously
reduced through the same agency, viz., Cockerham,
Halton, Tunstall, Melling, Tatham, Claughton, Walton,
Whytington, Dalton, Ulverston, Aldingham, Urswick,
Pennington, Cartmel, Kirkham, St. Michael's-on-Wyre,
Lytham, Garstang, Poulton, Ribchester and Chipping;
except the two latter, all these are in Amounderness, and
north of the Ribble; into none of the other parts of the
county do the Scots appear to have penetrated. In
some cases the reduction amounted to something like
fifty per cent.; in fact, the invaders must have set fire to

[1] See "Popular History of Cumberland," p. 231.

buildings and laid waste the land all along their line of
march.

Clitheroe Castle, though perhaps never a very extensive
fortification, is one of the oldest foundations in the county,
probably dating back to Saxon times. It stands in a commanding situation on the summit of a rock rising out of
the plain, about a mile from Pendle Hill; in Domesday
Book it is described as the Castle of Roger (Roger de
Lacy). Of the original building nothing is now left but
the keep, a square tower of small dimensions. The honour
dependent upon this castle extended over a very large
area, part only of which is in Lancashire; it included
Whalley, Blackburn, Chipping, Ribchester, Tottington
(in Salford Hundred), and Rochdale, and consequently
the manors of all these places were at one time held
of the castle of Clitheroe. Henry de Lacy, second Earl
of Lincoln and great-grandson of Roger de Lacy, was
born in 1250, and, like his ancestor, he made this castle
his Lancashire stronghold and residence, and here each
year his tenants and the stewards of the various manors
attended his courts to render in their accounts and offer
the suit and service required. The town of Clitheroe
must, on the occasions when the Earl was at the castle,
have put on a festive appearance, as the lord of the
honour is said to have assumed an almost regal state.
Several of the accounts of the stewards, parkers, and
other servants of the Earl have fortunately been preserved, and we are by them enabled to get a glimpse at
the social life of the Lancashire people between the years
1295 and 1305.[1] We find that, besides the forests of
Pendle, Accrington, Rossendale and Trawden, there were
parks at Ightenhill and Musbury, well stocked with deer.
There were over twenty vaccaries, or breeding farms, all
of which added to the Earl's income. On the estates

[1] The original rolls are in the Record Office. They have been
printed by the Chetham Society, vol. cxii.

were iron forges, and iron smelting was practised, and of course coal was dug up from the seams lying near the surface.

The following extracts from these rolls will serve to illustrate the historical value of the details furnished.[1] Full allowance must be made by the reader for the difference in value of money between the thirteenth and the nineteenth centuries;[2] and it must be remembered that labourers in addition to their wages generally received rations, and were sometimes housed.

	£	s.	d.
82½ stone of cheese and 27½ stone of butter - -	2	10	2
2 wagons, etc., and 2 axes - - - -	0	3	9½
Food and wages for a man leading the wagons and cart during one year, and carrying hay and fencing -	1	5	5½
Mowing 11½ acres of meadow - - - -	0	5	9
Threshing and winnowing 53 quarters - - -	0	3	10½
Rebuilding and roofing a house - - - -	0	19	0¾
Rent of Colne and Walfred Mill, less tithe - -	12	16	0
„ „ fulling Mill - - - -	1	13	4½
80 cattle of the Abbot of Whalley agisted[3] in Rossendale Forest - - - - - -	0	13	4
A forge for iron, framed out in Rossendale[4] - -	3	0	0
Tolls of fairs, markets, and stallage at Rochdale (1 year)	2	13	8
Old brushwood for a forge (for 13 weeks) - -	0	13	0
Winter herbage on Pendle Hill - -	2	13	0
Summer herbage there - · - - -	2	5	0
17 ash-trees - - - - - -	0	10	0

[1] All the extracts refer to the Lancashire part of the honour, and to the years between 1295 and 1305.

[2] Authorities differ on this point, but all agree that money in the thirteenth century was worth many times its present equivalent coin. At the very least, it requires to be multiplied by ten.

[3] *Agisted* = allowed to graze in the forest.

[4] In 1338 the Abbot of Whalley charged certain persons armed "with swords and bows and arrows" with having taken away his goods, and, *inter alia*, 300 pieces of iron, and from the evidence adduced it appears that near Whitworth (in Rochdale parish), which is adjoining Rossendale, the Abbot and others were accustomed to dig up the ironstone and smelt it. (See Fishwick's " History of Rochdale," p. 84.)

	£	s.	d.
A stray mare - - - - - -	0	3	0
80 wild boars - - - - - -	3	6	1
Rent of Burnley Mill (deducting tithe) - - -	10	0	0
Fishery of Northmeols - - - - -	1	6	8
Rent (in lieu of ½ lb. of pepper) - - - -	0	0	6
„ („ „ one pair of gloves) - - -	0	0	1½
„ 52 acres 1 rood of land at Accrington - -	1	11	9
Accrington Hall, Kitchen and Grange (rent) - -	0	4	0
3 vaccaries at Accrington (rent) - - -	5	3	1½
Brushwood and ore sold to a forge at Accrington for 27			
weeks - - - - - - -	1	14	6
Herbage of Clitherow Castle ditches - -	0	1	6
„ „ the garden and loft adjoining -	0	3	0
Toll of the Fair and Market of Clitheroe - -	8	0	6
Produce of 27 vaccaries let out - - -	81	0	0
Goods of Elias Thayn, a felon beheaded - -	6	10	0
Haymaking a three-acre meadow - - -	0	2	4½
Wages of the parker of Ightenhill Forest - -	2	5	6
The Abbot of Salley for finding a lamp for the soul of			
Earl John [de Lacy] - - - - -	0	6	8
Fulling Mill at Burnley, built anew - -	2	12	6½
For merchat[1] of 2 women - - - -	0	13	4
3 oxen - - - - - - -	1	16	0
Hides of 9 mares, 2 foals of the 3rd year, and 7 foals of			
the 2nd year - - - - - -	0	4	9
4 quarters of oates - - - - -	0	9	0
Mowing 60½ acres of meadow - - -	0	17	7¾
Making and stacking the hay - - -	0	12	7
Reaping, gathering and binding 16 acres of oats -	0	6	10½
Making anew 2 waggons - - - -	0	2	8
Food and wages of one harrower in seedtime -	0	3	4
Wages of 109 men reaping corn as if on one day -	0	17	7½
Wheat sold, 1 qr. 5 bus. - - - -	0	13	9
213 oxen sold - - - - -	105	13	2
168 cows, 5 bulls and 2 calves sold - -	67	8	4
Wages for the porter of Clitheroe Castle ½ a year -	1	2	9
2 pairs of gloves and 1 pair of spurs (for rent) -	0	0	5

[1] *Merchats* = fines paid to the lord for marriage of a daughter. The above sum was the sum returned to the tenant because it was found that the women were not daughters of villeins.

	£	s.	d.
Iron ore (in Clivacher) for 10 weeks (sold) - -	o	6	8
Expenses of 16 hawks at Clitheroe, and of grooms carrying them to London, with cocks bought for them -	1	o	5½
Carrying the Earl's bed to Denbigh - - -	o	1	8
Making and planting nine hundred five score and six perches of paling round Musbury Park, with the carriage of the said palings in part from Tollington Wood - - - - - - -	60	10	5¼
18 oxen bought for the carriage of the paling - -	8	17	9
91 loads 6½ dishes of ore bought of the miners : 9 dishes make a load ; price per load, 22d. - - -	8	8	1½
9½ fothers 7 pieces 1 stone of lead brought from the same (of which 6 stone make a piece, and 25 pieces make a fother) - - - - - -	13	13	3
Cutting down and cutting up wood for burning the said ore - - - - - - -	o	7	5
Making a pair of bellows anew for burning the said ore	o	7	8
Making and binding with iron a pair of scales for weighing the lead, and making other necessary utensils -	o	2	6
Making a shed for the lead and an enclosure for the ore	o	5	8

From these references to smelting of lead it is quite clear that the operation was being performed here for the first time—probably as an experiment; but where did the ore come from? A reference is made to carrying ore from Baxenden (near Accrington) to Bradford (in Salford), but there is no evidence that lead was ever worked or discovered there, so probably the ore was imported from some lead-mining district.

Sea-coal (*carbones maris*) is thrice mentioned as being paid for in the Cliviger and Colne district, where it had no doubt been dug up.

The Compotus of the Earl of Lincoln contains many details referring to the various vaccaries in his holding; each of these was looked after by an *instaurator*, or bailiff, who lived generally at the Grange, whilst his various assistants occupied the humbler " booths." Accrington vaccary may be accepted as a sample; there were there when the stock was taken on January 26, 1297, 106 cows, 3 bulls, 24 steers, 24 heifers, 31 yearlings, and 46 calves.

In this, as in all the other vaccaries, many cattle died from murrain, and some fell victims to the wolves which infested all the forests.

Toward the end of the year 1349 Lancashire was visited with the pestilence known as the Black Death, which about this time broke out again and again in almost every part of the civilized world. By a fortunate accident a record of the dreadful ravages made by this disease in the Hundred of Amounderness has been preserved.

It appears that the Archdeacon of Richmond (in whose jurisdiction was the whole of Lancashire north of the Ribble) and Adam de Kirkham, Dean of Amounderness, his Proctor, had a dispute relative to the fees for the probate of wills and the administration of the effects of persons dying intestate; the matter was referred to a jury of laymen, whose report furnishes a return of the number of deaths from the plague, and other details which may be accepted as at all events fairly correct, although the district must have been at the time in such a state of panic as to render the collection of statistical facts extremely difficult.

In ten parishes in Amounderness, 13,180 died between September 8, 1349, and January 11, 1349-50, and nine benefices were vacant in consequence. The chapel of the hospital of St. Mary Magdalen at Preston was without a priest for eight weeks, and in that town 3,000 men and women perished; of these, 300 had goods worth £5, and left wills, but 200 others with the like property made no wills. At Poulton-le-Fylde the deaths amounted to 800; at Lancaster 3,000 died, at Garstang 2,000, and at Kirkham 3,000, whilst the other less thickly populated places each lost more or less of its inhabitants.[1] How the rest of

[1] Treasury Receipts, ²¹ᵃ⁄₃ Record Office; also *English Hist. Review*, 1890.

Lancashire fared under this dreadful visitation is uncertain, but Manchester and a few other places in the south of the county are said to have suffered very heavily.

We have already seen that Edmund Crouchback, the favourite son of the King, had given to him the honour of Lancaster, which was confirmed by Henry III., who granted (in 1267) to him the castle of Kenilworth, the castle and manor of Monmouth, and other territories in various parts of the kingdom. The founder of the house of Lancaster died at Bayonne in May, 1296, and Thomas, his eldest son, succeeded to his vast possessions in Lancashire and elsewhere; and in 1297-98 he passed through the county in company with his royal master on his way to Scotland; in 1310 he married Alice, the sole daughter of Henry de Lacy, Earl of Lincoln, and then got possession of the great estates in the county which had for several generations belonged to the De Lacy family.

In 1316-17 one of the followers of the Earl of Lancaster, in order, it is said, to ingratiate himself with the King, invaded some of the possessions of the Earl, and the result was a pitched battle, which took place near Preston, in which Banastre and his army were completely defeated.

The subsequent quarrel between this celebrated Earl of Lancaster and the King is well known, and need not be repeated here; finding himself unable to meet the royal forces, he retired to his castle at Pontefract, where he was ultimately retained as a prisoner, and near to which town, after suffering great indignities and insults, he was executed as a traitor, March 22, 1321-22. Thomas, Earl of Lancaster, was succeeded by Henry his brother, who, on the reversion of the attainder of the latter, had granted to him, in A.D. 1327, the issues and arrearages of the lands, etc., which had belonged to the earldom of

Lancaster and Leicester. On the death of Henry, Earl of Lancaster, the title went to his son Henry (called Grismond), who became Earl of Lancaster, Derby, and Lincoln, and was, as a crowning honour, for his distinguished military services, created in 1353 the first Duke of Lancaster, for his life, having his title confirmed by the prelates and peers assembled in Parliament at Westminster. He was empowered to hold a chancery court for Lancaster, and to issue writs there under his own seal, and to enjoy the same liberties and regalities as belonged to a county palatine,[1] in as ample manner as the Earl of Chester had within that county. Henry, who for his deeds of piety was styled "the Good Duke of Lancaster," obtained a license to go to Syracuse to fight against the infidels there ; but being taken prisoner in Germany, he only regained his liberty by the payment of a heavy fine. Towards the close of his life he lived in great state in his palace of Savoy, and became a great patron to several religious houses, one of which was Whalley Abbey (see Chapter IX.). He died March 24, 1360-61, leaving two daughters, one of whom (Blanch) was married to John of Gaunt, Earl of Richmond, fourth son of Edward III. ; and to her he bequeathed his Lancashire possessions, and on the death of her sister Maud, the widow of the Duke of Bavaria, in A.D. 1362, without issue, she became entitled to the remainder of the vast estates of her late father.

After the death of the Duchess of Bavaria, John of Gaunt was declared by Parliament to be Duke of Lancaster in the right of his wife—to have and to hold the title and honour to him and his lawful heirs male for ever.

John of Gaunt was born at Ghent, in Flanders (hence his surname), in March, 1340. In A.D. 1369 he was sent over to France with a considerable force, but owing to

---

[1] Lancashire is said to have enjoyed the privilege of a palatinate in the time of Roger de Poictou, but the evidence is not convincing.

sickness in his camp he returned to England, to find that his wife had during his absence died of the plague, and been buried in great state in Westminster Abbey. In 51 Edward III. (1377), a grant of a chancery in his dukedom and all the rights appertaining to a county palatine was made to him; and he was ordered to send (when required) two knights to Parliament "for the commonality," two burgesses for every borough in the said county. Previous to this John of Gaunt had taken to himself a second wife—Constance, one of the daughters and heiresses of Peter the Cruel, King of Castile and Leon, whose arms he impaled with his ducal coat; his attempt by force of arms to obtain a right to the kingly title, however, failed. The life of the illustrious Duke of Lancaster is written in the pages of English history: his many military exploits, his bold bearing in opposing the bishops in the Wickliffe case, the many offices which he held under the King, his unpopularity at the time of the insurrection of Wat Tyler, his doings in Scotland and in Spain, are all incidents in the career of one whose name must for ever be remembered in the county where he held such power.

For his duchy he obtained in 13 Richard II. (1390) a right to have an exchequer in the county, with barons and officers appertaining thereunto, and also the right to appoint justices itinerant for the pleas of the forests.

John, named Plantagenet King of Castile and Leon, Duke of Lancaster, Earl of Leicester, Lincoln and Derby, Lieutenant of the King in Aquitaine, and High Steward of England,[1] died in the year 1399.

Under this Duke, Lancaster Castle was partly rebuilt, and a considerable portion of the gateway tower (which still bears his name) added.

Henry Bolingbroke, who was now Duke of Hereford, was the next heir to the dukedom, but as he was in exile

[1] So described on his tomb in Westminster Abbey.

for his supposed treason, the King (Richard II.) seized the possessions of the late John of Gaunt, and shortly afterwards proceeded to Ireland, where he learnt that during his absence Bolingbroke had returned to England, and that the whole kingdom had received him with open arms. The King's flight to Wales, his surrender, first of his person and then of his throne, followed in rapid succession, and on September 29, 1399, the head of the House of Lancaster became King of England under the title of Henry IV.

It must be remembered that the County Palatine and Duchy of Lancaster are not identical, as the latter comprises many places which are not in Lancashire, but are scattered over fourteen counties in England and Wales. The Duchy of Lancaster was held by Henry IV. as heir to his father, but his right to the Crown of England was by no means of such an indefeasible character. To remedy this defect, the King obtained several Acts of Parliament, declaring that neither the inheritance of his Duchy of Lancaster nor its liberties should be affected in consequence of his having assumed the royal dignity ; also that all ecclesiastical benefices in the county should be conferred by himself or his heirs ; that the right of succession to the duchy after his death should belong to his eldest son, Henry, Prince of Wales, and his heirs, or, in default of such heirs, to his second son, Thomas.[1] He also established the duchy court of Lancaster, which was held at Westminster.[2] The county also held its Star Chamber, the decrees of which were certainly not in accordance with the provisions of Magna Charta. This court, with others of the same character, was abolished in 1640-41 by Act of Parliament. Henry V., who succeeded to the dukedom, confirmed all that his father had done respecting the duchy. Henry VI., being pressed for

[1] Baines' " History of Lancashire," i. 45 (second edition).
[2] The records of this court are preserved in the Record Office.

money, mortgaged the revenues of his duchies of Lancaster and Cornwall for a term of five years, and on their reverting to the Crown in 1460-61, several new officers were appointed—amongst others, a chancellor, a receiver-general, an attorney-general for the duchy, and one for the county palatine.[1]

In 1461 Edward IV. obtained an Act of Parliament " for incorporating and also for confiscating the Duchy of Lancaster to the Crown of England for ever," and since then the ruling monarch has held the duchy with all its liberties and privileges. In the time of Philip and Mary, in an Act for enlarging the duchy, it is styled " one of the most Princeliest and Stateliest peeces of our Sovereigne Ladie, the Queenes, auncyent inheritance."

From the time of the creation of the palatinate, all justices of assize, of gaol-delivery, and of the peace, have been made under the seal of the county palatine, as are also the sheriffs for the county ; an almost complete list of the latter from A.D. 1156 to the present time has been preserved.[2]

One of the privileges of a county palatine was that none of its inhabitants could be summoned out of their own county except for certain offences. This exemption, it appears, was not always observed, and its non-observance led to several serious riots, and resulted in the passing of an Act of Parliament in A.D. 1449, which declared that anyone making a distress where he had no " fee, seigniory or cause " in the Duchy of Lancaster should be treated as a felon. Another Act passed in 1453 directed

---

[1] In 1850 the revenue account of the duchy shows a very long list of estates in many counties. One half of the whole yearly income was, however, derived from Salford, the largest rent being £285 for land in Pendleton. The Corporation of Salford still pay in lieu of tolls a fixed rent of £5 a year. In 1850 the payments from the duchy to the Queen amounted to £12,000, which in 1893 had increased to £48,000.

[2] See Baines' " History of Lancashire," i. 57 (second edition).

that, if a person was outlawed in Lancashire, only his goods and lands in that county were to be forfeited ; this law was, however, repealed two years afterwards.

The population of Lancashire shortly before the Black Death in 1349 was no doubt very much greater than it was for many years subsequently, notwithstanding the very heavy levies made upon it for the various wars in which the three Edwards were engaged. For the war in Wales, in 1282, the Sheriff of Lancashire was instructed to call upon every person owning land or rents worth £30 a year to provide a horse and armour and to join the royal forces ; whilst William le Boteler, of Warrington, was ordered to meet the King at Worcester, and with the assistance of others he was to raise in Lancashire 1,000 strong and able men to serve in the Welsh war. Amongst the accounts of this campaign we find an entry referring to this : "To Master William le Boteler for the wages of one constable, two hundred and six archers, with ten captains of twenties, from Saturday, January 16 [1283], to Wednesday, the 27th of the same month, for twelve days, £22 4s."[1]

The Crusaders also had many followers from this county, whilst for the wars with France and Scotland writ followed writ in quick succession, all calling for men and arms. And again in the fifteenth century the drain continued to be heavy, and culminated with the War of the Roses, which began in 1455. None of the battles between the Houses of York and Lancaster were fought within this county, but during the struggle Lancashire must have sent some of her bravest sons to perish in that ignoble strife between the roses red and white.

It should also be noted that in 1422 a second visitation of the plague appeared in the north of Lancashire, which, though not so widespread as it was in 1349, appears to have been quite as deadly, for on June 24, 1422, a precept

[1] Meyrick's "Ancient Armour," i. 137.

was sent to the Sheriff to make proclamation in all the market towns and elsewhere within the county, that the sessions fixed to be held at Lancaster on Tuesday, the morrow of St. Lawrence, would be adjourned to Preston, because the King had heard both by vulgar report and the credible testimony of honest men, that in certain parts of Lancashire, and especially in the town of Lancaster, there was raging so great a mortality that a large portion of the people there, from the corrupt and pestiferous air, infected with divers infirmities and deadly diseases, were dying rapidly, and the survivors quitting the place from dread of death, so that in many cases the land remained untilled, and the most grievous desolation reigned where late was plenty.[1]

The Parliamentary representation of Lancashire began in the thirteenth century. Previous to this the King had three times a year called together his Council, consisting of the barons, the heads of the Church, and the military chief tenants of the Crown; but in 1213 King John directed the sheriffs of counties to send four men of each shire to confer with him on national affairs.[2] In 1254 the number was reduced to two for each county; in 1261 Henry III. summoned three, which was shortly afterwards again reduced to two. In 1265 Simon de Montford, Earl of Leicester, in the King's name summoned to Westminster two knights from each shire and two burgesses from each town. The exact character of these meetings is unknown, as is the method of the selections of the knights of the shire; but in 1290 they were formally summoned to Parliament, and in 1294 became a necessary part of the national council chamber.

From the earliest returns extant, we find that Lancashire only sent two knights to Parliament. The first Lancashire returns extant are for the Parliament of 1259,

[1] Report of Deputy-Keeper of Public Records, xxxiii. 21.
[2] Stubbs's "Select Charters," p. 40.

6

when the county was represented by Mathew de Redman
(who a year before had been the Member for Cumberland)
and John de Evyas, the lord of the manor of Samlesbury,
in the parish of Blackburn.   For 1296 there are no
returns, but in the following year the knights of the shire
were Henry de Kighley (probably one of the ancestors of
the Kighley of Inskip, in St. Michael's-on-Wyre) and
Henry de Boteler, eldest son of William de Boteler,
Baron of Warrington.   From this time to the present a
fairly complete list has been preserved.[1]   To the Parliament of 1295 were also summoned two burgesses from the
boroughs of Lancaster, Preston, Wigan and Liverpool ;
and the Sheriff in making his returns volunteered the
statement that there was no city in the county.   The
first recorded members for these four enfranchised
boroughs were, respectively, for Lancaster, William le
Despencer and William le Chaunter ; Preston, William
FitzPaul and Adam Russell ; Wigan, William le
Teinterer and Henry le Bocher ; Liverpool, Adam Fitz-
Richards and Robert Pynklowe.   The sending of representatives to Westminster was at this time not always
looked upon as a coveted honour, but rather as a binding
obligation to be got rid of at the first opportunity.   True,
the members were paid for the whole time they were
absent from home, a knight getting four shillings a day,
and a burgess two shillings ; but this amount and the
long journey to and from London, with the danger and
difficulties to be encountered on the way, did not offer a
strong inducement for a burgess or a knight to leave his
own home for sometimes a considerable period.   The
fact that these early members were selected from a class
comprising the dispencer, the dyer, the butcher and the
"chaunter," shows that the title of " M.P." was rather at
a discount than a premium in this county, at all events.

[1] See "The Parliamentary Representation of Lancashire," by
W. J. Pink.

Lancaster and Preston sent members until 1331, and did not again do so until 21 Henry VIII. (1529). Liverpool and Wigan ceased to return to Parliament after 1307, and the privilege was not renewed until 1547; in the interval the Sheriff's returns were to the effect that there "was no city or burgh from which any citizen or burgess can be sent by reason of their low condition and poverty." From this practical disenfranchisement it may be inferred that after the visitation of the plague (see p. 74) the towns of Lancashire were slow to recover their former position, and that such trade as there had been in the early part of the fourteenth century had not returned.

It has been frequently stated that soon after the Act passed by Edward III. (in 1337), by which Flemish weavers and others were invited to settle in England, a large number of them came to Lancashire and established their trades in Bolton, Rochdale and other towns. This statement is not borne out by facts; the trade of these districts did not at, or soon after, this time rapidly develop, neither is there any marked influx of foreign names, such as would naturally have followed such an invasion,[1] and which are very noticeable in some of the more southern parts of the country. In Lancashire were found now, as in "The Vision of William concerning Piers Plowman," in 1362:

> Bakers, Bochers, and Breusters monye,
> Wollene websteris: and weveris of lynen,
> Taillours, tanneris, tolleres in marketes,
> Masons, minouis, and mony other craftes,
> Dykers and Delvers.

and "Cokes [cooks] and knaves crieden, 'hote pies hote.'" There were also drapers, needle-sellers, ropers, and various other traders, and ale-houses in plenty.

The food of the poorer classes consisted of cheese, curds, therf-cake (oat cake), beans, flavoured with leeks,

---

[1] See "History of Rochdale," p. 33.

parsley or cabbages, with occasionally a little bacon or pork, and less frequently fish. The more well-to-do classes fared much more sumptuously, as flesh, game and fish were all obtainable. Lancashire had yet no seaport of any great importance; the only two worth recording were Liverpool and Preston. In 1338 all the ports in the country were required to furnish ships according to their size and commerce. Liverpool could only send a single barque with a crew of six men, and 200 years later this port had only twelve vessels, carrying 177 tons and navigated by 75 men;[1] yet in 1382 the port was important enough to warrant the issue of a precept to the Mayor and Bailiffs of the town prohibiting them from exporting corn.[2]

The ships which went to the port of Preston in the middle of the fourteenth century (see p. 66) could not have been of large dimensions.

Though Liverpool as a town had not in the fifteenth century grown much in size or importance, yet its castle, seated upon the rocky knoll commanding the entrance to the Mersey, was of some importance; built probably in the time of the Conqueror, it had ever since been kept available for purposes of defence. In 1351 Henry, Duke of Lancaster, appointed Janekyn Baret, his esquire, to be Constable of Liverpool Castle, with an annuity of ten marks sterling for the term of his life, and in 22 Henry VI. (1442-43) the duchy receiver accounted for £46 13s. 10¼d. which had been expended on repairs to this castle; it was about this time that a new south-east tower was erected. During the reigns of Henry V. and Henry VI. considerable sums were spent in keeping this stronghold in repair, yet in a report made on its state in 1476 it is described as being in a somewhat ruinous condition; the east tower wanted repairing, for which

---

[1] Baines' "History of Lancashire," ii. 359 (second edition).
[2] Report of Deputy-Keeper of Public Records, xxxii. 354.

purpose the walls of the bakehouse were to be taken down, and the elder-trees growing on the walls within and without the castle were to be cut away.

In 1476 further repairs were done, but the object of these appears to have been rather of a domestic than military character. At this time three towers are named: the new tower, the prison tower, and the great tower.[1]

Besides the castles already mentioned, there were a few others of minor importance. Hornby Castle, in the parish of Melling, may possibly date back to the time of the Edwards, and is several times referred to in the thirteenth and fourteenth centuries. On the western side of the peninsula of Furness, which is separated from Cumberland by the waters of the Duddon, lies the Island of Walney, which has near to it several other small islands, on one of which was built the ancient castle or peel long known as the Pile of Fouldrey. The waters near to its site formed a natural harbour capable of floating, even at low tide, the largest vessels at that early period in use, and to protect that and the adjacent country this castle was erected. It is of great antiquity; it was certainly there in the twelfth century, as appears from a precept issued on March 13, 1404 to the escheator for the county to " amove the King's hands from the island called Wawenay [Walney], the cause of the seizure being insufficient." The reason why the King had taken possession is then clearly stated, viz.: " That King Stephen, having granted to the Abbot and Convent of the Monastery of St. Mary of Furness certain lands and tenements in the island called Wawenay [Walney] in Furness on condition of sustaining and keeping in repair a certain castle or fortress called La Pele de Fotheray for the defence of the country there, the said castle was now prostrated by

---

[1] See detailed account of the plan of this castle in *Lanc. and Ches. Hist. Soc.*, vol. vi., new series.

John de Bolton the Abbot and the Convent of Furness, to the great fear of all the country."[1]

It was here that Lambert Simnel, the pretended son of the Duke of Clarence, landed in 1487, and was joined by Sir Thomas Broughton. The subsequent history of this stronghold is very obscure; in 1588 it is described as an old decayed castle.

In the parish of Tunstall, Sir Thomas Tunstall, in the time of Henry IV., built Thurland Castle on a rising piece of ground between the Greta and the Cant.[2]

Of the religious houses and churches which had sprung up since the coming of the Normans, it need only here be stated that they had now spread all over the county, and that the Christian creed had become the religion of the entire community (see Chapter IX.).

The impending final struggle between the rival Houses of York and Lancaster would probably not excite any very great interest in the minds of the people of this county, except that they had again been called upon to find men for Lord Stanley's army, which the King had commissioned him to raise in the counties of Lancashire and Cheshire; this force is supposed to have been about 5,000 strong, and it virtually decided the battle, as Lord Stanley, on the field, turned against the King, and led his troops to the support of Richmond.

With the death of Richard III., the last Plantagenet King, on the field of Bosworth, came an end of that system of government which had existed for nearly 300 years, and the old feudal chain was soon to be broken, and Englishmen were to become more their own

---

[1] Record Office, Roll of Fines, etc., chap. xxv., A 7, No. 14; also Coucher Book of Furness.

[2] Turton Tower, near Bolton, claims to be a very ancient foundation, but as its name never occurs in the ancient charters heretofore discovered, it appears doubtful if it dates back beyond the fifteenth century. ¦

masters and less the blind followers of their social superiors; and, moreover, they were soon to find themselves free from the tyranny of priestcraft and superstitions, and prejudices were to be gradually dispersed by the increase of civilization and freedom.

Towards this end the introduction of printing was a powerful lever, for when John Caxton, in 1472, set up his press in London, the priest could no longer prevent the spread of knowledge, and it was not long before the printed books found their way into Lancashire.

With the spread of literature and knowledge came the spirit of adventure and enterprise, which soon raised the country to a position which it had not heretofore occupied.

CHAPTER VII.

LANCASHIRE IN THE TIME OF THE TUDORS
(A.D. 1485-1603).

A S soon as Henry VII. was firmly seated on the throne, he proceeded to reverse the attainders which his predecessor had passed against certain of the prominent adherents of the House of Lancaster, and at the same time confiscating the estates of (amongst others) Sir Thomas Pilkington, Lord Robert Harrington and Sir James Harrington, all of whom took part in the battle of Bosworth Field, and were natives of Lancashire, their properties were nearly all at once given to Lord Stanley, who was at the same time created Earl of Derby, and elected a member of the King's Privy Council. Not ten years after this, Sir William Stanley, brother of the Earl, became mixed up with the Perkin Warbeck rebellion, and notwithstanding the influence of the latter, he was arraigned upon a charge of high treason, and, being found guilty, was executed on February 15, 1495; his chief seat was at Holt Castle, in Denbighshire.

It seems strange that, in the same year that this tragedy was enacted, the King came in state to pay a visit to his mother, who was now the second wife of the Earl of Derby. To entertain their Majesties (for the Queen came also) with becoming dignity, the Earl spared no expense, even erecting a new bridge across the Mersey, near Warrington, for his special use, which bridge has since been used by the public. The expenses incurred by the royal journey from Chester to Knowsley were duly recorded, and are of interest:

July 18 [1495]. At Winwick, 20th at Latham: To Sir Richard Pole for 200 jucquetts, price of every pece, 1s. 6d., £15. 100 horsemen for fourteen days, every of them 9d. by day, £52 10s. For their conduyt for 3 days, every of them 9d. by day, £11 5s. For the wages of 100 footmen for fourteen days, every of them 6d. by day, £35. For their conduyt for four days, every of them 6d. by day, £10. For shipping, vitailling and setting over the see the foresaid 200 men, with an 100 horses, £13 6s. 8d. To the shirif awayting upon Sr Sampson for the safe conduyt of the foresaid souldeours, 2s.

Aug. 2. To Picard a herrald of Fraunce in reward, £6 13s. 4d. To the women that songe before the Kinge and the Queene in rewarde, 6s. 8d.

3rd. At Knowsley. 4th. At Warrington. 5. At Manchester.

Lancashire, in 1485, is said to have suffered considerably from the "sweating sickness" which was at this time very prevalent in many parts of the kingdom; but in the absence of contemporary notices of it it may be assumed not to have appeared here in its severest form.

Towards the £40,000 granted by the Parliament of 1504 to the King, Lancashire's share was a trifle over £318; and the commissioners appointed to collect it in the county were Thomas Botcler, John Bothe, Pears Lee, Richard Bold, John Sowthworth, and Thomas Lawrence, knights, and William Thornborough and Cuthbert Clifton, esquires.

We have now seen the close of the fifteenth century, which has been described as "a blustering, quarrelsome fellow, who lived in a house with strong barricades all round it, his walls pierced with narrow holes, through which he could shoot his visitors if he did not think they were approaching him in a friendly manner," and we are entering on the sixteenth century, which "improved a little on this, but still planted his house with turrets which commanded the entrance door, and had an immense gate studded with iron nails, and unsurmountable walls round his courtyard."

The days of building castles and strongly fortified houses was indeed over, but still everyone looked with some suspicion on his neighbour, and the old English saying,

> Let him keep who has the power,
> And let him take who can,

was not quite forgotten.

Of the class of fortified houses erected about this date, a good example is afforded by Greenhalgh Castle. By a royal license granted to Thomas, Earl of Derby, in 1490, he was authorized to erect in Greenhalgh (in the parish of Garstang) a building or buildings with stone or other materials, and to "embattle, turrellate or crenelate, machiolatte," or otherwise fortify the same ; authority was at the same time given to enclose a park, and to have in it free warren and chase. Camden says that the Earl built this to protect himself from certain of the nobility of the county whose estates had been forfeited to the Crown and bestowed upon himself. This account of the origin of this castle is probably correct.

The great religious changes in Lancashire, brought about by what has been called the anti-Papal revolt, and the subsequent Reformation, will be reserved for a future page (see Chapter IX.).

The old strife between England and Scotland had now again been renewed, and the conflict culminated in the battle of Flodden, where the Lancashire archers, led by Sir Edward Stanley, almost totally destroyed the Highlanders who composed the right wing of the Scottish army. The other Lancashire leaders were Sir William

Mollineux of Sefton, Sir William Norris of Speke, and Sir Ralph Ashton of Middleton.

No wonder that this decisive victory should become a favourite theme of the poet and the minstrel. There are several old poems referring to the Lancashire men and the field of Flodden; one of these, which is certainly 300 years old, has been printed by the Chetham Society;[1] it consists of nearly 700 lines, of which the following will serve as a sample :

> Lancashire, like lyons
>   layden them aboute !
> All had been lost by our Lorde !
>   had not these leddes [lads] bene.
> For the care of the Scottes
>   increased full sore
> For their King was downe knocked
>   and killed in their sight,
> Under the banner of a bishop
>   that was the bold Standley l
> Ther they fetilde[2] them to fly
>   As fast as they might.

Another long poem on the same subject is preserved in the Record Office ;[3] it gives also a glowing account of how the " lusty lads," led by the " lusty Stanley stout," went forth " in armour bold for battle drest," and how—

> From Warton unto Warrington,
> From Wigan unto Wiresdale,
> From Weddecon [Wedacre] to Waddington,
> From Ribchester to Rochdale,
> From Poulton to Preston, with pikes,
> They with Stanley out went forth.
> From Pemberton and Pilling dikes,
> For battle billmen bold were bent.

In Middleton Church there was a brass to the memory

---

[1] Vol. xxxvii.

[2] *To fettle* is an old Lancashire word.

[3] Harl. MSS., Cod. 3526. See Harland's " Ballads and Songs of Lancashire."

of Sir Ralph Assheton and his bowmen, and a painted window still remains to commemorate the event. Of the general state of some of the larger towns of the county, we have a brief record from the pen of that careful antiquary John Leland, who went through Lancashire in 1533. Manchester he says was "the fairest, best built, quickest [*i.e.*, liveliest] and most populous town in Lancashire; well set a worke in makinge of clothes as well of lynnen as of woollen, whereby they have obtained, gotten and come vnto riches and welthy lyuings, and have kepte and set manye artificers and poor folkes to work;" and in "consequence of their honesty and true dealing, many strangers, as wel of Ireland as of other places within this realme, have resorted to the said towne with lynnen yarne, woollen, and other wares for makinge clothes." So great a name had Manchester now got for the making of woollen cloth that in an Act passed in 1552 Manchester "rugs and frizes" are specially named; and in 1566 it became necessary to pass another Act to regulate the fees of the queen's *aulneger* (measurer), who was to have his deputies at Bolton, Blackburn and Bury. The duty of these officers was to prevent "cottons, frizes and rugs" being sold unsealed. Cottons were not what is now meant by this term, but were all of woollen.[1] Cotton manufacture did not begin until a century later. Manchester at this time probably consisted of some ten or a dozen narrow streets[2] and lanes, all radiating from the old church; its water was from a single spring rising in what is now Fountain Street, and which flowed down Market Street to Smithy Door. The town business was conducted in a building called the "Booths," where the court of the lord of the

[1] "Cottons" is probably a corruption of "coatings."

[2] Market stede Lane, Deansgate, Mylne Gate, Wething Greve, Hanging Ditch, Fenell Street, Smythy Door, and St. Mary's Gate, are all named in the Court Leet Records 1552-54.

manor was held, and near to which stood the stocks, the pillory and whipping-post, and not far distant was the cucking-stool pool. These streets were narrow, ill-paved, or not paved at all; the houses were of wood and plaster, with the upper stories projecting and mostly roofed with thatching. The only church in Manchester was the collegiate or parish church, which stood on the site of the present cathedral in the time of Edward VI.; the lord of the manor of Manchester was Sir Thomas West, Knight, ninth Baron de la Ware. The early records of the Manchester court leet[1] have been preserved, and furnish some interesting details of the life of the dwellers in the town at this period.

In 1522, amongst the officers of the court, were two ale-founders (or, as they are generally called, ale-tasters or conners), two byrlamen (lawmen) to overlook the "market stede," two for Deynsgate and four for the mylne gate, wething greve, hengynge dyche, fenell street, and on to Irkes brydge, and a score of people were named as " skevengers," whose duty it was to see that the streets were kept clean. At the same court an order was made that persons were not to allow their ducks and geese to wander into the market-place, and certain other regulations were enforced, showing that even at that date the sanitary arrangements of the place were to some extent attended to.

In 1554 we have, beside the other officers, market overlookers for fish and flesh, leathersellers, and men to see that no ox, cow, nor horse goes through the church-yard; and it was ordered that all the middens standing in the streets, between the conduit (which supplied the town with water) and the market-cross, and all swine-cotes in the High Street, should be removed. The

---

[1] From 1522 to 1686, and from 1731 to 1846. The whole have been printed by order of the Corporation, and edited by J. P. Earwaker, Esq., F.S.A.

authorities appear to have had some trouble to persuade the people that the street, or the front of their own houses, was not the place for dunghills or middens, as the orders to remove them appear at almost every court, in some cases the order only being to erect a pale or hedge round, so that there be no "noyance nor evil sight in the street."

In 1556 warning was to be given in the church that the inhabitants were to bring their corn and grain to be ground at the Free School Mill.

Ale and bread in 1558 were to be sold only by the regulation measures and weights. Archery had long been one of the recreations of the people, so we are surprised to find that in 1560 the inhabitants were ordered to have put up before the Feast of St. John the Baptist (June 24) a pair of butts in Marketstede Lane, and another pair upon Colyhurst Common; in the same year it was ordered that no person should allow any carding or bowling in his house or garden, fields or shop, "whereto any poore or handiecrafts men shall come or resort."

Provisions were also made for the traveller whose business brought him to Manchester, for no man was allowed (in 1560) to brew or sell ale unless he was able to "make two honest beddis [beds]," and he was also to "put furth the syne of a hand." Later on it was ordered that this sign was only to be used when the innkeeper had ale to sell. It is curious to find an old Act passed in 1390 still enforced, viz., that no one not being a forty-shilling freeholder shall keep a greyhound nor any hound.

Ale was not to be sold to be drunk on the premises at more than 6d. a gallon; for outdoor consumption the price was not to exceed 4d. a gallon.

A singular order appears in the next year's record, to the effect that no one shall sell bread which has any butter in it, although he was permitted to bake it for his own use or to give to his friends.

About this time it appears to have been the custom at weddings and other festive occasions to invite people to the feast — which was held at an alehouse—and then collect from them a sum of money to defray the expenses, and to stop this practice the court ordered that no one should be called upon to pay more than 4d. for such entertainment.

No doubt the fairs of Manchester were now resorted to by considerable numbers, hence the order made in 1565 that every burgess was to find an able-bodied man, furnished with a bill (or axe) or a halberd, to wait upon the steward of the manor at these gatherings. At this time fruits, particularly apples, were sufficiently an article of commerce as to necessitate the appointment an overseer to regulate their sale. The manufacturers of "rugs" (a kind of coarse woollen cloth) were now forbidden to wet their good "openly in the stretes," but to do it either within their respective houses or behind the same.

Alehouses were frequently the subject of the court's regulation, gaming, selling of ale during "tyme of morning prayer," and the like offences being severely dealt with, whilst drunken men found abroad in the streets at night were not only imprisoned in the "dungeon," but had to pay 6d. to the constable for the poor, and the unfortunate ale-house keeper, if found in a state of intoxication, was "discharged from ale-house keeping."

The wearing of daggers and other weapons was found to lead to disorder, and forbidden, and the law forbidding the wearing of hats[1] on Sundays and holidays was enforced. Apprentices and male and female servants were to be fined if found in the streets after nine o'clock at night in the summer and eight o'clock in the winter.

The practice of archery towards the end of the century

---

[1] Act passed in 1570 requiring persons to wear woollen caps, made in England, on Sundays.

began to fall off, and notwithstanding the Acts of Parliament passed to encourage it here in Manchester, officers had to be appointed to see the burgesses " exceryse [exercise] shootinge accordinge to the statute."

Although Manchester was not at the time a borough, yet it is evident that the court leet was alive to many of the requirements of a growing town, and that, although its industries were now only in infancy, it had become a commercial centre, and was beginning to emerge from the obscurity to which it had been relegated during the feudal system.

The plague of 1565 was succeeded in the year following by a great dearth, when a penny white loaf only weighed 6 or 8 ounces.

Even at this date the Manchester church was often selected as the place to be married at, although neither the bride nor the bridegroom lived in the town, and on these occasions they were accompanied by " strange pipers or other minstrels," who played up to the church doors and after the ceremony at the ale-house. This raised the jealousy of the " town waytes," who persuaded the court to order that they should come no more.

After Manchester, the next largest town was Preston, which was the capital of the duchy and one of the oldest incorporated towns in the county. Before the time of Elizabeth it had had no less than ten royal charters, and within it were two religious houses and its very ancient parish church ; moreover, its " guild merchant " had been held every twentieth year for centuries. The guild roll of 1542 contains the names of over 200 burgesses, that of 1562 exceeds 350, and the one of 1602 gives 537 in-burgesses, and 561 foreign or out burgesses. In the lists for 1562 and 1582 we find enumerated drapers, pewterers, cordwainers, glovers, masons, websters (weavers), tailors, mercers, butchers, carpenters, barbers, tanners, saddlers, flaxmen, leadbeaters, cutlers, schoolmasters, and other occupations which accompanied a well-to-do town of this period. The sale of woollen cloth and fustians was at this time a branch of Preston trade. Here also strict regulations were enforced as to the accommodation at inns, no one being allowed to retail ale unless he could lodge four men and find stabling for four horses. It was such regulations as these that enabled Holinshead (in 1577) to record that " the inns in Lancaster, Preston, Wigan and Warrington " are so much improved " that each comer " is " sure to lie in clean sheets wherein no man hath lodged ; if the traveller be on horseback his bed-cloth cost him nothing, but if he go on foot he hath a penny to pay." Preston was one of the four Lancashire towns which in 1547 recommenced to send members to Parliament. Toward the end of the sixteenth century Preston had a population of something ike 3,000.

The chief town of the county for many centuries was Lancaster, though in size and importance it had now been excelled by several other towns. The old castle was the county gaol, and in this town until quite recently the assizes were held, and, moreover, it was the oldest corporate borough, dating back to the twelfth century ; yet for all this, in an Act of Parliament passed in 1544, it is reported as to Lancaster that though there were many " beautiful houses" there, they were all " falling into ruin," and in 1586 Camden reported that " it was thinly peopled and all the inhabitants farmers, the country round it being cultivated, open, flourishing, and not bare of wood." As a town it consisted of only eight or nine streets, but there was a school, fishmarket, pinfold, etc.[1] Lancaster returned two members in 1529, and from 1547 continued to send that number.

Liverpool in the time of Henry VII. had begun to fall off in importance, and we find that that monarch made a

[1] Speed's Plan.

grant of the "Town and Lordship of Litherpoole" at a
rental of £14 a year; this was renewed in 1528.

Henry VIII., always on the look-out for royal revenues,
ordered in 1533 a return to be made of the King's rental
in Liverpool, when it was found only to amount to
£10 1s. 4d., a sum equal to something like £150 of the
present money;[1] this was exclusive of Church property.
The streets of Liverpool were Water Street, Castle
Street, Dale Street, Moore Street, Chapel Street, Jugler
Street and Mylne Street.   The Act of Parliament of 1544
reports of Liverpool as it had done of Lancaster (P. 97),
both towns being put down as having fallen into decay;
and yet both towns in 1547 returned two representatives
to Parliament.   Why had these two ancient boroughs so
decayed?   One reason probably, in the case of Liverpool,
was its comparative isolation, as until centuries after this
there was no road to it for wheeled carriages, all inland
travellers having to go on horseback, and goods on
packhorses, or by barges on the Mersey, from Warrington.

All these ancient boroughs, provided they paid the dues
to the national exchequer, and to some extent carried out
the statutes of the realm, were at liberty to make their
own laws for self-government, and it is but natural to
suppose that this arbitrary rule in some cases resulted
in success, whilst in others it led to results disastrous to
the community.   Again, the visitations of the plague in
some towns carried away a large percentage of the population, whilst in others their effects were slight.   Either
or both of these causes would be sufficient to materially
reduce the prosperity of one of these small boroughs.
In 1540 Liverpool is said to have been nearly depopulated
by the plague; and in 1556 there were only 151 householders left, which could not represent a population of
much over 1,000;[2] and in 1558 the visitation of this

[1] Picton's "Liverpool Municipal Records."
[2] Corporation Records.

scourge was so severe that all who were attacked were ordered "to make their cabins on the heath," and to remain there for nearly three months, and after that (until they had permission to do otherwise) to keep on "the back side of their houses, and to keep their doors and windows shut on the street side." This plague carried off upwards of 240 of the already reduced inhabitants. At this time we find warehouses for merchants named, and the Corporation had a ferry boat to carry people and goods across the river. The port of Liverpool was now claimed to be a dependency of the port of Chester, and so indignant were the Corporation at this that they sent their Mayor to London to represent to the Chancellor of the duchy that to call Liverpool "the creeke of Chester" was not only to punish its inhabitants, but was against the jurisdiction and regal authority of the county palatine and duchy; and they also stated that Liverpool had heretofore been reputed the best port and harbour from Milford to Scotland, and had always proved so with all manner of ships and barks. From the return made in consequence of this appeal, it appears that Liverpool had only twelve vessels, the largest of forty tons burden.

The close of the sixteenth century did not find the town in a much better position, for even the keeper of the "Common Warehouse of the Town" was only to have £1 2s. 8d. for his wages, because of "the small trade and trafique" that there then was, and a pious ejaculation is added, "until God send us better traffique." The principal trade now carried on was with Ireland and Spain or Portugal; to the latter herrings and salmon were exported and wine brought back. Wool, coatings (cottons), and tallow were exported in small quantities. Many regulations referring to the sanitary arrangements of the town and the suppression of drunkenness and gaming were almost identical with those enforced by the court-leet of Manchester. A "handsome cockpit" was made by the

Corporation in 1567, and horse-racing was patronized ten years later.

The only other town in Lancashire which in 1547 returned representatives to Parliament was Wigan.

Leland, who paid a visit to Wigan about the year 1540, thus describes the town: "Wigan pavid as bigge as Warington and better buildid. There is one paroch chirch amidde the Towne, summe Marchauntes, sum Artificers, sum Fermers. Mr. Bradeshaw hath a place called Hawe a myle from Wigan; he hath founde moche Canel like se Coole in his ground very profitable to hym." The vast underground wealth, which was in the future to be of such importance to this county, would appear at this time to be unworked, if even its existence was known. Wigan was one of the few towns in the county with its Mayor and Corporation. The population of Wigan would scarcely be as great as Warrington (which was now about 2,000[1]), as in 1625 the number of burgesses entitled to vote at the election was only 138. Warrington was not incorporated, but was under the manor court. Its chief industry was the manufacture of sail-cloth. Clitheroe, though a borough, was still (except for its connection with the castle) a place of small importance, as was also Blackburn; at neither place had as yet any textile industry been introduced. At Bolton-le-Moors Leland found cottons and coarse yarns manufactured, and here also they were accustomed to use " se cole, of which the pittes be not far off." At Bury also yarns were made.

Rochdale was " a market of no small resort," says Leland, but he is silent as to its commercial doings; nevertheless, if manufacture was not carried on there, its inhabitants were doing a good business in the sale of wool and coatings, as is proved by the fact that several cases of dispute as to the non-delivery of goods of this kind were heard in the duchy court. In the reign of

[1] Beamont's " Annals of Warrington."

Elizabeth the manufacture of these articles soon followed, and before the end of the century this industry was well established here. Some of the coal in this district lying near the surface was now worked, and cutlery was also made in this wide parish, as were also hats. Foot-racing was a favourite pastime in Lancashire in the sixteenth century, and sometimes the stakes ran high, as in the case of a race run near Whitworth (Rochdale) on August 24, 1576, when the match was for twenty nobles a side.[1]

Before the introduction of the woollen and cotton manufacture, and the consequent rapid increase of population and buildings, this county was very far from being amongst the least beautiful of England's shires. Large unbroken forests, where still lingered the lordly stag, surrounded with game of varied kinds, were yet to be seen ; and the dense smoke from the tall factory chimney was not there to blast and wither with its poisonous breath the tender foliage of the stripling oak. Its rivers then meandered through miles of pleasant lands, where the lowing of cattle and the melodious songs of birds formed the only accompaniment to the gentle rippling of the waters ; no contaminating dyeworks, chemical works, or other followers in the train of commerce, had yet planted themselves along the banks ; and the salmon, the grayling and the trout, and other small fry, held undisputed possession, unless they were molested by the otters, which were then abundant.[2] In the northern parts of the county things still remained much as they had been for centuries, except, of course, in some districts a slight increase in population, and in all an improved state of civilization and culture. Amongst these towns in the north may be mentioned Kirkham, which claims to have been incorporated in the time of Edward I., by the name

[1] Fishwick's "History of Rochdale," p. 44.
[2] Fishwick's "Lancashire in the Time of Elizabeth" (Royal Historical Society, vii. 191).

of " the bailiffs and burgesses." This claim was ratified by James I. They had a market and fair, but did not send representatives to Parliament.

In the days when the monasteries and abbeys were young, no doubt the education of the people was one of their recognised duties, but when these religious houses became (as they often did) the homes of luxury and licence, this duty was unfulfilled; and it was only after the Reformation, when the religious excitement abated, that anything like an attempt at national education was made, and at this time schools of any kind were almost unknown in the county, and the mass of the people were alike ignorant, untaught, and superstitious.

Preston was probably the first town in Lancashire which had a free school regularly endowed ; it is said to have been established in the fourteenth century, but was certainly there in the time of Henry VI., as in 1554 a plaintiff in the duchy court spoke of it as having then been in existence for "the space of 100 years,"[1] and the incumbent of the chantry in the parish church, founded by Helen Houghton (about 1480), was required to " be sufficiently lerned in grammar " to teach the scholars. Manchester was indebted to Hugh Oldham, the Bishop of Exeter (a native of Lancashire), for its first free school. In 1515 the Bishop conveyed certain lands to the Wardens of Manchester for the purpose of paying a master and usher to teach the youth of the district, who had, as the indenture sets forth, " for a long time been in want of instruction, as well on account of the poverty of their parents as for want of some person who should instruct them in learning and virtue." Before his death, in 1519, he had built the school which has for so long done honour to its founder.

At Kirkham a free grammar school had been, or was just about to be, founded in 1551, when Thomas Clifton,

[1] Pleadings (Philip and Mary), Record Office.

of Clifton, bequeathed " towards the grammar schole xxˢ."
And in 1585 the parish authorities took possession of the
school-house in right of the whole parish. This school
appears subsequently to have fallen into decay or been
given up, for in 1621 Isabel Birley, who had been all her
life an alehouse-keeper in Kirkham, being "moved to
compassion with pore children shee saw often in that
town," went to the church (where the thirty sworn men
were assembled) with £30 in her apron, which she wished
to give for the building of a free school; her example fired
the others with enthusiasm, and the requisite sum was
soon raised. The history of this well-known school is
interesting.

When Queen Elizabeth ascended the throne, besides
these schools there were free grammar schools at Prescot,
Lancaster, Whalley, Clitheroe, Bolton, and Liverpool,
but within the next fifty years many more were added,
amongst them being those at Burnley, Hawkshead,
Leyland, Rochdale, Middleton, and Rivington (near
Bolton). To most of these early-founded schools libraries
were attached, in some of which still remain many
valuable sixteenth-century books.

The belief in witchcraft and its kindred superstitions
was firmly rooted amongst the people; on this subject
something will be said in another chapter, but *en passant*
it may be stated that in 1597 a pardon was granted to
one Alice Brerley, of Castleton (in Rochdale), who had
been condemned to death for slaying by means of witchcraft James Kershaw and Robert Scholefield.[1]

The condition into which Lancashire was thrown
through the religious crisis consequent upon the Reformation will be treated of elsewhere, but it must here
be noted that in the time of good Queen Bess churches
were said to be almost emptied of their congregations,
alehouses were innumerable, wakes, ales, rushbearing, bear-

---

[1] State Papers, Dom. Ser., cclxiii.

baits, and the like, were all exercised on the Sunday, and altogether a general lawlessness appears to have prevailed all over the county. In the reign of Henry VIII. the old commissions of array (whose duty it was to get together in each county such armed forces as were required from time to time) were done away with, and their places occupied by lord-lieutenants.

In 1547 the Earl of Shrewsbury was Lord-Lieutenant of the county of Lancaster and six other counties, but in 1569 the county had a Lord-Lieutenant of its own in the person of Earl Stanley, third Earl of Derby. The duties of these newly appointed officers of the Crown were manifold; but one of their chief services was to assemble and levy the inhabitants within their jurisdiction in the time of war, and to prescribe orders for the government of their counties; and from the proceedings of the Lancashire lieutenancy we may glean a few details relating to the civil and religious life of the period.[1] For the military muster of 1553 the quota required from the respective hundreds was: West Derby 430, Salford 350, Leyland 170, Amounderness 300, Blackburn 400, Lonsdale 350.

These numbers were to be raised by each town in the hundred in proportion to the wealth or number of its inhabitants: West Derby, Wigan, and Ashton, in the parish of Winwick, had to find 11 each, whilst Liverpool only sent 5. In Leyland the greatest number (10) came from Wrightington with Parbold; in Amounderness Preston found 26, whilst the parish of Kirkham contributed over 100. Blackburn parish sent 113 men, and the parish of Whalley 175; unfortunately, the particulars for the towns and parishes of Salford are wanting. In 1559-60 the county was called upon to raise no less than 3,992 soldiers.

During all these troubled times the highest hills in the

[1] *Chetham Soc.*, xlix.

district were used as beacon stations, where a system of signalling was practised; thus, in 1588 the hundred of Salford was called upon to pay £5 9s. 4d. for watching the beacon on Rivington Pike from July 10 to September 30.

Some further details about this particular are furnished in the original " accompt " of Sir John Byron, who was a Deputy-Lieutenant of the county:

1589.

	£	s.	d.
Paid for erecting a beacon - - - -	20	0	0
„ „ powder at Ormskirk for the trayninge -	4	0	0
„ „ two days trayninge of 300 soldiers - -	20	0	0
„ „ 18 rowles of matches - - - -	0	10	8
„ to Robert Pilkington at two severall tymes for repayringe and kepinge the beacon at Ryvington Pyke - - - -	5	7	4
„ for 210 pounds of powder for the saide two dayes trayninge - - - - -	14	0	0

Notwithstanding the wars and rumours of wars which were then so common, and notwithstanding the religious excitement created by the persecution, first of the Roman Catholics and then of the Puritans, people seem to have prospered in the county. The towns and villages greatly increased in number, size and importance, and the time of Elizabeth especially witnessed the erection and rebuilding of some of Lancashire's finest halls. The ancient domestic houses which had been the residences of the old feudal lords were now remodelled or entirely swept away, and the subdivision of the land brought out a new class of proprietors, who, though not descended directly from the old owners of the soil, soon took up the rank of gentry, and built for themselves those smaller though not less interesting mansions which at one time were found all over the county.

During the Tudor time were built such houses as Speke Hall, near Liverpool; Ordsall Hall, near Manchester;

Little Mitton, the home of the Sherburns; Ince Hall, Cleworth Hall, Smithell's Hall, Lostock Hall, Lydiate Hall, Rufford Hall, Belfield Hall, Rawcliffe, Rossal Grange, and a host of others far too numerous to mention. Many of these date back to very early days, and were originally built with a view to make every man's house his castle; but with the end of the sixteenth century other views began to obtain, and an Englishman, for the first time probably in the country's history, commenced to feel that his house was really his castle, and that it was defended for him by the strong arm of the law.

The houses of the middle and lower classes were nearly always built of wood and clay ("daub"); the richer people had houses which were usually divided on the ground-floor into a common hall, a small withdrawing room or parlour, and a kitchen, the upper stories being reached by wide staircases, often with ornately carved oak banisters. The higher class of houses or halls consisted of many chambers, and not infrequently there was a private chapel, and the rooms were wainscoted. Many views have been preserved of the exterior of most of our old halls (which were highly picturesque), but of the interior and general domestic arrangements we are left to glean such items as have been handed down to us through the medium of inventories and kindred records. These inventories, taken after the proving of wills, are often (where they exist at all) meagre and incomplete, yet they furnish particulars which we should look elsewhere for in vain. The inventory of the goods of Sir Thomas Butler, of Bewsey (near Prescot), knight, taken in 1579, will give some details of the contents of one of Lancashire's old houses. The following are selected items:

PLATE AND JEWELLERY.—Basin and ewer, silver engraved bowls, silver salts with covers, silver spoons, a crystal cross.

LINEN, ETC.—Table-cloths, damask work, towels, napkins, flax sheets, bed-hangings, quilted and woollen blankets, mattresses, curtains of taffeta, curtains of darynx (a kind of damask made at Tournay), green silk coverlet, etc.

FURNITURE, ETC.—Tables, chairs, stools, truckle beds, pair of playing tables, brass candlesticks, pewter in considerable quantities, and the usual kitchen and brewing apparatus.

APPAREL.—Velvet hose, satin doublets, taffeta doublets, velvet breeches, riding-cloak lined with unshorn velvet, Spanish leather jerkins, a long gown of silk grogram (a silk material), velvet cloaks, black jersey stockings, a taffeta hat, a black felt hat.

SUNDRIES.—Cross-bows, clock and bell, pictures of Christ and of the Queen's majesty, drinking glasses, "a sylver toth pyke," armour, weapons, guns, corslets, "cote of plate," daggers, bucklers, "a black brydd and her cage, bought by Sir Thomas in London," "the honey and wax of certen hyves," an English Bible and other books (valued at £4), etc.

As a contrast to this house, furnished with all the luxuries of the time, take the inventory of one John Rodes, a husbandman fairly well-to-do, who lived at Inchfield, near Todmorden. By his will, which was dated November, 1564, he left his goods to his children, together with £5 apiece; his wains, carts and implements were also to go to his children; he left over £25 in legacies, and he held a lease of a farm for an unexpired term of years; yet, besides his horses and cows, hay and corn, and other farm stock, all his goods consisted of:

Bedding, £4 6s. 8d. (valued at); pans, £2 os. 1od.; pots, 13s. 4d.; pewter, 3s. 4d.; a tub, 2d.; "in husslements" (odds and ends) belonging to the household, and in iron gear, 1os.

This was no doubt a fair sample of the contents of the house of a labouring farmer in these times; his household furniture was not worth £10. In some of the moorland districts sheep were kept in large quantities, and in some houses websters' looms were common enough pieces of furniture, as many of the clothes worn were now home-made, which also accounts for the presence of spinning-wheels and wool-cards. In many of the wills of this period, even where no inventory has been preserved, the bequests are often very numerous and defined, and consist of every imaginable kind of household goods, so that from them we are enabled to get a glimpse at the contents of the houses of the testators. Articles of plate, amongst the wealthier classes, were much prized, and often made the subject of special bequests, as was frequently the case with gold rings and other jewellery. There often occur such items as silver goblets, parcel-gilt goblets, salt-cellars with and without covers, silver spoons " with the image of the twelve apostles " and the like ; and hanging in the hall were nearly always old swords, old calverts, pistols, cross-bows and quivers with arrows, and not infrequently more or less complete suits of armour.

From the very rare mention of books in either the wills or inventories, it is evident that very few were among the possessions of the sixteenth-century Lancashire householders.   In the few instances where books are named, they are referred to in a manner showing that they were considered valuable and rare.   The Rev. Richard Jones, Rector of Bury, by his will, dated June 15, 1568, directed that his " four bokes of Crysostum be chened [chained] in the churche, there to remayne for ever."   Another testator, in 1574,[1] left " one litle bible," which he enjoined his son to see used every Sabbath day when there were no sermons nor sacraments ; and during the week-day this precious volume was to be lent to his " poorest kinsfolk."   Pictures were also very uncommon, and those which adorned the walls of the rich were nearly always sacred subjects ; one article of furniture appears in nearly every case—the old oak chest ; sometimes it is simply called " a chist," at other times the " carven oak chest," and it was used invariably as a store place for sheets and linen.

[1] Richard Entwysle of Foxholes. (See "History of Rochdale," p. 408.)

The representation of Lancashire in Parliament was slightly increased in 1559 by the addition of two members —one for Clitheroe and another for Newton-in-the-Willows; the latter was not a borough even by prescriptive right, and the selection of its representative rested almost exclusively with the lord of the manor as late as 1797, when a contested election resulted in a poll of only 66 votes. Except some slight alterations during the Commonwealth, the representation of the county remained unchanged until the passing of the Reform Act in 1832. As illustrating the everyday life in Lancashire in the time of Elizabeth, the following list of prices and wages is interesting. It is taken from the steward's accounts of the Shuttleworths, of Gawthorp Hall (near Burnley).

PROVISIONS.—A salt salmon, a fresh salmon, a salt fish and two salt eels, 2s. ; red herring and a hundred sprats, 1s. ; a quart of vinegar, 4d. ; a quart of wine, 6d. ; a pound of figs, 4d. ; a quarter of veal, 12d. ; a quarter of mutton, 1s. 6d. ; 10¾ gallons of claret wine, 14s. 4d. ; for three quarters of sack, 2s. ; five chickens, 6d. ; a pound of pepper, 4s. ; thirty-two snipes, 22d. ; four lapwings and two plovers, 8d. ; half a fat lamb, 2s. 6d. ; three geese, 15d. ; half a peck of pears, 6d. ; white wine, 2s. a gallon ; ten woodcocks, 22d. ; fine couple of rabbits, 3s. 9d. ; a peck of cockles, 4d. ; a pike and a bream, 3s. 8d. ; two dozen dace and a perch, 5d. ; a peck of apples, 2s. 4d. ; a peck of oysters, 6d. ; a fat pig, 2s. ; five eggs, 1d. ; eight gosling, 20d. ; a stone of butter, 3s. 4d.

WAGES.—A smith, per day, 6d. ; a day's mowing, 6d. ; for ditching, 4d. a rood ; working in the delph (stone quarry) six days, 15d. ; for blending and spinning 5½ stone of wool, 13s. 9d. ; for weaving and colouring part of the said wool, 3s. 8d. ; for fulling and dressing the said cloth, 4s. 10d. ; soleing a pair of shoes, 5d. ; spinning wool for blankets, 2s. a stone ; weaving pieces of blankets, ¾d. a yard ; white-washing, 2d. to 4d. a day; a stonemason, 4d. a day ; weaving 24 yards of canvas, 22d.

SUNDRIES.—A load of wheat, 10s. ; a cow, 26s. ; twinters (calves two winters old), 22s. ; an ox, £2 8s. ; 100 bricks, 1s. ; two sheep-skins for arrow-case, 10d. ; a quire of paper, 4d. ; six chaldrons (of 36 bushels each) of sea coal[1] at the ship, £4 16s. ; for bringing the same

---

[1] Local coal of very inferior quality appears to also have been used. Such entries occur as "four loodes of cole at Hilton delve, 4s.," but

to the house, 12s.; and for watching them one night, 1s.; three pairs of shoes for the children, 3s. 10d.

In considering the rate of wages, it must be borne in mind that at this period the labourer often had board as well as wages.

As bearing upon the social condition of the people, it may be noted that at the Herald's visitation of Lancashire in 1533 only forty-seven families entered their descent, and even these furnished very meagre genealogical particulars. This may in a great measure be accounted for by the fact that the visitation was made at a time when the King was struggling with the Pope for religious supremacy, and that the growing feeling in favour of the Reformers had not yet made much progress in this county, and consequently the Herald, though armed with a royal warrant, was received with coldness, some families point-blank refusing even to speak with him, whilst others, having granted an audience, dismissed him "with the utmost rudeness."[1] The Herald appears to have taken his revenge in full, and recorded of one well-known knight (Sir Richard Houghton) that he "hath putt away his lady and wife, and kepeth a concobyne in his house"; and he adds, "he gave me nothing nor made me no good chere, but gave me proude woordes"; of another gentleman (Robert Holt of Stubley) he reported "that he married an olde woman, by whom he hedd no yssue, & therefore he wold not have her name entered"; as for Sir John Townley of Townley, near Burnley, he "sogt hym all day rydinge in the wylde countrey, & his reward was ij^s of w^h the guyde hedde the most p'te," and he winds up with, "I hed as evill a jorney as ev^r I hedd"; in addition to all this, Sir John refused to tell him the name of his first wife, and asserted that there were no

this was probably only the cost of the carriage, as the coal would belong to the Shuttleworths, and be got in the quarry.

[1] "Bibliotheca Heraldica," p. 582.

gentlemen in Lancashire but Lord Derby and Lord Monteagle.

The next visitation was in 1567, when Elizabeth had been nearly ten years on the throne, and the Roman Catholics and Puritans in this county had become specially marked for persecution (see Chapter IX.); notwithstanding this, 129 families entered their pedigrees, and most of them claimed the right to bear arms. The marked increase between 1533 and 1567 bears evidence to the growing wealth and importance of Lancashire. Arising from a desire to add "field to field" and found county families, a custom had obtained a footing in Lancashire at this time to marry children when of tender age. Many examples might be quoted to illustrate this, but one will suffice. In 1562 two sisters, Elizabeth and Anne, co-heiresses of Ralph Belfield, of Clegg Hall, were married, at Middleton Church, respectively to Alexander Barlow of Barlow and Richard Leigh of Highleigh; twenty-two years afterwards both the couples applied for divorce, Barlow testifying that he did not remember any marriage having taken place, and Anne Leigh, *née* Belfield, declaring that at the time of her marriage she was only seven years old, and that after it was celebrated she went to live with her grandmother, whilst her youthful husband was sent to Shrewsbury School, and whilst he was there she sent him a "gilt book," and he sent her a knife, which she wore at her girdle: both marriages were dissolved.[1] There were, however, many other instances where divorce was neither obtained nor applied for.

The close of the Tudor age found Lancashire in a very different state to that which marked its advent. Commerce with other countries across the seas was beginning to show effects, and the wool and other products of the county found a ready market. The population had

[1] See "History of Rochdale," p. 352.

greatly increased, yet still there was no large town in the modern sense of the word, and the manufactures of the day were mostly carried on in the houses of the manufacturers, and the new fabrics composed of silk and wool, introduced by the Flemish exiles at Norwich, had not yet been added to any great extent to the trade of this district.

The social position was everywhere improved : a better class of domestic architecture had supplanted the old order, and now the people lived in fairly comfortable houses, built frequently of stone or brick, which, though internally not furnished with the luxurious appliances of a nineteenth-century villa, were yet princely palaces compared with the wretched dwelling-places which had preceded them.

The glorious literature which distinguished the reign of the Virgin Queen, and which embraced alike history, poetry, and the drama, must have had some effect upon the Lancashire people, although as yet we find no printing-press in any of her towns.

CHAPTER VIII.

THE SEVENTEENTH CENTURY.

ALLUSION has been already made to the superstitious side of the character of the Lancashire
people; their belief in omens, charms, witchcraft and
demoniac possessions lingered long. This is a fitting
place to tell the tale of the " Lancashire Witches " and
the so-called " demoniac possessions."

The belief that demons or evil spirits took possession
of human beings is of very great antiquity, and the
popular mind had firmly taken hold of this; whenever a
case of this kind occurred, the priest was called in to
exorcise the devil, and the Puritan divines were not slow
in asserting that if a Roman Catholic could perform a
miracle, they at least could turn out an evil spirit, and
thus the superstition appears to have been rather fostered
than rebuked. One of these demoniac cases[1] took place
at an old half-timbered house called Cleworth Hall[2]
(in the parish of Leigh), where there lived Nicholas,
the eldest son of Edmund Starkie of Huntroyd (near

[1] The author read a paper on "The Lancashire Demoniacs" before
the Hist. Soc. of Lanc. and Ches. (vol. xxxv.), in which this subject
is more fully gone into.

[2] This case does not belong to the seventeenth century, but it is
inserted here as bearing upon the subject, and only occurred four
years before the century began.

Burnley); he had issue a son John and a daughter Ann, who, with five others, were said to have become "possessed," when John Darrell was called in to exorcise the evil spirit. This Darrell was a graduate of one of the Universities, and was subsequently domestic chaplain to Archbishop Whitgift, and Rector of St. Mary's, Nottingham.

An account of this singular instance of ignorance and credulity was written by Darrell and secretly printed in 1600. The various symptoms described are not incompatible with many diseases now known to the medical profession, and need not be described; to cure the patients, however, a conjurer of the name of Hartley was called in, who for his services was to receive 40s. a year and bed and board; but this did not satisfy him long, and on being refused additional pay, in the shape of a house and the land it stood on, he so affected the possessed ones that (as Darrell puts it) they "sent forth such a strange supernatural and fearful noyse and loud whupping as the like was neuer hard at Cleworth nor in England."

Mr. Starkie was naturally not satisfied with the treatment, and having applied to a Manchester physician in vain, he went to the famous Dr. Dee, then Warden of Manchester, who advised him to consult "some godly preachers" and get them to call a public or private fast day. The eldest son's vagaries were certainly peculiar: he would at times act like a madman or a mad dog, and he and his sisters, we are told (by Darrell), would howl and bark and join in a chorus "like a ring of five bells." The whole affair was doubtless a fraud, but, nevertheless, it shows in a marked degree the dense ignorance even of some of the well-to-do classes at that time: for we find that Mr. Starkie, after his futile appeal to the Manchester physician, Dr. Dee, and others, could only resort to the justices of the peace, who in their wisdom sent Hartley to the Lancaster assizes, where he was in solemn manner tried, condemned and hanged, not for the evident im-position and fraud, but for witchcraft, the strongest evi-dence against him being that he had on several occasions "drawn magic circles." But perhaps the most curious circumstance about the case is that at his execution the rope broke, whereupon, probably thinking to save his neck, he confessed that he was guilty; the plea, however, failed, and he was quietly hung up a second time. After Hartley's execution, John Darrell and the pastor of Calke, in Derbyshire, were called to Cleworth (in 1596), and they with thirty others spent a day in fasting and prayer, the result being (so we are told) that the whole seven were dispossessed, the devil coming out of their mouths in various forms, as a crow's head, a hedgehog, a toad, etc.

This and other impostures practised by Darrell and his associates led to a prolonged controversy, in which several pamphlets were printed in London, the author of one of them being Samuel Harsnett, who was afterwards Archbishop of York. Not very long after this, King James issued his "Dæmonologie," in which he advocated the putting to death of all witches.

In Pendle Forest, in the parish of Whalley, in a small cottage near Malkin Tower, lived in the beginning of the century a woman known as "Old Demdike," and her daughter; the mother's real name was Elizabeth Southerns, her daughter was Elizabeth Device *alias* young Demdike. Old Demdike, who was over eighty years of age, was supposed to have made her house into a meeting-place for all the witches in the neighbourhood, and this led to a score of suspected persons (most of them women) being arrested and tried at Lancaster. Eight of these were known as the Witches of Samlesbury, the rest being associated with Pendle Forest. This trial created so much interest in the county that Thomas Potts, the clerk of the court, was ordered by the judges to collect and publish the particulars of the case. From this scarce book[1] may be obtained the full details of this notorious trial; for our present purpose a few particulars must suffice. The wretched old crone, Elizabeth Southerns, died in prison before the trial took place, having first made a confession to the effect that the devil had twenty years before appeared to her, and to him she had sold her soul, and had thus obtained her power; she also described the well-known method of taking away a man's life by means of the insertion of pins into a "picture of clay like unto the shape of the person" upon whom the revenge was sought. Anne Whittle, *alias* Chattox, before the assizes not only admitted that she was a witch, but gave the names of many persons whom she had "bewitched to death," and several of the others made similar confessions. It seems somewhat strange that these prisoners should so easily be led to condemn themselves, and the reason may be either that they expected by so doing to escape capital punishment, or, what is equally likely, that they, having so long lived by the profession of witchcraft, really did imagine that they had the power they claimed to possess.

The whole trial appears to have partaken far more of the nature of persecution than an attempt to ascertain the truth. The leader of this persecution was Roger Nowell, of Read Hall, who, according to the clerk of the court, was "one of his Majesty's Justices in these parts, a very religious, honest gentleman, painful in the service of his country." Another agent against the Samlesbury prisoners was a priest called Thompson, who tutored the principal witness, Grace Sowerbutts, a girl of fourteen years of age, to accuse three of the prisoners of

---

[1] "The Wonderfull Discoverie of Witches in the County of Lancaster, with the arraignment and trial of nineteene notorious Witches, etc., etc. ; London, 1613." Reprinted by the *Chetham Soc.*, vol. vi., old series.

having bewitched her. To strengthen the evidence for the prosecution, Roger Nowell produced the deposition taken before him at his house, and it appears that he did not scruple to make the sons and daughters condemn their parents, and thus make them instruments for their destruction.

On the indictment against Anne Whittle being read, she pleaded not guilty, whereupon " Mr. Nowell, the best instructed of any man of all these particular poyntes of evidence against her and her fellows," requested that the prisoner's own confession made before him should now be " published against her," and this was forthwith done. Of the character of the evidence given by the various witnesses, the following are samples: Anne Whittle, to spite the wife of one John Moore, " called for her Deuill *Fancie* and bad him goe bite a browne cow of Moore's by the head and make the cow goe madde ; and the Deuill then in the likenesse of a brown dogge went to the said cow and bit her, which cow went madde accordingly and died within six weekes." Alice Chattox " at a buriall at the new church in Pendle did take three scalpes of people which had been buried, and then cast them out of a grave, and took eight teeth out of the said scalpes," which were afterwards used for purposes of witchcraft. They were not only accused of causing the deaths of various people and cattle by charms, but also of being the means of bringing about evil of every description. In the case of Elizabeth Device (the daughter of old Demdike), her own child, nine years of age, was " set upon the table in the presence of the whole court," and there declared that she knew her mother to be a witch, for she had several times seen her spirit in the shape of a brown dog come to her at her house.

Another extraordinary piece of evidence was that of James Device, a son of young Demdyke's, who first put himself out of court as a creditable witness by confessing that he had recently stolen a sheep, and then swore that he had seen a number of witches at his grandmother's house, who first partook of the stolen mutton and then went out of doors, where they " were gotten on horse-backe, like unto foales, some one colour, some of another, and Preston's wife was the last, and when shee got on horsebacke they all presently vanished out of sight."

Amongst the witches was one Alice Nutter, of the Forest of Pendle, whom Potts describes as " a rich woman " with " a great estate and children of good hope, and in the opinion of the world of good temper, free from envy or malice," and he adds, " Whether by the means of the rest of the witches or some unfortunate occasion shee was drawne to fall to this wicked course of life I know not ; but hither she is now come to receive her triall both for murder and many other vile and damnable practices." The witnesses against this prisoner were the other accused and members of their families only.

At the conclusion of the trial, Alice Whittle, Elizabeth Device, Anne Redferne, Alice Nutter, Katherine Hewet, John Bulcock, Jane Bulcock, Aliza Device and Isabel Robey were found guilty and sentenced to be hanged, which sentence was duly carried out. Margaret Pearson was ordered to stand in the pillory in open market at Clitheroe, Padiham, Whalley and Lancaster, on four market days ; the other prisoners were acquitted.

But this did not stamp out the Lancashire witches, for so long as the people continued to believe in their super-natural powers, so long would the supply be equal to the demand. In 1633 another batch of seventeen witches of Pendle were commanded to take their trial at Lancaster assizes, and, singularly enough, one of the convicting justices was the John Starkie who in 1596 was himself the subject of demoniac possession (see p. 114).

The chief witness in this case was a stonemason, who on oath declared that he had seen two greyhounds, with which he tried to hunt a hare; but they refused to run, and on his beating them, they immediately became transformed, one into Dickonson's wife, and the other into a little boy; the former put a kind of bridle on the head of the latter, and he became a white horse, upon which she jumped, and, placing the witness before her, she rode away with him to a place called Hoarstones (in Whalley), which was about a quarter of a mile off, where he found a number of persons coming, all riding on " horses of several colours." After this interesting congregation had feasted in the house, they adjourned to the barn, where he saw six of them kneeling and pulling at six ropes fastened to the roof, "at or with which pulling came flesh smoakeinge, butter in lumps, and milk." Whilst they were thus exercised they " made such foule faces that feared him, so that he was glad to steale out and run home." Margaret Johnson, though not one of the accused, confessed that she had been at a meeting at Hoarstones, where there were present between thirty and forty witches; she also said that " men witches usually have women spirits, and women witches men spirits," and that Good Friday was the " constant day for a yearly meeting of witches." All these prisoners were found guilty by the jury, but the judge delayed the execution of the sentence, and the matter in the meantime coming to the ears of the King, four of the convicted were sent up to London to be examined by the royal physicians and surgeons, and ultimately were brought before the King himself. The result of all this was an acquittal of the lot. It was upon this case of witch-finding that Heywood and Broome founded their play of " The Late Lancashire Witches," London, 1634, and Mother Demdike is one of the characters in Shadwell's " Lancaster Witches," a comedy, London, 1682. Harrison Ainsworth's novel, " The Lancashire Witches," has the same subject. After this, the " profession " of witchcraft appears to have gradually died out, but the demoniac possession was harder to slay, as the exorcising of these spirits was a power highly valued alike by Roman Catholic priest and Puritan divine. At Downham, near Clitheroe, a case was reported, with the usual "godly minister" as voucher[1] again, in 1696, and the Vicar of Walton-on-the Hill furnished an account of another case which had taken place about half a century earlier, and in which the priest at Madame Westby's (of Mowbrick in Kirkham) and the Rector of Croston having failed to effect a cure, the possessed one was sent to Dr. Sylvester, of Liverpool, who physicked the "devil out of him."

Towards the end of the century several other cases are on record where the priest is said to have exorcised the spirit. But the most famous instance of this class of deceptions was what is known as the "Surey demoniac," from its hero having lived at Surey, in the parish of Whalley. The boy who was possessed was one Richard Dugdale, aged nineteen, the son of a gardener, and he apparently had all the symptoms required for the occasion, and acted the part required of him to perfection. Amongst other things he was seen to vomit stones, silver and gold curtain rings; he could make himself "as light as a feather bouster," or as "heavy as a load of corn"; he had ventriloquial powers, and could speak out of the earth, and all these were accompanied with the more violent signs, such as convulsions, contortions, shoutings, and the like. The curious part of this is the ready credence which was given to it. Amongst those who subscribed their names to the account of this youth's performances, and asserted their opinions that the whole was true, and that this was a genuine case of diabolical possession, which was beyond the reach of the medical man, and could only be dealt with by prayer and fasting, were : the minister of Toxteth Chapel, near Liverpool ;

[1] See *Lanc. and Ches. Ant. Soc.*, x. 215.

Samuel Angier, minister of Denton; Richard Frankland, M.A., sometime Vice-President of the Presbyterian College of Durham; Thomas Jolly, ejected minister of Altham; Henry Pendlebury, minister of Holcombe Chapel; Nathaniel Heywood, the ejected Vicar of Ormskirk; and Dr. Robert Whittaker, of Burnley; and besides these over thirty people gave evidence, many of them on oath, as to the truth of the details furnished before Hugh, Lord Willoughby, and Ralph Egerton, Esq., two justices of the peace. The first pamphlet, giving an account of "Satan's Strange and Dreadful Actings in and about the Body of Richard Dugdale," was published in London in 1697, and it called forth replies and counter-replies, the Rev. Thomas Jolly being one of the writers in support of the demoniac; and the Rev. Zachary Taylor, Vicar of Croston, one of those who believed the whole affair a "fanatical imposture."[1] For long years after this the belief in the efficacy of certain "charms," as well as the tales of the fortune-telling gipsies, lingered in the county, and even yet occasionally, on pulling down old barns and farmhouses, there are found hidden away amongst the rafters small boxes containing charms written on paper in a peculiar cipher, mixed up with signs of the planets, etc., the whole purporting to be all-powerful to drive away all evil spirits from the building;[2] these writings are probably not more than 150 years old.

The visit of James I. to Lancashire cannot be passed over, as it was in consequence of this visit that the King issued the famous "Book of Sports," which created such indignation in the minds of some of his subjects. Early in August, 1617, the King, on his return from Carlisle, reached Hornby Castle, the seat of Lord Monteagle, from whence he went to Ashton Hall, the home of Lord

[1] Some of these tracts are now very scarce.

[2] One of these was found near Rochdale a few years ago. (See "History of Rochdale," p. 535.)

Gerard, and after staying there one night he went on to
Myerscough Lodge, the seat of Edward Tyldesley, Esq.
Here, on August 12, Sir Richard Hoghton, with a retinue
of gentlemen, went to meet the King, who arrived in his
coach, and having had pointed out to him where the
forest began, his Majesty commenced to hunt, and during
the day he killed a buck. On the following day the King
again hunted in Myerscough Forest, and succeeded in
slaying five bucks, after which he made a speech to the
gentlemen present on the subject of "pipeing and
honest recreation." On the 14th the town of Preston was
in a high state of excitement, preparing for the royal
visitor, and the good old town was full of strangers, who
had come to welcome King James. On the 15th the
King arrived at Preston, and proceeded to the cross in
the market-place, where the Recorder made a speech and
the Corporation presented to his Majesty "a bowle."
Perhaps the good Prestonians were animated with a
better spirit than that which stirred the Mayor of Chester
on a similar occasion, when he exclaimed :

> A cupp with gold unto your grace I'll bringe,
> In hope to us you'll give a better thinge ;
> For Ile be sworne itt did not goe near our heart
> When from so manie gold angells wee did parte.[1]

The Corporation then feasted the King at the Guild-
hall, probably at mid-day, as immediately afterwards the
royal party repaired to Myerscough, where another stag
was killed. The next day James I. stayed at Hoghton,
where Sir Richard had invited a great company to meet
him. Before dinner, notwithstanding the great heat of
the day, they went out hunting, and after dinner (about
four p.m.) the King went to look at the alum-mines which
his host had recently opened. After an hour thus spent,
they returned to the forest, and had varied fortune until
evening, when they returned to a late supper. The

---

[1] Satirical poem, Hopkinson's MSS., xxxiv. 85.

following day was spent at Hoghton; there was no hunting. The Bishop of Chester preached before the King,
and after dinner there was a rushbearing and piping in
the middle court. This form of Lancashire wakes has
often been described. This was probably a simple rush-
cart, with its accompanying morris-dancers, etc., got up
to entertain the King. In the evening there was a mask,
in which many "noblemen, knights, gentlemen, and
courtiers" took part; there were also some speeches and
dancing, including "The Huckler," "Tom Bedlo and the
Cowp Justice of Peace."[1] On this day a petition of the
Lancashire people was presented to the King. In this
it was represented that "they were debarred from lawful
recreations upon Sunday after evening prayers, and upon
holy days, and praying that the restriction imposed in
the late reign might be withdrawn."

In May, 1618, King James issued a proclamation, in
which he refers to his progress through Lancashire, where
he had "found it necessary to rebuke some Puritans
and precise people." These people, he thought, were
Jewishly inclined, because they affected to call Sunday
the Sabbath day. And the proclamation ends by declaring that his pleasure was that in Lancashire, after the
end of Divine service, the people were not to be let
or hindered or discouraged from any lawful recreation,
such as dancing, either men or women, archery, leaping,
vaulting, May games, Whitsun ales, morris-dancers, may-
poles, or other sports. Those recusants and others who
did not attend Divine service were, however, to be
debarred from the sports. The latter clause was, no
doubt, introduced to please the Bishops and the clergy,
who were highly indignant at the proclamation itself.
This order led to the issue in 1618 of "The Book of
Sports." Charles I. made a somewhat similar order as
to the due observance of wakes and fêtes on the anni-

[1] "Nicholas Assheton's Journal," *Chetham Soc.*, xiv.

versary days of the dedication of churches. From
Hoghton the King went to stay with the Earl of Derby
at Lathom House, from thence proceeding to Bewsey
Hall, the seat of Thomas Ireland, Esq.

During his visit he knighted William Massy, Robert
Bindloes, Gilbert Clifton, John Talbot, Gilbert Ireland,
and Edward Olbaldeston. Frederick, the son-in-law of
James, was crowned King of Bohemia in October, 1619,
but after a very brief tenure he was dethroned in 1620,
and after the battle of Prague fled to Holland. The
Puritan party in this county had strong sympathy with
the ejected "winter-king" as he was styled, and James
seized the opportunity to urge Parliament to grant him
two subsidies, one involving an assessment of 4s. in the
pound on land, and 2s. 8d. on goods and chattels; and
when the new Parliament met in 1624 a grant of £300,000
was made to recover the palatinate lost by Frederick.
For the war with the Roman Catholic Powers which
followed the Puritans were responsible.

Half the army raised for this service perished from
sickness, and altogether the result was disastrous; and
just when the feeling of discontent was beginning to
manifest itself, the King died.

Charles I. was not slow to follow in the steps of his
father in his manner of rule: subsidy followed subsidy,
sometimes with the authority of Parliament, and sometimes without. And thus came about the contest
between the King and the Commons, which led to the
attempt to rule England without a Parliament. In
1635 the attempt was made to levy the tax known
as Ship - money, for the equipment of a naval force.
Humphrey Chetham was at that time High Sheriff of
Lancashire, and to him was sent the writ for the collection within the county; on the back of this writ he wrote:
" If you shall tax & assesse men according [to] their
estate, then Liverpool, being poore and now goes as it

were a beginge, must pay very little : letters patent are now forth for the same towne."[1]   The whole county was assessed at £475, of which Liverpool had to find £15. In the same tax for 1636, Lancashire was put down to find one ship of 400 tons burden, 160 men, and £1,000 ; towards this, Preston was to raise £40, Lancaster £30, Liverpool £25, Wigan £50, Clitheroe and Newton £7 10s. each.   Comparing these figures with some of those for the Yorkshire towns, it would appear that in this county there was no borough as rich as either Hull, which paid £140, or Leeds, which was called on for £200. In this same year (1636) Lancashire was ordered to find 420 foot soldiers and 50 dragoons.

After eleven years' interval a Parliament was again summoned to meet, on April 13, 1640, which only sat for three weeks ; but on November 3 following the Long Parliament was convened, when Lancashire was repre- sented for the county by Ralph Ashton (Parliamentarian) and Roger Kirby (Royalist) ; Lancaster, John Harrison and Thomas Fanshaw (both Royalists) ; Preston, Richard Shuttleworth and Thomas Standish (both Parliamen- tarians) ; Newton, Peter Leigh and Sir Roger Palmer (Royalists) ; Wigan, Orlando Bridgeman (Royalist) and Alexander Rigby (Parliamentarian) ; Clitheroe, Ralph Ashton and Richard Shuttleworth (both Parliamen- tarians) ; Liverpool, John Moore (Parliamentarian) and Sir Richard Wynn, Bart. (Royalist).   If its members of Parliament represented the county, parties here must have been equally divided, as there were seven Parlia- mentarians and seven Royalists.

Amongst the first enactments of this Parliament which concerned this county was the abolition of the Duchy Court of Star Chamber and the repeal of the forest laws. The knights, squires, merchants, gentlemen and free- holders of Lancashire at this time presented a petition to

[1] Liverpool Municipal Records.

Parliament representing that undue influence had been brought to bear at the election of knights of the shire, and they prayed that those who had been instrumental in bringing on arbitrary government should be dismissed from office. The next step was taken in 1641, when Parliament resolved to take command of the militia, and with this in view Lord Strange was removed from his office of Lord-Lieutenant of the county and Lord Wharton put in his place; at the same time a considerable number of justices of the peace known not to be well affected to the Parliament were struck off the commission and others appointed in their stead; and Mr. Ashton, Mr. Shuttleworth, Mr. Rigby and Mr. Moore, members of Parliament (all Parliamentarians), were despatched to Lancashire to see that the ordinance of the militia was put into force. We now find ourselves on the eve of those domestic struggles which ever since have been known as the Civil Wars, and in which Lancashire was destined to play no small part. At this time most of the old castles and fortresses had long ago been allowed to fall into disuse and ruin, but there still remained tenable the castles at Lancaster, Clitheroe, Greenhaugh and Liverpool, and the smaller fortified houses of Thurland, Hoghton, Latham and Greenhaugh, all of which were utilized to the utmost. In 1641 the revolt in Ireland was causing considerable anxiety in the minds of the Lancashire people, insomuch that they entreated Parliament to appoint a fleet of small ships to guard their coast, to prevent the Papists giving intelligence to the rebels, and to act as a defence for the "petitioners and other Protestants who inhabited the maritime parts opposite to Ireland."

The breach between the King and his Parliament gradually became widened, and early in 1642 Charles removed his Court to York, where he received a petition from Lancashire signed by 64 knights, 55 divines,

740 gentlemen, and about 7,000 freeholders, in which they express their satisfaction that the measures taken by the King had "weakened the hopes of the sacrilegious devourers of the churches patrimonie, and provided against all Popish impieties and idolatries and the growing danger of Anabaptists, Brownists, and other novellists," and then proceed to say that there is one thing which "sads our hearts," which is "the distance and misunderstanding between Your Majesty and Your Parliament."

To check the strong party of Royalists in the county, orders were issued to levy fines on the estates of the so-called "malignants," and other means adopted to, if possible, render them powerless when the struggle actually began. These precautions, however, were taken too late to be really effective.

On January 20, 1642, the King made a last attempt to come to terms with the House of Commons, and failing to arrive at a satisfactory conclusion, Parliament ceased to seek for the royal assent to their Bills, and by an "ordinance" of their own took the entire control of the militia. In the meantime the King went to Yorkshire, but was refused admission to Hull. Both parties were now making active preparation for an appeal to arms, and when the King on June 2 indignantly refused to hand over all his powers to Parliament and become a King in name only, the negotiations between the two came to an end, and practically the Civil War began. On August 22, 1642, Charles reared his standard on the walls of Nottingham Castle, and his herald made the proclamation of war. Parliament now appealed to the King to lower his standard, but it was of no avail, and on September 9 the Commons published a declaration setting forth their view of the causes of the war.

The great civil strife which followed was not one war, but many wars. In Lancashire these were for the most part carried on by officers and troops raised in the various districts, assisted sometimes by the local militia ; sometimes they besieged a town, and at other times only attacked a private house, but in every case the issue was one and the same—the King or the Parliament. Some time before actual war was declared at Nottingham and London, the troubles had begun in Lancashire.

The first outburst appears to have taken place at Preston, on June 20, 1642, when Sir John Girlington, the High Sheriff of the county, had convened a meeting at which to read the King's declarations and his answers to the Lancashire petition. The number of people attending this meeting was so great that it was adjourned to Preston Moor (just outside the town), and amongst those present were Lord Strange, Lord Molineux, Sir George Middleton, and Sir Edward Fitton. The meeting broke up in confusion ; the High Sheriff and some 400 others rode up and down the moor crying, " For the King, for the King !" whilst the greater number rallied round the opposition party, and remained to pray for the uniting of King and Parliament.

From a letter addressed to the Speaker of the House of Commons, dated June 27, 1642, and signed by Ralph Ashton, John Moore, and Alexander Rigby, we learn that the High Sheriff had surprised the garrison at Preston and carried away all the powder in the magazine there, and that Lord Strange had taken away thirty barrels of powder and a great quantity of matches from Liverpool, and had also, with many armed forces, " repaired to a towne called Bury, about 20 miles distant from his own house."[1] These proceedings alarmed the people of Manchester, who at once took up arms, and many volunteers from the surrounding districts were mustered

[1] The *Chetham Society*, vols. ii., xlii., and lxvi., contained full details of the Civil War in Lancashire. From this source many of the following particulars are taken.

and trained. These volunteers, together with the militia, numbered some 7,000 men, who were said to be well furnished with muskets and pikes, and when Alexander Rigby witnessed these training, they were dismissed with shouts of "For the King and Parliament!"

Whilst these warlike preparations were proceeding, it appears incredible that Lord Strange, with Thomas Tyldesley, of Myerscough, and a small retinue, should have paid a visit to Manchester; yet such was the case, the ostensible reason of this being to attend a banquet (on July 15)[1] in the house of Mr. Alexander Green, who lived in that town.

During the dinner, Captains John Holcroft and Thomas Birch, who were active Parliamentarians, entered the town with an armed force, and beat to arms. Lord Strange, with his small band of followers, turned out, and a riot ensued, in which a man called Richard Perceval, a weaver of Levenshulme, was killed. This is said to have been the first blood shed in Lancashire in these wars, but strictly speaking the great struggle had not yet commenced. After this, the people barricaded the chief approaches to the town with gates and earth-works, holding themselves ready to withstand an invading force. At the same time Lord Strange was busy muster-

---

[1] In a tract dated July 5, 1642, entitled "The Beginning of the Civil Warres in England, or Terrible News from the North," Lord Strange is reported to have approached Manchester with a considerable armed force on July 5, and drawing up at a little distance from the town, demanded that the inhabitants should deliver up their magazines. On their refusal to give them up, he marched against the town, outside of which he was met by "ten small companies set in a faire battalion," and a skirmish took place, which lasted several hours, and resulted in the withdrawal of the Royalist forces with the loss of twenty-seven men. The tract then states "that this is the beginning of the Civill Warre, being the first stroke that hath been struck, and the first bullet that hath been shot." There is much reason to doubt the correctness of this reported fight, as no mention of it is made by contemporary authorities.

ing men in the royal cause on the moors near Bury,
Ormskirk and Preston, in consequence of which he was
deprived of his Lord-Lieutenancy of Chester and North
Wales, and subsequently denounced as a rebel guilty of
high treason.   Amongst the King's supporters, none
were more zealous than the members of those old
Lancashire families who had, on account of their adherence
to the Roman Catholic religion, been deprived of the
right to bear arms.

Manchester, although it may have had within its
boundaries many stanch Royalists, was undoubtedly at
this time an important stronghold of the rebels, and it
was the first place in Lancashire which Lord Strange
received instructions from the King to recover.

Manchester was ready for the attack, the town having
been fortified in a rough-and-ready way.[1]   On the night
of Saturday, September 24, 1642, Lord Strange, accompanied by Lord Rivers, Sir Gilbert Gerrard, Lord
Molyneux, Sir John Girlington, and others, with some
4,000 foot, 200 dragoons, and 100 light horse, marched
to Manchester ; they had also with them six or seven
cannon, which were placed so as to rake the centre of
Deansgate and on the lower end of the old Salford Bridge.
The main body of the Royalists were stationed on the
south side of the river, in the grounds of Sir Edward
Mosley.   On the Sunday, in the middle of sermon,
people were called out of church to witness several " hot
skirmishes," which continued to break out during all that
day and on the Monday, when the siege really commenced, and continued during the whole week, and for
all that time (if we must credit the chronicler) the artillery
kept up a continual fire upon the town, yet did " little or
no harm," save " killing one which stood gazing on the

---

[1] These fortifications consisted of posts and chains, and barricades
of mud.   They were erected under the superintendence of Lieutenant-
Colonel Rosworm, a German engineer, at a cost of £30.

top of a stile." During this siege, Lord Strange's father died, and he then became Lord Derby. The command of the forces inside Manchester was given to Captain Bradshaw and Captain Radcliffe, who were assisted by Lieutenant-Colonel Rosworm; the inhabitants generally are said to have helped the soldiers, whilst some of the gentlemen were engaged night and day in making bullets. We are also told that the soldiers each day had prayers and singing of psalms at the street ends.

During the siege several attempts were made to force an entrance into the town; the troops in Salford made a vigorous attack on the old bridge, but were repulsed by Lieutenant-Colonel Rosworm, who maintained the post with thirty musketeers; another attack was directed against the head of Market Street Lane, but with no success. On the evening of the 27th Lord Strange sent a message to the townspeople, in which he offered to retire his troops if Manchester would give up its arms, and allow his force to march through the town, and give him £1,000 in money. To this a reply was sent to the effect that they were not conscious of any act committed by them which should "in the least kind divest" them of the "Royal protection, nor of any disobedience of his Majestie's lawfull commands;" they expressed their wonder that Lord Strange should come to them in this hostile manner to take away their arms; and, being by no means assured of the safety of their persons and goods if they delivered up their arms, they were resolved to retain them in their own custody. This decided refusal to yield resulted in a lessened demand, Lord Strange declaring that he would be satisfied if they gave up a part of their arms; this also was refused, and the siege was renewed.

On the last day of September the Earl of Derby, having received orders to join the King's army at Shewsbury, raised the siege, and after an exchange of prisoners

withdrew his troops. It is impossible to ascertain with
any degree of certainty how many were slain during this
siege, but a Parliamentary authority gives the numbers
as being on his side only five or six, whilst the Royalists
lost several officers and 200 common soldiers. Certainly
one of the slain was Thomas Standish, of Duxbury, a
captain of the trained band of Leyland; he was shot by
a bullet fired from the church steeple.

This, the first victory on the Parliamentary side,
brought forth a declaration of the Lords and Commons
assembled in Parliament, in commendation of the inhabitants of the town of Manchester for their valiant
resisting of the Earl of Derby, and at the same time
assuring them that payment should be made for all
disbursements or losses.

The Commons also ordered that a public thanksgiving
to God for the deliverance of Manchester should be
observed in all the churches and chapels in Lancashire.
The fortifications were now strengthened, and Manchester
became the recognised headquarters of the Parliamentary
army in this county, and the Earl of Derby, on his return
from Warwickshire, took up his position at Warrington,
and at the same time garrisoned Wigan. The Manchester
people now raised several troops in their immediate
neighbourhood, which were occasionally employed to
disarm any place which it was thought might be used
against them; thus the town of Bury was disarmed,
although it belonged to the Earl; and whilst accomplishing this feat, they took the surplice from the church
there and put it on the back of one of the soldiers, and
" caused him to rid in the cart the arms were caried in,
to be matter of sport and laughter to the behoulders."
Probably out of a spirit of revenge, the Manchester people
rased to the foundations the house of Sir Edward Mosley,
called the Lodge, where the Earl of Derby was quartered

during the siege. At the college they established a manufactory of gunpowder.

In December the Earl of Derby called a meeting of some of the leaders on his side, and they resolved to raise £8,700, to be assessed on the several hundreds of the county, and appointed collectors and treasurers for the same, and they also fixed the pay to be given to the forces raised; the rates were: captains of foot, 10s. a day; lieutenants, 4s.; "ancients" (*i.e.* standard-bearers), 3s. Horse soldiers received rather higher pay, varying from a captain's 15s. a day to a trooper's 2s. 6d. per diem, while sergeants were paid 1s. 6d., drummers 1s. 3d., corporals 1s., and common soldiers 9d.

During the rest of the winter, except here and there a skirmish, nothing of any great importance took place in Lancashire between the two parties, but in almost all the towns active preparations were made and garrisons stationed. Preston, Blackburn, Wigan, Bolton, and other boroughs, all assumed a warlike aspect.

Some of the miniature wars which took place have a comic aspect, as when Sir Gilbert Hoghton, on December 24, marched a body of men all the way to within a quarter of a mile of Blackburn in order to disarm that town, where they halted, when one of his men, having a small piece of ordnance, "plaied" most of the night; but the only damage he did was to knock the bottom out of a frying-pan. The recorder of this goes on to say, "they were afraid of coming near one another," and upon Christmas night Sir Gilbert withdrew his forces, and "his souldiers and clubmen were glad of it, that they might eate their Christmas pyes at home."[1]

Early in this month (December) there was a slight engagement at Chowbent, near Leigh, of which an account was sent (dated December 9, 1642) to a " Rev.

---

[1] A slightly different version of this is given in "Lancashire' Valley of Achor."

Divine in London " by one of the combatants, from which
it appears that as the people were going to church on
the previous Sunday a post rode through the country
informing them that the Earl of Derby's troops were
coming. Whereupon "the countrey presently rose, and
before one of the clocke" they had mustered about
3,000 horse and foot, who set out to meet the enemy,
"encountering them" at Chowbent, and driving them back
to Leigh, "killing some and wounding many." During
the attack some of the " youths, farmers' sons," allowed
their zeal to outrun their discretion, having " had little
experience of the like times before this." They, being
mounted, overrode their foot soldiers; and when the Earl's
forces, having retreated to Lowton Moor, discovered that
the enemy's infantry was left a long way behind, they
turned about and began another assault, but were ultimately obliged to fly, leaving many killed and a couple
of hundred taken prisoners. The scribe then goes on to
say, if the attack should be repeated, the people in the
district would be found to be on their guard, as the "naylers
of Chowbent, instead of making nayles," had been busy
making bills and battle-axes, and that they were determined to take as prisoners all the " greatest papists
and most dangerous malignants, and carry them to
Manchester to keepe house with Sir Cecil Trafford, that
arch-papist who is there a prisoner. For now the men of
Blackburn, Paduam [Padiham], Burnely and Colne, with
those sturdy churles in the two forests of Pendle and
Rossendale, have raised their spirits and have resolved to
fight it out rather than their beef and fatt bacon shall be
taken from them."

In the beginning of 1643 Sir Thomas Fairfax left
Yorkshire, and for a time made Manchester his headquarters, and from this time forward the war in the
county assumed a more serious aspect. Early in February
Sir John Seaton, the Major-General of the Parliamentary

troops, set out from Manchester, having under his command about 1,000 "firemen, horse and foot," and 600 "bill men, halberdiers and club men." The route taken for this march was by Bolton and Blackburn, from both of which towns additional troops were obtained. Preston had all along been held by the friends of the King—indeed, it had now become the headquarters of the Royalists, and the inhabitants had spared neither time nor money to render it, as they thought, safe and secure; around it they had thrown up an outwork of earth, within which was a wall of brick. As usual, we find considerable difference in the accounts of this attack on Preston. The Vicar of Dean, who was " an eye-witness " of the fight, writing to a divine in London, says that the assault was commenced by Sir John Seaton a little before sunrise; that the three companies from Manchester especially distinguished themselves, and that in an hour's time Preston was taken. The account ordered to be printed by the Commons in Parliament gives two hours as the time taken to effect an entrance, and states that the Major-General (Sir John Seaton) " behaved himself galantly at the end of Church Street, where the entry was made," there beating down the sentries and the soldiers stationed in the steeple of the church. Another authority[1] gives a more graphic picture : The Parliamentary force, he says, somewhat late in the evening of February 7, having passed the Ribble Bridge, drew up their main body in the fields, whilst some of their companies, led by some who knew the town well, were placed near the house of correction, so as to be ready to force an entrance through the Friargate Bars, whereas the forces generally were to assault the East Bars. The defending party fought well and bravely, but after the entrance was gained the invaders were allowed to march through the streets without resistance, yet as they passed

[1] Major Edward Robinson, "A Discourse of the Warr in Lancashire," *Chetham Soc.*, lxii.

along the soldiers with their muskets and pikes broke all the glass windows within reach.

The Parliamentary loss appears to have been slight, but of the Royalists over 200 were slain. Amongst the first to fall were the gallant Mayor, Adam Morte, and his son; the former was more than once heard to declare that before he would surrender the town he would set fire to it and begin with his own house.

Sir Gilbert Hoghton escaped and made his way to Wigan, but Lady Hoghton, Lady Girlington and Mr. Townley were all taken prisoners, and amongst the spoils taken were "three pieces of ordnance, a murdering piece, a great quantity of musquiets, and many horses, with two or three colours."

Most of the conquering forces remained in Preston and began to strengthen its fortifications, and erected a strong sconce upon the marsh outside Preston, so as to command the fords over the Ribble. To keep alive the enthusiasm of the soldiers, as well as to disarm a dangerous foe, an attack on Hoghton Tower was decided on, and with this object three companies were despatched from Preston on February 14. This fine specimen of a baronial residence was well situated and fortified; it was from its tower that Sir Gilbert Hoghton was wont to light his beacon to call musters of the friends of the King; on its walls were mounted "three great pieces of ordnance."

Sir Gilbert, as we have already seen, having escaped from Preston and gone to Wigan, and his wife being a prisoner, it is not to be wondered at that the little garrison at the Tower should be disheartened, and after a short parley give up the place.

The soldiers at once took possession, and whilst they were searching for arms and powder the place was blown up, and Captain Starkey and some threescore of his men were killed. This explosion was at the time put down as being caused by an act of treachery on the part of Sir

Gilbert's soldiers, but subsequently it appears to have been admitted that it was due to the carelessness of the victorious forces. The author of " Lancashire's Valley of Achor " distinctly states that it was "fired by their neglected matches, or by that great souldier's idoll, tobacco;" and he further adds that they were "burdened with the weight of their swearing, drunkennesse, plundering and wilfull waste at Preston."

Within a few days of the taking of Hoghton Tower, troops were sent to reconnoitre Lancaster, where, finding the inhabitants either unprepared to resist or more or less in sympathy with them, they at once attacked the castle and took it, and thereupon released all the prisoners they found there, whether they were in gaol for felony or debt. At the castle were Roger Kirby, M.P. for the county, and Sir John Girlington, who appears to have escaped on finding that the castle could hold out no longer.

The town of Bolton had been left with only some 500 men, and taking advantage of this, on February 16 the Earl of Derby and the Major-General marched from Wigan towards it with about 1,000 horse and foot and got within a mile of the place without being discovered by the garrison, which, it seems, was "at prayer in the church." And now the Earl's forces made a fatal mistake: instead of making straight for the town, they went round by Great Lever, and in doing so their presence was discovered, and the soldiers were at their posts ready to receive the besiegers. The first assault took place at Bradshaw Gate, where three forts had been erected. The contest was a severe one. The fortification consisted of certain outworks and a mud wall, 2 yards thick, on the inner side of which was an arrangement of chains, which has not been clearly defined. One account says that the invaders, with iron bullets of five or six pounds weight, shot through the mud walls; whilst another faithful narrator scornfully reports that "they played children's play, for they mortally hit but one lad," and he, common report said, was one on their own side.[1] The same authority adds that "hither their wittie malice brought a new invented mischievous instrument," which consisted of "an head about a quarter of a yard long, a staffe two yards long or more put into that head, twelve iron pikes round about and one in the end to stab with. This fierce weapon (to double their scorn) they called a *Roundhead*." The Royalists, having forced the outworks, got possession of several houses, to some of which they set fire; they were, however, ultimately driven back and retreated to Wigan, taking along with them, it is said, two or three cartloads of dead bodies.[2] When the fight was over, 1,700 men came from Middleton, Oldham, Rochdale and Manchester to the assistance of the besieged town. The officers in command of the garrison at Bolton were Colonel Ashton, Captain Buckley, of Oldham; Captain Scoffield, of Rochdale; Captain Holt, of Bury; and Captain Ashurst, of Radcliffe Bridge.

The rebels had now got into their hands Manchester, Preston, Lancaster, and Bolton, the Royalists having their headquarters at Warrington and Wigan, whilst most of the other towns (including Liverpool) had as yet not been called upon to take any prominent part in the struggle; but it may be assumed that almost invariably the Roman Catholics, the older gentry, and most of the freeholders, were on the King's side. About this time an event took place which caused great excitement in the northern part of the county, and which had some influence on the future course of the war in that portion of the county. On March 4 a large Spanish ship

[1] "Lancashire's Valley of Achor."

[2] "A punctuall relation of the passages in Lancashire this week" (February 14, 1642).

appeared in sight, and being driven by the wind into the waters of the Wyre near Rossall Point, the captain, not knowing where he could land, put out his anchor and fired his cannon as a signal of distress; on a pilot boat being sent out, it was discovered that the ship was laden with ammunition intended for the use of the Parliamentary forces. The ship, which was described as being of "a great burden, such a one as was never landed in Wyre watter in any man's memory," was forthwith seized by the Royalists and brought into the mouth of the Wyre; whereupon the Earl of Derby with a troop of horse came to Rossall, and finding there in or about the ship Colonel George Dodding, of Conishead Priory, and Mr. Townson, of Lancaster, both Parliamentary men, he took them prisoners and ordered the ship to be burnt, which was accordingly done. The Preston commanders, for whose use this ammunition was no doubt destined, in the meantime got to know what was being done, and despatched four companies of foot towards Rossall; they passed the night at Poulton-le-Fylde, and the next day, sending out scouts, they discovered that the Earl and his men were on Layton Hawes, and not liking to meet his horsemen, they marched on to Rossall, where from the opposite side of the river they witnessed the burning of the Spanish ship; this, as she was probably stranded, was not complete, so that most of the guns which she carried (some being of brass) were not destroyed, and this the Parliamentary officers were not slow to take advantage of, and they forthwith sent up boats and carried away the ordnance down the Lune to Lancaster, where they were stowed away in the castle.

Whilst the Earl was in the Fylde district he was instrumental in raising many more troops for the King's forces, and after doing so he decided to attack Lancaster, and if possible recover the guns which by his want of forethought had been taken by the enemy. Accordingly on March 18 the Earl (according to his own account) presented himself with a few forces before the town, and the Mayor having refused to surrender, he (the Earl) "made bold to burn the greatest part of the town, and in it many of their souldiers, who defended it sharply for about two hours, but we beat them into the castle, and I seeing the tower clear from all but smoke, spared the remainder of that town and laid siege unto the castle." This attempt to recover the castle he abandoned ; having been informed that Sir John Seaton with a large force was on his way from Preston, he resolved to steal a march on that town, now left almost defenceless. The account of this destruction of Lancaster as given by Major Robinson has a very different aspect ; he asserts that there were very few soldiers in the town, except those in the castle, and consequently the firing of the houses was an unnecessary piece of cruelty ; in the centre of the town many of the best houses were fired, and in one long street all the houses, barns, with the cattle in their stalls, were entirely burnt.

When the Earl left Lancaster he took with him many prisoners of war, amongst whom was the Mayor of that town. The Earl managed to march to Preston by a different route to the one taken by Colonel Ashton, who commanded the party sent to the relief of Lancaster, and thus on March 22 he reached Fullwood Moor, where he waited until after dark; in the meantime, however, the scouts from Preston had discovered his advance, and had alarmed the garrison. The Friarsgate Bar was strongly guarded, but the nearer the enemy came to it, it is said, the "weaker it waxed, for the townes men were generally disaffected to Parliament."[1] This is probably true, as after, according to one authority, two hours' fight[2] the

[1] This is Major Robinson's statement.
[2] Major Robinson says he "discharged that little pece of ordenance they carried with them divers times," and then walked into the town.

town was regained. The next day many people from the country around Preston came into the town shouting, " God bless the King and the Earl of Derby!"

The Earl seemed now to be bent on recovering all that had heretofore been lost, and within a week of the taking of Preston (on the 27th) Bolton was again attacked, the Royalist force about two o'clock in the afternoon being drawn up on the moor outside the town, and a message sent to demand a surrender : this was refused, and towards dark the " minister of the town prayed with a company of souldiers, most of them townsmen. The end of prayer was the beginning of the fight."[1] The enemy made several assaults during the night, and at one time got close to the mud wall, but some forces from Bury coming to assist the besieged, the enemy were finally repulsed. There was probably very little loss on either side.

Colonel Ashton only arrived at Lancaster to find the town partially in ruins; he then marched on to the neighbourhood of Whalley. On the road he was followed by the Earl of Derby and his forces, and a slight engagement took place, after which the Royalists took shelter in the abbey, but were afterwards forced to retreat through Langho Green to Ribchester. Colonel Ashton and his men then proceeded to Padiham, where, " having a good minister, some hours were spent in thanksgiving " for their great deliverance.

On April 1, Wigan, one of the headquarters of the Royalists, was stormed and taken after a very short struggle by Colonel Ashton's forces; but, according to Rosworm, owing to some treachery the place was vacated the same night, the soldiers having first taken some prisoners and much spoil, and having placed " great heaps of woollen cloth of the drapers in the streets." Wigan was again taken on April 28 by Colonel Ashton, who, having burnt the gates of the town, took an oath

---

[1] " Lancashire's Valley of Achor."

from the townsmen never again to bear arms against the King.

Warrington was now garrisoned by the Earl of Derby. It was defended on one side by the river Mersey, which was crossed by a bridge of four arches; over this bridge was a narrow roadway, and on the centre pier stood a watch-house which had formerly been used by the Austin Friars as an oratory. The other sides of the town were defended by mud walls, with gates at the principal entrances; outside these walls outworks had been thrown up. Against this stronghold Sir William Brereton's forces and a large detachment from Manchester laid siege on April 1 (1643), but they only succeeded in getting possession of Sankey Bridge and "a fayre large house of one Mr. Bridgeman's."[1] They withdrew their troops after a three days' siege and some smart fighting, the reason alleged for this being that the Earl of Derby set fire to the centre of the town, and threatened to burn down the whole place rather than it should be taken.

Lancaster towards the end of April was again taken by the Parliamentary forces, and the pieces of ordnance from the Spanish ship (see p. 139) were removed to Manchester, and very shortly afterwards (May 19) Warrington, after withstanding a week's siege, was obliged to surrender, partly, it is said, because provision ran short. After these various warlike proceedings, it is not astonishing that funds began to fail, and for want of the sinews of war, many preferred to return to their usual occupations, and thus the leaders of both parties were surrounded with difficulties. Whilst the Parliament could and did order the estates of the delinquents to be confiscated, the Royalists could only levy voluntary rates, which fell heaviest on those whose estates had thus been seized. The tide of war seemed now to have turned against the Earl of Derby, who, to add to his other defeats, made an

[1] Edward Bridgeman, late M.P.

attempt, and failed, to regain the magazine in Liverpool. The Royalists were further disheartened by the removal from their midst of the Earl of Derby, who was ordered by the Queen to betake himself to the Isle of Man, which was then menaced by the enemies of the King ; here he landed on June 15, 1643. Shortly after this Hornby Castle[1] was taken by the Parliamentary forces, and there now only remained Thurland Castle and Lathom House in the hands of the Royalists; and as the Earl of Derby, Lord Molyneux, and Colonel Thomas Tyldesley were all out of the county, the enemy began to realize that they were almost in possession of the whole county. Before the departure of these leaders much plundering by the soldiers was reported in the Fylde district, where Lord Molyneux and Colonel Tyldesley were for a time stationed; at Kirkham, Clifton, St. Michael's and Laton, cattle were taken and houses sacked. About this time Colonel Alexander Rigby (whose name hereafter appears more prominently) came armed with a commission from the Commons to raise forces in the hundreds of Leyland and Amounderness, and to get the soldiers so raised ready for war in the least possible time. His efforts were successful, and in nearly every parish in the district he met with some support. Encouraged by this, he, about midsummer, undertook to take Thurland Castle, which was then held by Sir John Girlington,[2] who had around him " many disperat caviliers;" his castle was well fortified and provisioned. Colonel Rigby was supplied (in addition to the men he had raised) with forces from Salford and Blackburn Hundreds. Alexander Rigby's

[1] This castle was afterwards ordered to be dismantled. Its position rendered it difficult to attack, as it stood on an eminence from which the ground sloped rapidly in every direction. It was entered by the large windows on the east side, and the entrance thus gained, the victory was assured.

[2] This castle was first taken by Colonel Ashton, in June, 1643, but Sir John Girlington, having got hold of it, reoccupied it.

own account of this siege is that during the greater part of the conflict, which lasted seven weeks, he was threatened by the forces of Westmorland, which were drawn up within his view ; to these forces were added the Royalists from the Cartmel and Furness district. Having decided to deal with these forces before attacking the castle, he took " 500 foot, 2 Drakes, and 3 small troops of horse " (part of his army which lay before Thurland), and marched thirty miles " over mountain and sea, sands and water," and when in sight of the enemy (near Dalton) they " committed themselves to God's protection and began their worke with publike prayers." From some cause, which is not recorded, he goes on to state that the enemy, before a blow was struck, began to retreat, and were soon dispersed, throwing away their arms, and leaving their guns and ammunition behind them. Colonel Rigby took some 400 prisoners, including Colonel Huddle- ston, of Millom. After this exploit the little band of soldiers turned back to Thurland in the best of spirits, and endowed with such enthusiasm that in a very short time Sir John Girlington surrendered, on condition that he and his wife should be allowed free passage into Yorkshire. The castle was at once demolished. A portion of the ancient walls and an entrance doorway are all that now remains of this fortified house of the Tunstall family.

The next step to be taken was, of course, to attack Lathom, which was now the refuge and headquarters of the few Royalists left. This strong fortress was built on the site of an older building in the time of Henry VI., and according to the ballad of " Flodden Field," " this bright bower of Lathom " had " nine towers on high : above these rose what was known as the Eagle Tower ; it stood on a flat, boggy piece of ground, and was surrounded with a wall some 2 yards thick, on the outside of which was a moat 8 yards wide and 2 yards deep. On each of the nine towers there were six pieces of ordnance. Into this stronghold a few faithful followers of the Earl of Derby (who was now in the Isle of Man) had retreated, and were determined to assist the Countess in maintaining it against all comers; with this in view, they proceeded to garrison it and to procure from the surrounding neighbourhood provisions to enable them to withstand a prolonged siege. These precautions were not taken too soon, for on February 24, 1643-44, a meeting was held in Manchester, when it was resolved that forthwith an attack should be made on Lathom, the conduct of which was given to Colonel Alexander Rigby (a lawyer), Colonel Ashton of Middleton, and Colonel Moore of Bankhall.

On February 27, 1643-44, the Parliamentary forces took up their position about two miles from the house, and on the following day a letter from Sir Thomas Fairfax requiring the delivery of Lathom was sent to the Countess, to which she replied that she " much wondered that he wold require her to give up her Lord's house without any offence on her part done to the Parliament," and she asked for a week's consideration, " both to resolve the doubts of conscience and to advice in matter of law and honor."[1] This modest request was not at once granted, but after some further parley, and various proposals having on both sides been made and rejected, her ladyship ended the matter by saying " that though a woman and a stranger divorced from her friends and rob'd of her estate, she was ready to receive their utmost vyolence, trusting in God both for protection and deliverance."

The siege was now begun in earnest, though the object seems to have been rather to starve out the garrison than to take the place by storm; sorties were frequently made by the cavaliers, and from time to time shots were fired at the walls and towers by the enemy. One

[1] For full details of these two sieges see "Civil War Tracts," *Chetham Soc.*, ii.

chronicle adds they were intended either to " beate down pinnacles and turretts, or else to please the women that came to see the spectacle." After the siege had continued for nearly a month, Colonels Ashton and Moore appear to have begun to despair of success by ordinary weapons of war, and thereupon addressed a letter to the ministers of Lancashire asking them to " commend their case to God," so that "the Almighty would crowne their weake endeavours with speedy success."

Towards the end of April another summons was sent to the Countess demanding immediate surrender, to which she replied in person to the messenger, " Carry this back to Rigby; tell that insolent rebell he shall neither have p'sons, goods nor house ; when our strength and p'visions is spent, we shall find a fire more mercyfull than Rigby, and then if the providence of God p'vent it not, my goods and house shall burne in his sight; myselfe, children and souldiers, rather than fall into his hands, will seale our religion and loyalty in the same flame."

During the last few days the only thing that gave any anxiety to the gallant band within Lathom was a large mortar-piece from which the besiegers were continually sending fireballs and grenades into their midst. To get possession of this a sally was made, and after some smart fighting it was captured and dragged within the walls.

After this the spirits of the invaders appear to have been somewhat daunted, and at the end of nearly four months Rigby, hearing that Prince Rupert was coming to Lancashire, withdrew his troops to Eccleston Green, and ultimately marched them to Bolton. During this siege Rigby is said to have lost 500 men. Prince Rupert, on his arrival in the county, kept clear of Manchester, and marched straight towards Bolton, near to which town he was met by the Earl of Derby. Bolton was probably not well prepared to receive such a force as that led against it by the Prince and the Earl; the town was also destitute of ammunition, and had it not been for the timely appearance of Colonel Rigby with the remains of his forces, resistance would have been out of the question; but even as it was, the Boltonians gallantly and successfully drove back the enemy on the first assault, who, however, shortly rallied, and, returning to the attack, soon effected an entrance into the town, where little or no opposition was offered. This latter attack[1] was led in person by the Earl of Derby with 200 men, and after he had entered the town the other forces poured in on every side. Rigby fled, leaving some 2,000 of his men behind him, many (if not most of them) being slain on the spot, the Prince having ordered that no quarter was to be given to any person in arms. Another account accuses the Cavaliers of having "killed, stripped, and spoiled" all the people they met with, regarding "neither the dolefull cries of women nor children," and also of having brought out some "husbands on purpose to be slaine before their wives' faces." Many other outrages are said to have been perpetrated. All the records of this siege agree that the return of killed and wounded was very heavy, and it may safely be assumed that at least 1,500 were slain.[2] The colours from the Bolton soldiers were sent in triumph to Lady Derby at Lathom. Prince Rupert now marched on to Liverpool, where he found that Colonel Moore, the governor of the town, was prepared to resist him, having a strong garrison, and also being able to rely on the assistance of the sailors in port. To find provisions for this garrison Colonel Clifton is said to have taken all the sheep he could find on Layton Hawes (in Bispham). In the early part of June the siege began, but not for three weeks was the Prince able to take the town. The assaults were frequent, and resulted in serious losses to

[1] Seacome's "Memoirs of the House of Stanley."

[2] In Salford Chapel, "for poor distressed Bolton," the very large sum of £140 was collected ("Vicar's Chronicle").

the leaguers, but at last it became evident that further resistance was useless, so the wary governor, having first shipped off his arms, ammunition, and goods, left the north entrance to the town undefended, and thus admitted the enemy, who (according to Seacome) put to the sword all they met on their way to the high cross (where the exchange now stands). A large number of prisoners were taken, and the Prince seized the castle.

After a flying visit to Lathom, Prince Rupert continued his march to York[1] at the head of 20,000 men, where he joined the Duke of Newcastle. On July 2 the great battle of Marston Moor was fought, which, if it did not decide the contest between the King and the Parliament, left the cause of the Royalists in the North of England utterly ruined and hopeless. After this event, Lord Fairfax, taking advantage of the turn of tide in his favour, sent 1,000 horse into Lancashire to join the forces from Cheshire and Derbyshire, for the purpose of keeping a watch upon the movements of Prince Rupert, who had withdrawn the King's army into Westmorland and Cumberland.

Parliament was not slow to perceive the importance of retaining Lancashire, and at once ordered a grant of £3,000 for the soldiers there, and provisions were made to provide pensions for widows and children of those who had been slain; but this money was not to come out of the general exchequer, but "out of the several sequestrations of papists and delinquents within the respective hundreds of Blackburn, Leyland and Amounderness, or out of the assessments provided for that purpose; and no one was to receive more than four shillings and eightpence

[1] By way of Blackburn and Colne; at the latter place a slight skirmish took place on June 25. At Kirkham, between May and September, 1644, no accounts of the vestry were kept, because "Prince Rupert's army" had command of the county, and many of the parishioners had fled. In 1642 the soldiers "pulled asunder the organ pipes in the church."

per week." Prince Rupert again put in an appearance in Lancashire, and engagements of a not very serious character took place at Ormskirk, Up-Holland, near Wigan, and Preston. Liverpool being in great danger of being lost to the Royalists, Lord Derby made an attempt for its relief, but was repulsed with a heavy loss, and on November 1, 1644, the town was surrendered to Sir John Meldrum.

The close of the year 1644 found the Parliamentary forces in possession of all the fortified places in the county, except Lathom House, and in the following year the Royalists were defeated at Naseby and at Rowton Heath, near Chester, the latter entirely putting to an end the King's design, which was to march into Lancashire and attempt to regain what had there been lost. In the meantime, the Parliamentary party were determined to wrest from the Royalists their last holding in the county, and for this purpose, in July, 1645, General Egerton, with 4,000 men, began the second siege of this apparently invincible stronghold; for a long time they were unable to approach near enough to the house to enable them to use their heavy guns against it, but were content to lie behind a ditch at some distance from the walls. After withstanding this siege all the autumn, the garrison, for want of provisions, was obliged to yield, and on December 4 Lathom House, which was described as the glory of the county, was given up to the enemy. The greater portion of the house was pulled down and cast into the moat. The Earl and his Countess were now in the Isle of Man.

A little before this second siege, another of the Earl of Derby's strongholds was taken and destroyed—Greenhaugh Castle, in Garstang parish. Though small, this was said to be " very stronge, and builded so that it was thot impregnable with any ordenance whatsoever," and, moreover, it had only one door, and the "walls of an

exceeding thickness."[1] This castle was entirely demolished. As far as Lancashire was concerned, the war for
the present was over, but its effects upon the people had,
as may easily be imagined, been very severe, and this
fact was fully recognised by the Parliament, for on the
occasion of a general fast (September 11, 1644), it was
ordered that one-half of the money collected in London
and Westminster was to be sent for the relief of Lancashire, "where, in some parts, the people had nothing
left to cloathe them, or bread for their children to eat, in
consequence of the unheard-of spoil, rapine and cruelties,
lately committed by the enemie." In this year, the
Parliament took to itself the patronage of all the church
livings in the duchy, and as the Royalists had forcibly
taken the duchy seal from the Vice-Chancellor (Christopher
Banister), a new seal was made.

The cause of the King was now considered as hopeless;
nevertheless, one further attempt was made to revive the
spirit of loyalty to the Crown. General Sir Marmaduke
Langdale, having collected a considerable number of men
in the north of Lancashire and in Westmorland, joined
them to the forces raised in Scotland, and placed them
under the command of the Duke of Hamilton; this
united army, consisting of 15,000 foot and 6,000 horse,[2]
crossed the Border on July 4, 1648, and shortly afterwards
marched through Kendal, *en route* for Lancaster and
Preston, with a view of ultimately reaching Manchester.
In the meantime Cromwell had started for the North,
gathering forces as he went, and on August 16 he reached
Stoneyhurst. The Duke of Hamilton's army was now
stationed near Walton-le-Dale, on one side the Ribble,
and Sir Marmaduke Langdale's forces on Ribbleton
Moor on the other, so that the latter held a position
between the two main forces. Cromwell at once

---

[1] "A Discourse of the Warr in Lancashire."

[2] Another authority gives 32,000 (Burghall's "Civil War in Cheshire").

advanced against Sir Marmaduke; the manner of doing so will be best told in his own words[1]: "There being a lane very deep and ill up to the enemies army and leading to the town, we commanded two regiments of horse, the first whereof was Colonel Harrison's, and the next my own, to charge up that lane; on the other side of them advanced the Battel, which were Lieutenant-Colonel Reads, Colonel Deans, and Colonel Prides on the right, Colonel Brights and my Lord Generals on the left, and Colonel Ashton with the Lancashire regiments in reserve.

"We ordered Colonel Thornhaugh and Colonel Twisletons regiments of horse on the right, and one regiment in reserve for the lane, and the remaining horse on the left; so that at last we came to a Hedge dispute, the greatest of the impression from the enemy being upon our left wing; and upon the battel on both sides of the lane, and upon our horse in the lane, in all which places the enemy was forced from their ground after 4 hours dispute, until we come to the town, into which our troops of my regiment first entered, and being well seconded by Colonel Harrisons regiment, charged the enemy in the town and cleared the streets. . . . Colonel Deans and Colonel Prides outwinging the enemy, could not come to so much share of the action. . . . At the last the enemy was put into disorder, many men slain, many prisoners taken, the Duke with most of the Scots horse and foot retreated over the bridge, where, after a very hot dispute betwixt the Lancashire regiments, part of my Lord Generals and them being at push of pike, they were beaten from the bridge, and our horse and foot following them, killed many and took divers prisoners, and we possessed the bridge over Darwent and a few houses there, the enemy being driven up within musquet-shot of us where we lay that night. . . . In this posture did the enemy and we lie the most part of that night; upon

---

[1] Lieut.-General Cromwell's letter to the Hon. William Lenthall.

entring the town, many of the enemy's horse fled towards Lancaster, in the chase of whom went divers of our horse, who pursued them near ten miles, and had execution of them, and took about 500 horses and many prisoners. We possessed in the fight very much of the enemy's ammunition; I believe they lost four or five thousand arms. The number of slain we judge to be about a thousand, the prisoners we took were about four thousand."[1]

During the night the Duke, with the remnant of his army, retreated towards Wigan, and though they were hotly pursued, after some fighting by the way they got into that town, where they remained for the night, and on the morrow continued their flight towards Warrington. Wigan, Cromwell describes as " a great and poore town, and very malignant," and he adds that the Duke's army plundered the inhabitants " almost to their skins." Cromwell followed the retreating foe, and the two armies again engaged near Winwick, when another 1,000 of the enemy were slain, the rest being driven on to Warrington Bridge, which they found so well fortified that they faced about, and again prepared to meet their pursuers. Cromwell, considering (as he put it) " the strength of the pass," agreed to give quarter and civil usage, on the surrender of the officers and soldiers of the town as prisoners of war; these terms being accepted, the Duke and his army marched off into Cheshire.

The account of the fight at Preston given by Sir Marmaduke Langdale does not materially differ from that of the Parliamentary leader, but he frankly admits that his forces were utterly beaten, his foot soldiers being totally lost. The inhabitants of the various districts in which these battles had taken place again suffered most acutely, so much so that the Mayor and Bailiffs of Wigan

---

[1] Burghall put the killed and wounded at 4,000, and adds that they took 6,000 prisoners !

and several ministers in the county sent to London an appeal for immediate relief. This appeal refers to "the lamentable condition of the county of Lancaster, and particularly of the towns of Wigan, Ashton, and the parts adjacent," and sets forth that these districts had borne the heat and burden of both the wars "in an especial manner above other parts of the nation"; that the plague of pestilence had been raging for three years; that there was a scarcity of all provisions, grain the most in use being six times its usual price. All trade was utterly decayed, and it "would melt any good heart to see the numerous swarms of begging poore and the many families that pine away at home not having the faces to beg." Some of the poor, being on the point of starvation, had eaten carrion and other unwholesome food, "to the destroying of themselves and the increasing of the infection," the plague being entirely attributed to the "contagion from the wounded souldiers left there for cure."

Liverpool also suffered much from the wars. In July, 1648, letters were received by Parliament from the Governor of Chester, representing the sad condition of that garrison, especially as to the convenience of the harbour and the revolt of the ships. The town itself was said to be but small, "and much decayed," by reason of the war and the loss of the Irish trade, and also by "the free quarter of the soldiers."[1] The plague, also, about this time appeared in Liverpool and Warrington. During the next month the Deputy-Lieutenants were ordered to keep some horse soldiers near Lancaster, as that town was considered of special importance from a military point of view.

In the early part of 1649 the danger of further disturbance in the north appeared to have passed, and an order was given to demolish Clitheroe Castle and to disband

[1] Cal. State Papers, Dom. Ser., 1648-9, p. 219.

the forces in the county; but as some of them refused to be broken up, Major-General Lambert was despatched with orders to disband them, by force if necessary.

On January 30, 1649, the King was executed for high-treason, and the Commonwealth established, and thus the long struggle was brought to a close; but Lancashire had not yet seen the last of the Civil Wars; for in August, 1651, Charles II., the uncrowned son of the " martyr King," passed through the county on his way to Worcester; and, as was no doubt foreseen, this passage was not effected without a struggle with the strong Commonwealth party in the county.

The young King's forces marched over Ellel Moor to Lancaster, where he was proclaimed King at the market-cross; through Preston and Chorley, and on to Warrington bridge, where their progress was opposed by a company of foot, who were soon overwhelmed by numbers and forced to retreat, allowing the King and his followers to pass over into Cheshire. Cromwell in the meantime was in pursuit with an army of some 10,000 men, which at Preston was increased by another 6,000 under the commands of Generals Lambert and Harrison. On the other side, the Earl of Derby, having been sent for from the Isle of Man, was endeavouring, but almost in vain, to raise men in Lancashire. With such forces as he could get together (probably not more than 1,500 men), the Earl marched to Wigan, where he was met (in Wigan Lane) by Colonel Lilburne, and after a short but sanguinary battle he was slightly wounded and his followers utterly routed. The fighting was so severe that the Earl lost five colonels, the adjutant-general, and four lieutenant-colonels. With some thirty men as an escort the Earl escaped and made his way to Worcester to join the King. After the battle of Worcester the Lancashire Earl was again a fugitive, and on his way to Knowsley he was taken prisoner on the road, about half a mile from Nantwich in Cheshire, by Captain Oliver Edge, and lodged in the castle at Chester. Notwithstanding that Captain Edge, on the Earl's surrendering, had given him a promise of quarter, he was tried by court-martial at Chester, and found guilty, the sentence being that he should be beheaded in the market-place of Bolton, which sentence was carried out on October 15 (1651), in the presence of a large crowd of people, who are said to have been " weeping and crying and giving all expressions of grief and lamentation."[1]

The Civil Wars were now over, and attention was again turned to local matters. Manchester was one of the first towns to dismantle its forts, throw down its outer walls, and remove its gates; this was done in 1651. In the same year the court-leet ordered a gibbet, which had been erected in the corn market-place " for the punishment of the souldiers," to be taken down. Manchester, as a reward for her adhesion to the Parliamentary cause, was allowed to return a member of Parliament in 1654.

One would have thought that the dire troubles through which Lancashire passed would for a time at least have removed all desire to again take part in the contest between King and Parliament; but the spirit of some of the old Royalists still remained, and on the death of Cromwell (September 3, 1658) a league was formed to restore the monarchy, in which Lancashire was to have taken a prominent part; the son of the renowned Sir Marmaduke Langdale was to command the forces of this county, and amongst his supporters were the son of the " martyr Earl," Sir Thomas Middleton, and others. This crude attempt was frustrated by a signal defeat in a short engagement at Northwich, where the fugitives were scattered in all directions, some to Manchester and some to

[1] For full details of this historic incident see " Stanley Papers," "Civil Warr in Lancashire" (Chetham Society), Seacome's " Memoirs," Hughes' " Boscobel Tracts," etc.

Liverpool, where they found no sympathy but met with hard blows.

The religious condition of the county during the Commonwealth will be dealt with hereafter (Chapter IX.). Amongst the other effects of the events of the last ten years was the lowering of the whole social tone, the retarding of anything like education, or mental or material progress. Art, science, trade, commerce, and every branch of industry, must have been almost stagnant, whilst sickness, poverty, and crime were enormously increased. It was reported in 1655 that alehouses had become the very bane of the county. In the hundred of Blackburn alone over 200 of these had "to be thrown down."[1]

Manchester having been all through the Civil Wars a stronghold of the Parliament, it probably did not suffer quite as much as some of the other towns, and we are therefore not surprised to find that many improvements were made there very shortly after the close of the troubles; thus, in August, 1653, was established there the first public library, the origin of which was the gift by John Prestwich "of severall Bookes unto the inhabitants of the towne of Manchester, to be kept in some convenient place for a liberarie for the use of the said towne."

From an indenture bearing the afore-mentioned date, it will be seen that the Pendleton or Jesus Chapel, on the south side of the collegiate church, had been selected for the repository for these books; but being now in "great ruine and decay, the roofe thereof being fallen," the holders of the inheritance of it conveyed it to trustees, to the intent that it should be repaired and afterwards used for a library. This collection of books has now long ago been dispersed, and was probably never a large one.

---

[1] State Papers, Dom. Ser., iv. 240.

In 1656 the first town-hall was built; previous to that date the old wooden booths were used for the court-leet, etc. In these days, when football has become such a popular game as to render it one of the great national sports, it is interesting to find that in 1655 the Manchester Jury ordered all persons to be prosecuted who were found playing football in the streets. Nearly fifty years before this it had been found necessary to have " officers for yᵉ football " regularly appointed. This playing in the streets was not confined to Manchester; indeed, at Kirkham on Christmas Day, until quite a recent date, the streets were entirely given up to the followers of this popular pastime.

At the Restoration Manchester was prepared to welcome the newly-crowned King, and on April 22, 1661, the train-bands, under John Byrom, and the auxiliary band of Nicholas Mosley, together some 360 men, assembled in the field " in great gallantrie and rich scarffes, expressing themselves with many great acclamations of joy." They afterwards marched to the collegiate church, preceded by forty boys, " all cloathed in white stuffe, plumes of feathers in their hats, blew scarffes, armed with little swords hanging in black bells and short pikes shouldered." In the church was a large concourse of people, who, says the chronicler,[1] " civilly and soberly demeaned themselves all the whole day, the like never seen in this nor the like place." A sermon was preached by the Warden, Richard Heyrick, and a civic procession afterwards paraded the town. On arriving at the conduit which supplied the town with water, there was a long halt, in order that the "gentlemen and officers " might drink his Majesty's health "in claret running in three streams from the conduit." This stream afterwards ran for the public use until after sunset. Lancaster celebrated the event by presenting to the King

[1] Heawood's " Coronation."

" their small mite as a token of their joy by surrender of their fee farm rents of £13 6s. 6d., which they purchased of the late powers."

On October 7 following, 582 of the inhabitants took the oath of allegiance. In 1688 an assessment for the town gives the names of 500 ratepayers, who lived in seventeen streets or lanes ; eighteen years later (in 1679), when the oath of allegiance was again taken, there were about 800 attestors. These figures give some idea of the population of Manchester at this period. The trade of the town was now very much extended, a considerable business being done with Ireland and London. From the former yarn was purchased, which was woven and returned; and from the Metropolis cotton wool was purchased, which came from Cyprus and Smyrna, and was manufactured into fustians, dimities and other fabrics. The appearance of the town towards the end of the century underwent a great change; its old narrow streets and lanes were somewhat widened, and the time-worn houses of wood and plaster gave place to more substantial erections of stone and brick. There had also been established, by the bequest of one of Manchester's merchants, Humphery Chetham, of Clayton Hall and Turton Tower, the Chetham Hospital and Chetham Library, the latter being the first really free library opened in England.

Preston had now greatly increased, and was a prosperous town of about 6,000 inhabitants. In 1682 Kuerden describes it as being " adorned with a large square or market-place," and its streets as being " so spacious from one end thereof to the other, that few of the corporations of England" exceeded it. In the centre of the town was " an ample, antient and well-beautifyed gylde hall," under which were " ranged two rows of butchers' shops, and here once a week was a market for linen cloth, yarn, fish, and general agricultural produce, as well as cattle, sheep and pigs, and here and there were the houses of the wealthy, mostly built of brick and "extraordinarily addorning the streets." Preston had also its workhouse, public almshouse and school, and the old building formerly occupied by the Grey Friars served as a kind of reformatory for "vagabonds, sturdy beggars, and other people wanting good behaviour."

During the reign of Charles II. two guilds were celebrated at Preston, to which people came from all parts of the county. Liverpool towards the end of the reign of Charles II. began rapidly to develop. Blome, writing in 1673, states that Liverpool was a bold and safe harbour, in which ships at low water could ride at 4 fathoms, and at high water 10 fathoms, and that amongst the inhabitants were many eminent merchants and tradesmen, whose commerce with the West Indies made it famous. Emulating Manchester, it had then recently erected a town-hall, which was "placed on pillars and arches of hewn stone," having under it an exchange for merchants. This hall was built on the site where the old market cross had stood for a very long period. In the middle of this century (1650) the town consisted of Water Street, near to which was the tower, owned by the Stanley family, the Custom-house, Dale Street, Castle Street, Chapel Street, Tithebarn Street, Oldhall Street, and Jaggler's Street, and on its rocky eminence, looking down upon the town, still stood the castle. In 1654 the first attempt to light the streets was made, the order given by the authorities being that "two lanthorns with two candles burning every night in the dark moon [*i.e.,* when there was no moon] be set out at the High Cross and at the White Cross, and places prepared to set them in every night till eight of the clock."

A very large portion of the land on which Liverpool stood at this time belonged to Edward Moore (afterwards

Sir Edward), of Bankhall, and from his "rental"[1] we may gather much curious detail as to the tenure and character of the various lessees; the rent appears to have been paid partly in cash and partly in kind or service— thus, one tenant paid £1 a year, three hens, and three days' shearing; another, £1 6s. 8d. and the same boon hens and service. The pool from which the town took its name is frequently mentioned, and a note singularly foreshadows a branch of trade which subsequently became very advantageous to Liverpool. Moore called one of his tenements Sugar House Close, because a great sugar merchant from London came to treat with him for it; and it was agreed that he was to build up to the front street a goodly house four stories high, and at the back a house for boiling sugar.

At a little later period the establishment of extensive potteries in Liverpool introduced a new trade, but as early as 1665 a coarse kind of earthenware was made at Prescot, and the carting of it through the town was said so to "oppresse and cut out the streets," that the Corporation levied a toll of 4d. for every cartload. The Liverpool potteries are said to have been the earliest works of the kind in England.

The question of what to do with the wandering beggars appears to have met with a rough-and-ready answer from the Liverpool authorities, and in 1686 they sent round the bellman to warn the inhabitants not to relieve any foreign poor, and, to prevent any mistake, they ordered that all those on the relief list should wear a pewter badge; and so strictly were these regulations enforced, that a burgess was fined 6s. 8d. for harbouring his own father and mother without giving due notice to the officials.

The first regular post-stages between the various parts of Lancashire and the rest of England were slow in developing, as we may infer from the fact that in 1653

[1] Published by Chetham Society, vol. xii., old series.

three merchants (two Londoners and a Cornishman) made a proposal to the Government to work the inland and foreign letter office, and to establish a stage between Lancaster and Carlisle. This arrangement was probably not carried out. The roads all over the county were at this period in a dreadful state, and were not materially improved until the establishment of the turnpike system.

The educational advantages had now somewhat improved, the increase in public schools towards the close of the century being considerable. The experience of one boy will serve as a sample of how, no doubt, fared others. William Stout, the son of a well-to-do farmer, who lived at Bolton Holmes, near Lancaster (where his ancestors had lived for generations), records[1] that he was first sent to a dame school, and afterwards to the Free School at Bolton (about the year 1674), but when he was between ten and twelve years of age he was, especially in the spring and summer season, taken away for the " plough time, turf time, hay time and harvest, in looking after the sheep, helping at plough, going to the moss with carts, making hay and shearing in harvest;" so that he made small progress in Latin, and what he learnt in winter he forgot in summer; as for writing, he depended upon a writing-master who came to Bolton during the winter.[2] One of the earliest recollections of the writer just quoted was of his sister being sent up to London to be touched by Charles II., on which occasion she received a gold token worth about 10s., which she afterwards wore round her neck, "as the custom then was." The royal touch was not in this case efficacious. William Stout afterwards settled in Lancaster as a kind of general dealer and merchant, especially in groceries

---

[1] "Autobiography of William Stout"; London, 1851.

[2] A few years afterwards he was sent to a school in Westmorland, where he was taught both Latin and Greek.

and ironmongery, and from his diary may be gleaned
several interesting details of the state and trade of
Lancaster, which at that time (end of seventeenth
century) did a considerable shipping business to London,
Ireland, Virginia, Barbadoes, and other ports.

In 1689 the war with France much interfered with this
trade, and the cheese from Cheshire and Lancashire,
which required twenty ships yearly to carry it to London,
had all to be taken by land.   The rate for the carriage in
this way was from 3s. to 5s. a hundredweight in summer.
Iron was obtained in the crude state from the bloomeries
of Cartmel and Furness.   Tobacco was largely imported
into Lancaster directly from Virginia, the trade being
carried on partly by exchange of goods; thus, one John
Hodgson, of Lancaster, sent out £200 value of English
goods, for which he obtained in Virginia 200 hogsheads
of tobacco, and made by the barter a net profit of
£1,500, tobacco then selling at 1s. a pound.   Sugar
bought at Bristol and Liverpool was refined at Lancaster,
but none seems to have been imported at this time.   Our
diarist in 1695 was collector of the land-tax of Lancaster,
which was 4s. in the pound, and amounted to £120, so
that the rateable value was only about £600.

One curious funeral custom is worth recording.   " I
went" (writes Stout) "to Preston fair to buy cheese," the
market for cheese being mostly at Garstang and Preston
fairs.   "At this time we sold much cheese to funerals in
the country, from 30 lbs. to 100 lbs. weight, as the deceased was of ability; which was shrived into two or three"
(slices or pieces) "in the lb., and one with a penny
manchet given to all attendants.   And it was customary
at Lancaster to give one or two long biscuits, called
Naples biscuits, to each attendant, by which from 20 to
100 lbs. was given."   The providing of the penny manchet
at the funeral often formed a paragraph in the deceased

person's will, and the doles given to the poor on these occasions were often considerable.

The last Herald's visitation to the county was made in 1664-65 by Sir William Dugdale, and from it we discover that many old families of the last century have entirely died out, whilst others of more humble origin have succeeded them. The incompleteness of the pedigrees (to say nothing of their glaring inaccuracies) is striking, and one is surprised to find how many families, undoubtedly entitled to bear arms, neglected to enter their descents. The seventeenth century saw the birth of a new order of men in Lancashire, who in many cases rose to opulence and became the founders of what developed into county families; there were the clothiers—they in many instances sprang from the lowest social grade, but by industry and thrift acquired their positions. The clothier purchased the wool (or kept large quantities of sheep), and delivered it to persons who took it to their own homes, and having there made it into cloth, returned it then to their employers. This business was usually carried on in the towns of the county, which were now rapidly springing up, and the demand for the kind of labour required quickly drew workmen from the surrounding agricultural districts. Amongst the most prominent centres for this trade were Manchester, Oldham, Bolton, Rochdale, Ashton, Bury, and Blackburn. In the manorial and other records of this period we find frequent references to "loomhouses," "bleachouses," "woolmen," and "clothmakers." These pioneers of the wool trade, the clothiers, often lived in large town-houses, adjacent to and communicating with which were their warehouses for the wool and manufactured goods. The contents of one of these establishments is furnished by the inventory attached to the will of Anthony Mosley, of Manchester, clothier, proved at Chester, April 30, 1607. The will itself, after providing for the family of the testator and bestowing several hundred pounds for charitable purposes, concludes with a clause to the effect that the testator's "walke millers" (*i.e.*, fullers) shall each have a cloak of 10 or 11 shillings a yard; that every one of his servants shall have 40s. each; that at the funeral a dinner shall be provided, and "a dealing to the poor of 2d. a piece"; and finally that the parson who shall make the funeral sermon is to be rewarded with 20s. for his pains. The dwelling-house consisted of the hall, the parlour, and the kitchen, with chambers over them; also a chamber over the ware-house, a brewhouse, a "bolting-chamber,"[1] an upper loft, and cellars. The stock of cloth in the warehouse was valued at £255, and the stock at various fulling-mills was estimated at another £740, whilst the various trade debts owing to the deceased amounted to £1,260. The household effects are not given in detail, but are given as "household stuffe and cloth," and valued at nearly £600, beside £22 of plate. In 1613 there was a heavy decline in the wool trade, to remedy which a Royal Commission was appointed, and subsequently Acts of Parliament passed to remove the impost on cloth, which had been put on by the Merchant Adventurers' Company, who for some years had an almost complete monopoly of dyeing cloth. The establishment of a free trade in dyeing once more revived the trade, and dyers were found in all our Lancashire towns where woollen cloth was manufactured, and alongside them were found fulling, or, as they were then called, walk mills. Coal, ironstone, and flags where obtainable also now began to find a ready market. Towards the close of the century the making of fustian and other so-called cotton[2] goods, which had almost been confined to Manchester, began

---

[1] The place where the meal was bolted = sifted.
[2] The cotton trade had not yet arisen. These goods were coatings, and made of wool.

rapidly to be taken up by the surrounding towns, one of the first of these being Bolton.

Lancashire had not yet established a printing-press,[1] though booksellers and stationers were not unknown in the larger towns; and a fair number of authors from this county had furnished materials for the printers of the Metropolis, amongst whom were Isaac Ambrose, Vicar of Preston and Garstang; John Angier, pastor of Denton; Nehemiah Barnet, minister of Lancaster; William Bell, minister at Huyton; Seth Bushell, Vicar of Preston; Henry Pigott, Vicar of Rochdale; Charles Earl, of Derby; Edward Gee, minister at Eccleston; John Harrison, minister of Ashton-under-Lyne; William Leigh, Vicar of Standish; Charles Herle, Vicar of Winwick; Richard Hollingworth, a Fellow of Manchester College; and Richard Wroe, Warden of Manchester; Joseph Rigby; Alexander Rigby; William Moore, Vicar of Whalley; Jeremiah Horrox, the astronomer; Nathaniel Heywood, Vicar of Ormskirk; and a number of writers for and against Quakers (see Chapter IX.). One reason, perhaps, of this absence of the printing-press was that not until 1695 was the censorship of printed matter swept away.

On the restoration of Charles II., as a reward for faithful services to the House of Stuart during the Civil War, it was intended to establish a new order of knighthood; this intention was ultimately abandoned, but those in Lancashire who were to have been honoured were Thomas Holt, Thomas Greenhalgh, Colonel Kirby, Robert Holt, Edmund Asheton, Christopher Banastre, Francis Anderton, Colonel James Anderton, Roger Nowell, Henry Norris, Thomas Preston, — Farrington, — Fleetwood, John Girlington, William Stanley, Edward Tildesley, Thomas Stanley, Richard Boteler, John Ingleton, and

[1] One solitary book, "A Guide to Heaven from the Word," is said on doubtful authority to have been printed at Smithy Door, Manchester, in 1664.

C. Walmesley, all of whom had an estate of the value of at least £1,000.

William III., on his way to Ireland, before the battle of the Boyne, embarked from Liverpool on June 14, 1690, and he probably met with but a poor reception from the Lancashire people, as everywhere in the county the Roman Catholics were dissatisfied at the expulsion of the Stuarts by the House of Orange.   The unpopularity of the King gave rise to many plots against him, the last of which was known as the " Lancashire Plot," which, according to one authority,[1] was not only the parent but the companion of all the other conspiracies, and its origin was owing to the politics of James II., who, hoping to regain the crown, concerted with his friends, before his departure for France, that they should raise a ferment in England, and that some trusty person should be commissioned to carry out this scheme.

The person selected for this commission was Dr. Bromfield, who, to suit his purpose, passed himself off as a Quaker,[2] and passed rapidly through the North of England to Scotland, sowing the seeds of discontent as he went along.   From Scotland he proceeded to Ireland, and then returned to Lancashire, intending to make that county the centre of action.   Caryl, Lord Molyneux, had, in 1687, been appointed Lord-Lieutenant of Lancashire in the place of Lord Derby; and it was to his house at Croxteth that Dr. Bromfield first proceeded on his return from Ireland; and here he found at all events a sympathizer, if not an active partisan.

[1] Kingston's "True History of the Several Designs and Conspiracies against his Majesty's Person and Government, as they were carried on from 1688 to 1697."

[2] For full details of this "plot" see the late Mr. Beamont's introduction to "The Jacobite Trials in Manchester, 1694" (*Chetham Soc.*, xxviii.), and also Dr. Abbadie's "True History of the Late Conspiracy," etc. ; London, 1696.

From Croxteth he went to an inn at Rhuddlan, in Flint-shire, where he stayed for some time, and soon had a considerable number of visitors. From this place he made frequent visits to Ireland, by this means keeping up a safer communication with the exiled King and his friends in Lancashire. Suspicion having fallen on him, the vessel in which he crossed to Ireland was seized, but with the assistance of the landlord of the inn at Rhuddlan he made his escape and repaired to Ireland, where King James made him a Commissioner of the Mint. The Lancashire Plot included the murder of the King, and Colonel Parker, according to De la Rue, was the person who first propounded this portion of the plot to Lord Melford. Dr. Bromfield now found it absolutely necessary to have an active agent, who was to be at once un-scrupulous and trustworthy. Such a man he thought he had secured in John Lunt, an Irishman by birth, but who was successively a labourer at Highgate, a coachman, a licensed victualler at Westminster, and one of King James's Guards, with a promise of a captaincy. More-over, he was not a man of good character, as he had been tried for bigamy.

This Lunt, having followed the King to France soon after his abdication, was sent from thence with the rest of the guards to Ireland in May, 1689, and there renewed his acquaintance with Bromfield. Being assured that the people in Lancashire only waited the King's com-mission to rise in arms on his behalf and restore him to the throne, he at once undertook to be the bearer of the commission. Meanwhile the conspirators in Lancashire, evidently being eager for the rising, sent over to Ireland Edmund Threlfall, of Ashes, in Goosnargh, to fetch the needful commissions, and accordingly he and two others embarked in a " pink " (*i.e.*, a small ship) called the *Lion of Lancaster,* and sailed down the Lune by night without any Custom-house certificate. This vessel had been used to fetch cattle from the Isle of Man for the Earl of Derby, and the sailors were led to believe that this was again their destination on this occasion; but Threlfall induced the captain to make for Dublin, where they duly arrived, and having received the commission and obtained a passport from Lord Melford, they re-embarked on board the pink, which, to prevent suspicion, was laden with iron pots and bars and other commodities, and they anchored in the Lune near to Cockerham on the morning of June 13, 1689. Whilst in Dublin, Threlfall and Lunt had met, and had now returned together in the pink, and as soon as she was anchored in the Lune they were put ashore, before the arrival of the Custom-house officers, whose practice and duty it was to go on board every vessel as she entered the harbour. Lunt, with that carelessness which so often distinguishes conspirators, left on board his saddle-bags, which contained some of the commissions, and finding out after he got ashore that he had done so, he asked one of the sailors who was returning with the cock-boat to the ship to bring them after him to Cockerham; but before this could be done the officers came on board, and discovering the papers, set off in pursuit of their owners; but not finding them, they handed the documents over to the authorities.

The discovery of these papers caused considerable excitement, and they were carefully examined by the Earl of Devonshire, the Earl of Macclesfield, the Earl of Scarborough and Lord Wharton, who were all in Manchester on army business, and they recommended that warrants should be issued to apprehend Lunt and Threlfall. In the meantime the two conspirators had taken shelter at Myerscough Lodge, near Preston, where lived Thomas Tyldesley, who was one of the foremost supporters of their cause. Here they divided such of the commissions as they had brought with them, Lunt setting off to deliver those for Lancashire, Cheshire and

Staffordshire, whilst Threlfall took those for Yorkshire and Durham.

Lunt afterwards went to London to buy arms and enlist men to be sent to Lancashire. At this time Irishmen came into the county in such numbers as to rouse suspicion, and in October the justices of the peace at the adjourned quarter sessions at Manchester sent a letter to the Secretary of State, in which it was stated that the gaols were full of Irish Roman Catholics, that many others were staying at Popish houses, and that boxes with scarlet cloaks, pistols and swords had been sent from London to Roman Catholic gentlemen now absent from home.

The warrants against Lunt and Threlfall were, no doubt, issued, but it was not until August that an arrest was made, when Lunt and Mr. Abbot, the steward of Lord Molyneux, were apprehended at Coventry when they were returning from London. They were cast into prison as enemies to the King, and soon afterward Charles Cawson, the master of the ship which brought Lunt and Threlfall from Ireland, was arrested on a similar charge. Cawson was taken from Coventry to London, where he gave evidence before the Privy Council as to his taking Threlfall to Ireland, and bringing him and Lunt back, also as to the papers left in the pink at Cockerham. Meanwhile Threlfall, having despatched his business in Yorkshire and Durham, where he assumed the name and title of Captain Brown, and probably not knowing that a warrant had been issued against him, returned home to Goosnargh, where he remained for some time concealed, waiting for a chance to get away to Ireland. Ashes, which had been the home of this family for several generations, was well adapted for a place of concealment, not only from its retired situation, but from its peculiar structure, its centre wall being at least 4 feet thick, and containing two cavities large enough to

hide half a dozen men in; add to these advantages that
the house was surrounded by a moat, and on every side
were sympathizing neighbours.

All things considered, perhaps Threlfall was as safe
here as anywhere had he used ordinary caution, but on
August 20 (1690) he was surprised near his house by a
party of militia, and as he offered to resist, he was killed
by a corporal who was one of the party. At the trial in
Manchester in 1694, one John Wilson, of Chipping, made
a deposition that Threlfall had told him that he had
twenty Irishmen ready for his troop, who had been at his
house and in the county waiting for several months.

In the February following a deposition was made
before the Mayor of Evesham, in Worcestershire, that
divers persons in that neighbourhood had received commissions from King James to raise two regiments of
horse, two of dragoons, and three of foot for Lancashire,
and that in various places were hidden arms, etc., especially in the houses of Mr. Blundell, of Ince, and John
Holland, of Prescot ; and further, that the deponent had
seen and heard read a letter from the late Queen in the
hand of Lord Molyneux's son, which gave assurance from
the French King of assistance in arms and men. This
information led to the imprisonment of several leading
Lancashire Roman Catholics.

In the May following, Mr. Robert Dodsworth declared
on oath to the Lord Chief Justice Holt that the troops in
Lancashire were to be joined by the late King's forces for
Ireland, while the French were to land in Cornwall, and
the Duke of Berwick was to cause a diversion in Scotland, but that no rising was to take place until the late
King landed in Lancashire, which he had promised to do
within a month.

John Lunt in November was committed to Newgate,
where he was kept for twenty weeks, and then bailed out
to appear at the Lancaster Assizes, where he appeared in

August, 1690, and was then committed to Lancaster Castle on a charge of high-treason. Here he remained until April, 1691, when he was brought to trial and acquitted, partly because the Custom-house officers were unable to swear to the papers, and partly because Charles Cawson, the master of the ship, had in the meantime fallen sick and died. Lunt, notwithstanding his long imprisonment and narrow escape from the scaffold, appears almost immediately to have set about raising men and collecting arms for the proposed insurrection. The destruction of the French fleet off the Hague on May 20, 1692, dispersed all thoughts of an invasion and for awhile partially arrested the designs of the conspirators.

The progress of the conspiracy was now slow and spasmodic, and was seriously checked in May, 1694, by the arrest and committal to the Tower of Walter Crosby, on whom were found papers containing many details of the proposed insurrection ; but more fatal even than this was that Lunt turned traitor, and on June 15, 1694, made a full confession of all he knew to one of the Secretaries of State. This, then, is the Lancashire Plot as given by the Court advocates, who, if they erred at all, would certainly not do so in favour of the conspirators. As far as Lancashire is concerned, the whole matter was at an end, except that the following gentlemen were all tried at Manchester in 1694, viz.: Caryl, Lord Molyneux, Sir William Gerard, Sir Rowland Stanley, Sir Thomas Clifton, William Dicconson, Esq., Philip Langton, Esq., Bartholomew Walmsley, Esq., and Mr. William Blundell.[1]

It is but fair to add that the various accounts published regarding this so-called Lancashire Plot contain many variations and inconsistencies, and it is no easy matter to decide which of these various writers is correct ; a full

[1] All well-known Lancashire men, except Sir Rowland Stanley, who lived in Cheshire.

account of the trials is now, however, in print, to which the curious reader is referred.[1]   The result of these trials was that the prisoners were acquitted, the witnesses not being considered worthy of credit ; but subsequently the House of Commons, by a vote of 133 to 37, resolved that there were grounds for the prosecution of the gentlemen at Manchester, as it appeared that there was a dangerous plot carried on against the King and his Government ; this resolution was also confirmed by the House of Lords.

The Lancashire gentlemen at the next assizes prosecuted Lunt and two others, who were the chief witnesses against them, and they were all three convicted of perjury.

During the reigns of James I. and Charles II. several towns applied for and got fresh powers by royal charter ; this was the case with Preston and Liverpool and several smaller towns—amongst the latter were Kirkham and Garstang.   At a very early period a market was held at Garstang, but it was not incorporated until 1680, when Charles II. granted a charter whereby the inhabitants were declared to be a "body corporate by the name of the Bailiff and burgesses of the Borough of Garstang."   From 1680 to the present time the Bailiff has regularly been elected.

The birth of many new trades in Lancashire dates from the seventeenth century, although many of the national industries were followed here at a much earlier period.   We now find numerous references to various trades on the tokens, which were somewhat extensively issued in Lancashire in consequence of the great scarcity of small change shortly after the execution of Charles I. Some of these local tokens were of superior workmanship, and of material calculated to stand the wear to which they were subjected.   They represented pennies, half-pennies and farthings.

[1] *Chetham Soc.*, xxviii.

About 150 varieties of these Lancashire tokens were issued before the close of the seventeenth century,[1] some of which indicate the trade followed by the issuer, and thus furnish some clue to the spread of certain industries within the county. A study of them gives the following results:

SEVENTEENTH-CENTURY TOKENS.

TOWN.	NUMBER ISSUED.	TRADE INDICATED.
Ashton-under-Lyne	4	1 mercer, 1 tallow-chandler, 2 unclassed.
Blackburn	6	4 mercers, 2 apothecaries.
Bolton	5	2 dealers in tobacco, 3 unclassed.
Burnley	1	a mercer.
Bury	1	? a saddler.
Chadderdon	1	an innkeeper.
Cheetham	1	a farrier or blacksmith.
Chorley	5	1 dealer in tobacco, 1 cordwainer, 3 unclassed.
Chowbent	1	a woolman.
Clitheroe	5	1 dealer in tobacco, 1 grocer, 1 draper, 2 unclassed.
Colne	1	a merchant.
Crosby	1	a draper.
Garstang	1	a tallow-chandler.
Halliwell	2	1 dealer in tobacco, 1 unclassed.
Halton	1	unclassed.
Haslingden	1	unclassed.
Heaton	1	a tallow chandler.
Holland	1	unclassed.
Huyton	1	a grocer.
Kirby	1	a vintner.
Kirkham	2	1 grocer, 1 unclassed.
Lancaster	8	1 apothecary, 1 woolman, 6 unclassed.
Little Lever	1	unclassed.
Liverpool	12	1 sugar merchant, 2 merchants or shop-holders, 1 grocer, 1 apothecary, 1 draper, 6 unclassed.
Manchester	15	1 chapman, 4 grocers, 2 apothecaries, 1 innkeeper, 7 unclassed.
Milnrow	2	1 shoemaker, 1 unclassed.
Newton	2	1 dealer in tobacco, 1 unclassed.
Oldham	1	unclassed.
Ormskirk	6	1 grocer, 1 draper, 4 unclassed.
Poulton-le-Fylde	1	a draper.
Prescot	2	1 mercer, 1 unclassed.

[1] See *Lanc. and Ches. Ant. Soc.*, vol. v.

Town.	Number Issued.	Trade Indicated.
Preston	8	7 grocers, 1 apothecary.
Risley	1	a dealer in tobacco.
Rochdale	6	1 grocer, 1 dealer in woollen goods, 4 unclassed.
Shaw	1	unclassed.
Tarleton	1	unclassed.
Turton	1	unclassed.
Warrington	17	2 clothiers, 2 woollen-drapers, 2 apothecaries, 1 sugar-dealer, 1 draper, 1 grocer, 8 unclassed.
West Houghton	1	unclassed.
Whalley	2	unclassed.
Wigan	8	1 apothecary, 1 armourer, 1 grocer, 1 tallow-chandler. 4 unclassed.

Amongst the unclassified several tokens bore religious emblems, such as " the bleeding heart " and the " dove and olive branch"; and the "eagle and child" was a favourite design. Crests or family arms were also often used, but in these cases there is nothing to indicate the occupation of the person who issued the token.

During the century to which the Lancashire plot just recorded formed a fitting close, Lancashire had witnessed many stirring events—the monarchy had been destroyed, the Commonwealth set up, and the rule of kings again established ; Roman Catholics had persecuted Protestants, and Puritans had tried their best to repress Roman Catholicism ; and in each and every case this county had done its share : if battles were to be fought, the Lancashire lads were in the thick of them ; if religious creeds had to be repressed, in their mistaken zeal, there again were the people of this county to the fore. But, notwithstanding wars, plagues, persecutions, insurrections, and a host of minor evils, Lancashire still progressed, her towns increased in number and in size, and her sons were leading the van in all matters of trade, commerce and enterprise. Manchester, Liverpool, Preston, and other large towns were attracting to them men, not only from the surrounding districts, but from all civilized countries; whilst the woollen and other goods manufactured in the county had already obtained a world-wide fame. Amongst other industries introduced during this century was bell-founding, which trade was carried on in Wigan with considerable success as early as 1647, and many church bells in the surrounding districts came from this foundry.

CHAPTER IX.

RELIGION.

OF the non-Aryan tribes who at some remote period lived in the North of England we do not know sufficient to even conjecture what was their religion, if they had any; but judging from analogy, it may be presumed that they had some kind of belief in a super-human power.

The tribes who next succeeded these rude savages in effecting settlements in this country were all of the Aryan race, and all that we are able to ascertain as to their religious faith is that when Julius landed in Britain he found that the inhabitants were pagans, and followed a mysterious kind of worship known as Druidism, and that their priests were called Druids, and were not only the arbitrators in disputes, but also judges of crime.

One of the tenets of this religion was a belief in the immortality of the soul, and also in its transmigration. As to the nature of their gods we know little or nothing, except that to them were offered human sacrifices, who were sometimes criminals and at other times prisoners of war. Of temples they appear to have had few, but to have performed their mystic rites in the secluded groves of oak which were then found on every side. The Druids were exempt from military service, and were at once priests, lawgivers, and teachers. From the time the

Romans penetrated into Northumbria (see p. 15) near the beginning of the fifth century, the religion of the people of that district (which includes, of course, Lancashire) must have undergone a gradual change, as the polytheism of the Romans made itself apparent.

At all their large stations the conquerors erected temples dedicated to their gods, and altars to their various deities were put up in every direction, and thus, no doubt, year by year the influence of the Druidical priesthood diminished, and was probably finally extinguished by the more attractive worship which found favour in imperial Rome.

After the Romans vacated Lancashire, the conversion of Constantine the Great to Christianity (see p. 17) had no doubt some effect upon religious thought even in Northumbria. But long after the Roman Empire became a Christian State, the tribes which were then struggling for supremacy in Britain still adhered to the old pagan worship, and *Thor*, the god of thunder, *Wodin*, the god of war, *Eostre*, the goddess of spring, and a host of others, were numbered amongst their deities. They believed, however, in a future state, as their warriors slain in battle were supposed to inhabit a bright and happy palace called *Valhalla*. Near the end of the sixth century, King Æthelbert, who ruled in Kent, married the daughter of King Charibert of Paris, and by the terms of her marriage contract she was to be allowed to enjoy the exercise of Christian worship, which she did in a small chapel near Canterbury. With her, from France, came a Frankish Bishop named Liuhard, who was soon followed by a Roman Abbot named Augustine, who came by instructions from Pope Gregory I., accompanied by some forty monks, who were to establish the Christian religion in Kent; they ultimately persuaded the King to be baptized, and this event may be regarded as the foundation of the Christian religion in England. Little by little the new

12

religion spread, and in A.D. 627 Edwin, the King of
Northumbria, became a convert through the instru-
mentality of his wife, who was a daughter of Æthelbert,
(see p. 42), and Paulinus, one of the company who came
to Britain with Augustine. He had been consecrated to
the episcopate by Justus, Archbishop of Canterbury, "in
order that he might be to Ethelburga, in her Northern
home, what Liuhard had been to her mother in the still
heathen Kent."[1]   On the authority of Bede, Paulinus was
a man of striking appearance, being tall, though slightly
stooping, with black hair, but of worn and wasted visage;
his nose thin, but curved like an eagle's beak, and altogether a presence to command respect and veneration.

The tale as told by Bede, of the dramatic events which
led up to the conversion of Edwin, must be received with
caution, mixed up as it is with such incidents as a
spiritual visitor with whom the narrator held familiar
converse; nevertheless, the main facts of the story are
probably correct, allowing for the fact that the account
was written nearly 100 years after the events took place,
and by one who was prone to mix with history incidents
which would only at the present time be classed with
legends and superstitions.   The story, briefly told (omit-
ting the apparition), is that Edwin for a long time
refused to abandon his old faith, but after an attempt
had been made to assassinate him, the birth of a
daughter and a victory over his enemy, the King of the
West Saxons—all of which events were turned to account
by the wily Bishop (who was trying to convert him)—he
consented to call a council of leading men and to lay the
matter before them, and if they agreed with him they would
together be baptized and admitted into the Church.

At this meeting, a chief priest of one of the pagan
temples, Coifi by name, declared himself against his old
faith on the simple grounds that after all his long devotion

[1] Bright's "Early English Church History," p. 111.

to his gods he was still without that worldly success for which his soul thirsted; and, therefore, as he had nothing to lose and everything to gain, he should vote for giving the new religion a trial.

Another of the council spoke, and in simple but striking words reminded his hearers how they had often on a winter's night, gathered round the fire, when all outside was dark and dreary, the wind howling and the rain beating against the latticed windows, when a door for a moment opened admitting a poor little bird seeking shelter from the storm. But a moment only it stays, flies across the hall, and is gone. This, he continued, is a fit emblem of man's life; he appears for a little season, and having finished his appointed course is gone; but no earthly wisdom has told us from whence he came, or has illuminated his departure. And so, he concluded, if the new teacher can tell us anything with assurance of certainty as to man's origin or future destiny, his words ought to be received and accepted. Paulinus then addressed the assembly, at the conclusion of which Coifi, with all the fanatic zeal which might be expected from such a man, volunteered to enter the temples of the gods and to take therefrom what he heretofore had held to be sacred, and having been armed and mounted he rode to Goodmanham, a place of the highest pagan sanctity, and there tore down the idols of Thor and Wodin with shouts of joy and gladness. Bede adds, the people stood awe-struck, and thought that their chief priest had gone mad. But Coifi knew what he was about; he had only determined (like many a better man had done before) to keep himself on the winning side, for he saw clearly enough that paganism had received its death-blow, and however little his gods had done for him in the past, they would certainly do less in the future. Edwin, with the enthusiasm of a new convert, now set about erecting a small church, or more probably an oratory, in the city of York. This was made of wood, and within this building the Northumbrian King was baptized by Paulinus on Easter Day, A.D. 627 (April 12). This oratory was not long afterwards enclosed within a larger structure which was built of stone, and upon the site of which was afterwards erected the stately Minster of York. It is said that shortly after the baptism of Edwin a large number of his barons and subjects followed his example. Paulinus and his friends now lost no time in spreading through the length and breadth of Northumbria the tenets of the Christian religion, and under the patronage of the King and Queen no doubt many proselytes were obtained, not a few of whom were dwellers on Lancashire soil. This missionary work proceeded uninterruptedly for six years, but was then destined to receive a very severe check by the war between Edwin and Penda (see p. 42), in which the King of Northumbria was defeated and slain on October 12, A.D. 633, and subsequently the whole of his kingdom was overrun by pagan soldiers, who, according to Bede, slaughtered the Christians without regard to either age or sex. The head of Edwin was taken to York by some of his friends, and placed within the church which he had so recently built. Ethelburga, the Queen, and her two children, escorted by Paulinus, fled into Kent, and Paulinus was afterwards presented to the See of Rochester.

He was never Archbishop of York (as by some supposed), although the Pope offered that dignity to him ; the letter was addressed to Edwin, who was dead before it was delivered. Paulinus died at Rochester October 10, A.D. 644. Cædwallon ruled over Northumbria for only a few years, and his successor, Oswald, who had probably passed some years in the monastery of Iona very early in his reign, sent over to that community for help towards the revival of Christianity in this kingdom.

The first priest who was sent returned reporting that the people were impracticable and refused to be converted, whereupon a priest called Aiden was consecrated Bishop, and despatched to Northumbria in the year 635.

Oswald did not, as might have been expected, place Aiden at York, but gave to him a small island on the coast of Durham known as Holy Island, and here was founded the abbey of Lindisfarne, which was destroyed by the Danes in A.D. 795 ; from this centre the missionary work in the North of England emanated. The basilica at York was finished by Oswald, and by erecting other churches and granting lands for the sites of religious houses this King did much to establish the Christian religion in the North. But after eight years of comparative peace Northumbria again passed into pagan hands (see p. 43), and not .until Penda in A.D. 655 was defeated and slain did paganism receive its death-blow. Oswy, on gaining this final victory, fulfilled the vow which he had made—that if he was successful in this war he would give twelve sites for as many monasteries, and give his infant daughter to serve the Lord in holy virginity. The monasteries were founded, but none of them appear to have been on the western or Lancashire side of the Pennine Hills. Early in A.D. 665 the bishopric of York was re-established, when Wilfrid was consecrated as Bishop at Compiègne in France ; but having delayed his coming to his see for nearly twelve months, he was not a little astonished to find that in the meantime Chad's consecration had taken place and he was already in possession. ˉFor a few years only he held the office, and on his retirement to the monastery of Lastingham, Wilfrid took his place.

Of the dispute with Theodore, Archbishop of Canterbury, and the temporary expulsion of Wilfrid from the See of York and his subsequent visit to Rome, where he saw the Pope, and obtained from him a decree which was to reinstate him, little need here be said, except that on his return to York, and a " witan " having been called, the Pope's order was treated with scorn by the assembly, and Wilfrid was cast into prison, where he remained for nine months.

The real point at issue was the supremacy of the Pope, Egfrid, the King of Northumbria, being strongly opposed to it, whilst Wilfrid and his friends were just as firmly decided in its favour. Wilfrid had for some years been the sole Bishop of Northumbria, his diocese extending from the Firth of Forth to the Humber, and from the Firth of Clyde to the Mersey. Through the entreaty of an aunt of the King's, who was Abbess of Ebba, Wilfrid was at length liberated, but banished from the kingdom. Whilst these disputes were going on, Bosa occupied the episcopal chair of York, and was followed by John of Beverley, who died May 7, A.D. 721. Before this date several monasteries are believed to have been established in Lancashire. Wilfrid II. held the see from 718 to 732, when he was succeeded by Egbert, to whom Bede, now an old man, addressed a letter, the contents of which show clearly that already many abuses had crept into the Church, and that in some of the so-called religious houses luxury and license were more the rule than the exception. Land granted for purely religious purposes, and thus free from secular claims, was used to erect houses, religious in name, but really only dwelling-places for the founders and their people. Egbert, in A.D. 735, was appointed by Pope Gregory III. Archbishop of York, and thus became Primate of the Northern Province, and a few years afterwards his brother, Eadbert, became King of Northumbria. Towards the middle of the ninth century began the invasions of the Danes (see p. 44), which continued until A.D. 867, when the whole of Northumbria was in their possession, and for many years before and after this event the ecclesiastical history of the kingdom is almost a blank. The new occupiers of Northumbria were mostly from Denmark, and were a wild, lawless set of pirates, distinguished for courage, ferocity, and a violent hatred to the newly-established faith. The religion these tribes professed was a worship of Odin and other kindred gods. A great point of difference between the conquerors and conquered (who had both descended from the same race) was that whilst the Danes had continued to worship the gods of their forefathers, and had not forsaken their old profession of sea-pirates, the settlers in Britain had devoted themselves to peaceful pursuits, and had to a great extent adopted the new religion.

It may therefore be taken for granted that amongst the first objects upon which they wreaked their vengeance would be the newly-erected churches, and in all probability not one was left untouched. Persecution would follow as a natural consequence, and the religious progress made during the last two centuries was not only arrested, but almost annihilated. During the troubled times which intervened between this period and the election of Edward the Confessor Christianity made some progress, as even the Danes to some extent yielded to its influence, and a Bishop of Danish blood (Oskytel) occupied the episcopal chair of York, and his kinsman Oswald, in A.D. 972, was Archbishop, and held the see until his death in A.D. 992.[1] With the Conquest came another change, and the Bishops of York were selected from Norman ecclesiastics. Up to this period, except as part of the Diocese of York, we have found but scanty records referring to the religious history of Lancashire, but, nevertheless, it is absolutely certain that in some few of its scattered villages churches were built and Christian colonies established. But in considering this question it must be borne in mind that in what we call

[1] Lancashire was subsequently included in the Diocese of Lichfield and Coventry until the establishment of the See of Chester, in 1541, the northern portion being in the Archdeaconry of Richmond, in the Diocese of York.

Lancashire there were at that time no large towns, nor even any number of considerable-sized villages ; the inhabitants were mostly engaged in agricultural pursuits, and the religious requirements were administered from York. In Yorkshire and other parts of ancient Northumbria we know that churches and monasteries had been so long established that into the latter many abuses had been introduced even as early as A.D. 732, but we have no evidence to lead us to suppose that such was the case in Lancashire.

In the middle of the eleventh century, on the reliable testimony of the so-called Domesday Survey, we have positive evidence that in Lancashire there were then at least a dozen churches ; however many more were left unnoticed, or had existed and been destroyed by the ravages of the Danes, we can only conjecture, but there are not wanting indications in that direction which leave little room for doubt that, at all events, some half-dozen others are wanting to complete the list. The Great Survey was not in any way intended to furnish such a list, and its object might have been attained almost without the mention of a single ecclesiastical building ; it is therefore not improbable that other churches existed, of which no trace, nor even tradition, has been handed down to us. Beginning with the early churches in the north of the county, and coming down to the Mersey, we shall be able in some measure to trace the local rise and development of the Christian religion in the county. In the Lancashire part of Lonsdale no church is named as a building, but as we have after the word Lancaster[1] *Church Lancaster (Chercaloncastre)*, it is evident that this ancient town had at that time, at all events, its church (to which we shall refer again hereafter) ; and from the fact that to the four manors of Bentham (in Yorkshire), Wennington, Tatham and Tunstall were attached

[1] Lancaster parish is partly in Lonsdale and partly in Amounderness.

three churches, it is clear that not less than two of them were in Lancashire, and these were at Tatham and Tunstall. The church at Tatham, like many others of these early foundations, has now no village near to it, but stands at the extreme north of the parish; it is mentioned in the *Valor* of 1291, and it has been more than once rebuilt, but a Norman doorway remains, and an archway said to belong to the Saxon period.

Tunstall was the site of a small Roman station (see p. 36), and therefore the more likely to be afterwards used as the settlement of a Saxon community. The early history of this church is obscure, but it was recognised in 1291, and shortly afterwards appears to have belonged to the Abbot of Croxton Keyrial, in Leicestershire; it has been at least three times restored; it was originally dedicated to St. Michael, but the more modern dedication is to St. John. Thurland Castle, which is not far from the church, is supposed to have taken its name from a Saxon Thane. At Kirkby Ireleth one can scarcely avoid coming to the conclusion that at some time during the Saxon Heptarchy a church existed, though all material trace of it was soon afterwards swept away. The present parish church is dedicated to St. Cuthbert, who, in A.D. 685, had given to him by the King of Northumbria "the land called Cartmel and all the Britons there" ("terram quæ vocatur Cartmel et omnes Britannos cum eo"),[1] and as Kirkby Ireleth is only some ten miles from that place, it is at least probable that here Cuthbert erected a church, which afterwards being destroyed, left only a tradition of its founder.

A few miles to the west of Lancaster, at Heysham, on high ground overlooking the waters of Morecambe Bay, undoubtedly once stood a Saxon church, on the site of which, in Norman times, was erected the present building, portions of which, notably a doorway and part of the

[1] Symeon of Durham's "Life of St. Cuthbert," *Surtees Soc.*, li. 141.

north wall, are of undoubted Saxon architecture. In the churchyard is a very ancient runic cross with a richly carved scroll and rude figures of the Virgin and Child, and on the bare rock, a little above the church, are several excavations of coffin-like shape, in which at some very distant date human bodies were interred. The hog-backed stone in the churchyard, with elaborate carvings, has formed the subject of much learned argument, but whilst there are several opinions as to the correct story intended to be represented by the sculptor, all agree that this relic is of very great antiquity, and probably belongs to the sixth or seventh century.[1] The original church, which was only 24 feet long and $7\frac{1}{2}$ feet wide, was dedicated to St. Patrick, and has, on that account, been thought to have been established by a colony of Irish monks who, about that period, are said to have visited this district.

Coming back to "time-honoured Lancaster," the only vestige of the Saxon church which has been preserved is a small stone cross discovered in 1807 in the churchyard; it is almost complete, and bears an inscription in Anglian runes, of which the generally accepted reading is (when translated): "Bid" (*i.e.* pray ye) "for Cunibalth Cuthbœrehting" (Cuthbert's son). This is, by the best authorities, ascribed to the seventh century. At the time of the Conquest Lancaster had fallen from its former high estate, and was returned in the Domesday Book as a dependency of Halton. The church, which stood not far from the castle and some little distance from the town, was no doubt of small dimensions, and was the property of Roger de Poictou, who just before the close of the eleventh century (A.D. 1094) conveyed it to St. Martin of Sees, in Normandy, by the name of the church of St. Mary of Lancaster, with all things pertaining thereunto, including part of the land of the *vill*, from

---

[1] See *Lanc. and Ches. Ant. Soc.*, vol. ix.

the old wall (of the town) to the orchard of Godfrey and as far as Prestgate, and near to Lancaster two mansions, Aldcliffe and Newton.[1] The charter which made this grant to the monastery of Sees was, in fact, the charter which established the alien priory of St. Mary of Lancaster, which consisted of a Prior and five monks, with three priests, two clerks, and the usual servants—the monks were all drawn from the parent Norman monastery.

Amongst other endowments of this religious house, given to it by its founder, were the patronage and temporalities of a number of churches, many of which had only been recently erected in Lancashire; these were Heysham, Croston, Eccleston, Childwall, Preston, Kirkham, Melling, Bispham, Bolton (near Lancaster), and Poulton-le-Fylde. By charter dated March 26, 1200, King John took into his hands the custody, protection and maintenance of the church of St. Mary of Lancaster, and the Prior and monks there "serving God and St. Mary," with all their lands and possessions.

In 1260 Pope Alexander issued a Papal Bull in which he expressed a desire that "the church of the Monastery of Lancaster, of the Order of St. Benedict, of the Diocese of York," might be "filled with fitting honours," to accomplish which, "in the mercy of God and the authority of the blessed Peter and Paul his apostles, he mercifully" remitted to all "true penitents and the confessed" who approached the church for the sake of devotion annually on the feast of the Blessed Virgin Mary, "to whose honour it was asserted the church was dedicated," a hundred days of the penance enjoined on them. And in the 10 Kal., March, 1292, Pope Nicholas granted relaxation for one year and forty days of the enjoined penance to those penitents who visited the church of

---

[1] Aldcliffe Hall is on the south of the river. Of Newton all trace is lost. See "Materials for History of the Church of Lancaster," *Chetham Soc.*, xxvi., new series.

Lancaster on the feasts of the Blessed Virgin and St. Nicholas, in their octaves, and on the anniversary of the dedication.[1]

In 1246 a dispute was settled between John Romanus, Archdeacon of Richmond, and the Abbot and convent of Sees. The matter had been referred to the priors of Kirkham and Bridlington by the Pope, and through this intervention a compromise was arrived at, the terms of which were that the right of patronage with the pension of three marks, and all right which the Abbot and convent had in the church of Bolton in Lonsdale, should be yielded up for ever, and that the moiety of the church of Poulton, with the appurtenances which Alexander de Stanford possessed, when it became vacant, should be ceded to the priory of Lancaster to its own uses, provided that in the said church the vicarage should be taxed "by good men chosen by each party" from the goods of the same church to the value of 20 marks; to the vicarage the Abbot and convent of Sees to present their own clerk for ever, who shall find hospitality for the Archdeacon and support all other due and customary burdens.

It was also settled that the Archdeacon should confirm the church of Lancaster to the priory for ever as they formerly held it, and that neither he nor his successors should "compel" those so appointed to the vicarage, unless it shall please them, saving, nevertheless, to the Archdeacon and his successors in all things their archidiaconal rights in the same. This agreement was afterwards confirmed by the Archdeacon and the Archbishop of York. A few years later we find Gerard de Wipensis (or Vyspeyns), Archdeacon of Richmond, granting to the Abbot and convent, Prior and monks, at Lancaster, that they may in future hold and possess in full right the church of the Blessed Mary at Lancaster, with all lands,

---

[1] Calendar of Papal Reg., A.D. 1193-1304, and chartulary of the priory.

tithes, possessions, and chapels belonging to it, namely, the chapels of Gressingham, Caton, Overton and Stalmine. Also, as the monks by themselves or by fit chaplains administered continually day and night in the said church of Lancaster and the parish of the same, and laboured perpetually in the cure of souls, so they should not be compelled by anyone to make or ordain a vicarage or vicar in the said church against their will, as none existed therein. From this it is clear that at this time no vicar was appointed, the entire duties being executed by the monks or their chaplains.

The number of grants made in the thirteenth and following century to the church of Lancaster, and the Prior and monks there serving, is considerable, and it is impossible here even to catalogue them ; one or two will, however, serve to show how strong the influence of the religious men had become. By deed dated at Caton in 1256, Roger, son of Vivian de Heysham, granted to God and the church of the Blessed Mary of Lancaster, and to the Prior and monks, etc., for the safety of his soul and the soul of Wymark his wife, and for the souls of his ancestors and successors, the third part of his corn-mill at Caton, also of his fulling-mill there, with the pond and free water-course to the said mills, with free common in the wood of Caton for repairing the said mills, to be held for ever.

By another charter, without date, but executed in either 1261 or 1272 (one of the witnesses being Ralph Dacre, the High Sheriff, who held that office in those two years), John, son of Roger Gernet, of Caton, for the safety of his soul, etc., gave a piece of land in Caton, lying from the north corner of Cottescroft, going northwards as far as the root of the burnt oak, next to the sun, and so to the stream running between the land of William de Bensted and the land of Adam de Lee, to the priory to be held for ever free of all customs. About the same date, Helewise, daughter of Adam, son of Gilbert de Bolton, gave the church of the Blessed Mary of Lancaster, and the Prior and monks servin tghere, all the land in the vill of Bolton which she had received from her father, to be held by them for ever, but subject to the usual services to the lord of the fee.

One of the large landowners in Bolton (in Lonsdale) at this time was Thomas de Capernwray, who about A.D. 1261 gave to the church of Lancaster and the Prior and monks all his lands, buildings, services, and rents in the vill of Bolton, except certain land previously granted to Adam, son of Robert Kellet. Many other similar grants followed, and, as already stated, the advowson of nearly all the churches in the district fell into their hands.

After the alien houses were suppressed in 1414, most of the possessions of this priory went to the monastery of Syon in Middlesex, the foundation-stone of which was laid on February 22, 1415, by the King in person, who endowed it with £110 a year, to be paid out from the farm of the Lancaster Priory lands. Giles Lovell, the last Prior of Lancaster, died in 1428. The priory itself was granted to Syon in frank almoigne in 1432. Thus the Abbot and convent of Syon became the patrons of the Lancashire churches held by the priory. Probably Syon appointed Richard Chester Vicar of Lancaster, who in 1430-34 also held the rectory of South Wollyngham in Lincolnshire, and had protection granted to him on going in that year to the Council of Basle, in the retinue of Robert, Bishop of London.[1]

At Lancaster there was also founded, late in the twelfth century, a small hospital of the Augustine Order; it was dedicated to St. Leonard's in or about the year 1357. It was annexed to the nunnery of Seton in Cumberland; at one time its accommodation was limited to a

[1] Calendar of French Rolls; 48th Report of Deputy-Keeper of Records.

master, his chaplain, and nine persons, three of whom were to be lepers. There was also here a small monastery of the Grey Friars, about which little is known. The century succeeding the Conquest was distinguished by the rise of monasteries and convents, and with them rose many of the ancient churches in which Lancashire is so rich. It is, however, a mistake to suppose that the abbots built these; history rather shows that the monasteries absorbed the lesser ecclesiastical foundations, or, more frequently still, they received them as part and parcel of their own endowments.

The great monastic institution in this part of the country was Furness Abbey, which was not only a great religious centre, but from it sprang many other abbeys of note. Furness Abbey is near to the town of Dalton, but lies in a sheltered nook, so that it is cut off, as it were, from the neighbouring towns. The abbey of Savigni in Normandy was founded in 1112, and within a few years of its foundation (in 1126-27) Stephen gave Furness to this monastery, but only, it would seem, in order that St. Mary's of Furness should by this order be established; with this object, he endowed it with very large tracts of land, including the whole of Furness, Dalton, Ulverston, and Walney Island, in addition to such rights and privileges as made them veritable lords over all the district. And here was built that abbey which even in its ruins is majestic and beautiful. This institution was originally founded in July, 1123, at Tulket, near Preston, and the monks remained there for over three years, when, finding a more suitable site, they migrated to Furness. About the year 1148 the monks of Furness, with other followers of Savigni, joined the Cistercian Order. The monks of Furness were an immense power in the district, and, notwithstanding that they suffered like the rest of the people from the ravages of the Scots, must have enjoyed a very large revenue. Not only were they breeders of cattle and rearers of horses, sheep, and oxen, but they had on their demesne a considerable number of iron furnaces and salt works, all of which, if not worked by the community, were a considerable source of income. As in the case of other monasteries, as time went on, numerous benefactors arose, and lands and tenements all over the district were added to the possessions of the already opulent institution, and the patronage of Urswick Church and almost every other church for miles around fell to them. Very shortly after their settlement at Furness these monks began to send out colonies to other places; one of the earliest which they established was in Wyersdale, where, however, the monks did not remain very long, as about 1188 they removed to Withney in Ireland; but whilst they were in Lancashire they obtained the patronage of the church of St. Michael's-on-Wyre.

The last Abbot of Furness was Roger Pele, or Pile, who was elevated to that dignity in about the year 1532; he surrendered the abbey to the King, April 9, 1537. The suppression of Furness Abbey must have been for a time very severely felt by the inhabitants of the district, as from it emanated much hospitality, and to it all the natives looked for the education of their children and for such religious help as was usually obtained from these houses. Between the abbots and their tenants there appears to have been carried on a system of barter and exchange, some of the details of which are preserved in the evidence brought forward in support of a petition made in the duchy court in 25 Elizabeth (1582-83) by the tenants of Walney against the Queen's Attorney-General, who had obtained a lease of the late dissolved monastery. One of the witnesses, who was then seventy-eight years old, said that they (the petitioners) and their ancestors, whose estates they severally held, used to pay and deliver to the Abbot certain "domestical" provisions, such as calves, sheep, wheat, barley, oats, and the like, and for recompense they not only enjoyed their burgages or messuages, but also received from the abbey great relief, sustentation, and commodities for themselves and their children, viz., all the tenants had weekly one ten-gallon barrel of ale; the tenants of Newbarns and Hawcoat had all the worthings[1] of all the horse and oxen (except those at the Abbot's stables); the tenants had also a weekly allowance of coarse wheat bread, iron for their husbandry, gear and timber for the repairs of their houses. In addition to these grants, all tenants who had a plough could send two men to dine at the monastery on one day in each week from Martinmas (November 11) to Pentecost (Whitsunday); and the children of the tenants who had found the required provision were educated in the school of the monastery free, and allowed every day a dinner or a supper; and if any of them became good scholars, they were often made into monks. The question at issue between the tenants and the Attorney-General was that whilst he demanded the provisions, he claimed exemption from making the recompenses, alleging that the abbots had merely given the food out of benevolence and devotion to their neighbours. The result of the petition was in favour of the tenants.

The condition of the abbey itself in 1774 is thus described by West[2]: " The magnitude of the abbey may be known from the dimensions of the ruins, and enough is standing to show the style of the architecture, which breathes the plain simplicity of taste which is found in most houses belonging to the Cistercian monks which were erected about the same time with Furness Abbey.

" The round and pointed arches occur in the doors and windows. The fine clustered Gothic and the heavy

---

[1] Worthings = manure.
[2] " Antiquities of Furness."

plain Saxon pillars stand contrasted. The walls show excellent masonry, are in many places counter-arched, and the ruins show a strong cement.

" The east window of the church has been noble ; some of the painted glass that once adorned it is preserved in a window in Windermere Church (Bowness). The window consists of seven compartments or partitions. In the third, fourth and fifth are depicted, in full proportion, the Crucifixion, with the Virgin Mary on the right and the beloved disciple on the left side of the cross ; angels are expressed receiving the sacred blood from the five precious wounds; below the cross are a group of monks in their proper habits, with the Abbot in a vestment ; their names are written on labels issuing from their mouths; the Abbot's name is defaced, which would have given a date to the whole. In the second partition are the figures of St. George and the dragon. In the sixth is represented St. Catharine, with the emblems of her martyrdom, the sword and wheel. In the seventh are two figures of mitred abbots, and underneath them two monks dressed in vestments. In the middle compartment above are finely-painted quarterly the arms of France and England, bound with the garter and its motto, probably done in the reign of Edward III. The rest of the window is filled up by pieces of tracery, with some figures in coat armorial, and the arms of several benefactors, amongst whom are Lancaster, Urswick, Warrington, Fleming, Millum, etc. On the outside of the window of the abbey, under an arched festoon, is the head of Stephen, the founder; opposite to it, that of Maud, his Queen, both crowned and well executed. In the south wall and east end of the church are four seats adorned with Gothic ornament. The chapter-house is the only building belonging to the abbey which is marked with any elegance of Gothic sculpture; it has been a noble room of 60 feet by 45. The vaulted roof, formed of twelve ribbed arches, was supported by six pillars in two rows at 14 feet from each other.

" Now, supposing each of the pillars to be 18 inches in diameter, the room would be divided into three alleys or passages, each 14 feet wide. On entrance the middle one only could be seen, lighted by a pair of tall pointed windows at the upper end of the room ; the company in the side passage would be concealed by the pillars, and the vaulted roof that groined from those pillars would have a truly Gothic disproportionate appearance of 60 feet by 14. The northern side alley was lighted by four small pointed side-windows, besides a pair at the higher end, at present entire, and which illustrate what is here said. Thus, whilst the upper end of the room had a profusion of light, the lower end would be in the shade. The noble roof of this singular edifice did but lately fall in ; the entrance or porch is still standing—a fine circular arch, beautified with a deep cornice and a portico on each side.

" The only entire roof of any apartment now remaining is that of a building without the enclosure wall, which was the schoolhouse of the Abbot's tenants. It is a single-ribbed arch that groins from the wall.

" A remarkable deformity in this edifice, and for which there is no apparent reason or necessity, is that the north door, which is the principal entrance, is on one side of the window above it. The tower has been supported by four magnificent arches, of which only one remains entire. They rested upon four tall pillars, whereof three are finely clustered, but the fourth is of a plain unmeaning construction. The west end of the church seems to have been an additional part intended for a belfry to ease the main tower, but that is as plain as the east. The east end of the church contained five altars besides the high altar, as appears by the chapels, and probably there was a private altar in the sacristy.

" In magnitude this abbey was second in England belonging to the Cistercian monks, and the next in opulence
after Fountains Abbey in Yorkshire.   The church and
cloisters were encompassed with a wall, which commenced at the east side of the great northern door and
formed the straight enclosure ; and a space of ground to
the amount of 65 acres was surrounded with a strong
stone wall, which enclosed the mills, kilns, ovens and
fish-ponds.   The inside length of the church from east to
west is 275 feet 8 inches; the thickness of the east end
wall and the depth of the east end buttress is 8 feet
7 inches; the thickness of the west end wall 9 feet
7 inches; the extreme length of the church is 304 feet
6 inches ; the inside width of the east end is 28 feet, and
the thickness of the two side walls 10 feet.   The inside
width of the cloister is 31 feet 6 inches ; the area of the
quadrangular court is 338 feet 6 inches by 102 feet
6 inches."

Since this description was written many researches have
been made, and much light thrown on various points of
interest.   The church is ascribed to the time when John
de Cauncefeld was Abbot—*i.e.*, about A.D. 1160.   Of the
parts of the church still remaining in fair preservation,
the most conspicuous are the transepts, which are 126 feet
long, by 28 feet wide.   At the north end of the transepts
is a Transitional doorway which is rich in its ornamentation and mouldings ; above it is a magnificent window,
probably inserted in the fifteenth century.

Various monuments have been discovered, one of which
is probably the effigy of William de Lancaster, the eighth
Baron of Kendal, whose Inquisition is dated 31 Henry
III. (1246-47).

The beautiful groined roof of the chapter-house was
intact until the end of the last century.   Beyond the
chapter-house was the fratry, or monks' common room,
which was 200 feet long, and over it were the dormitories.

Near the western tower the walls of the hospitium, or guest-house, may still be traced. At the south end of the ruins there is a building with a groined room which has generally been called the school-house, but many authorities now consider that it was a small chapel, as it contains a large east window and a piscina ; if this be so, then it was without doubt the Abbot's private chapel. The date assigned to it is early in the fourteenth century.

Near to the abbey the Preston family, to whom the site was granted soon after the dissolution,[1] built their mansion, and part of this house now forms the Furness Abbey Hotel. In 26 Henry VIII. the rentals belonging to the abbey amounted to £942 per annum, of which tithe offerings and ecclesiastical fines came to £182. In 1540 these possessions were annexed to the Duchy of Lancaster, and were not finally alienated therefrom until the time of James I. From the Prestons it passed by marriage to Sir William Lowther, Bart., whose son and heir married Lady Elizabeth, the daughter of William, Duke of Devonshire; his son and heir, dying without issue in 1756, bequeathed all his estates to his cousin, Lord George Augustus Cavendish.

The coucher book of Furness is still preserved in London; it is a handsome volume containing 293 folios. On the seizure of the abbey in 1537 this volume and other memorials, trussed in three packs, were sent by Cromwell on the back of three mules to London, and £1 15s. 4d. was expended on their conveyance. It was afterwards placed in the duchy office, and ultimately handed over to the Record Office.[2]

Before the end of the twelfth century a new religious order was formed, of which the first house in England was the priory of SS. Julian and Botulph in Colchester, in

[1] Probably granted for a term of years.
[2] Printed by the Chetham Society (new series, vols. xiii., xiv., xv.).

1105 (or 1107). This was the canons regular of St. Augustine, who subsequently held 175 religious houses in Great Britain. At Cartmel a priory of this order was founded in 1188 by the Earl of Pembroke ; it was dedicated to St. Mary, and displaced the ancient parish church, which, if not of Saxon origin, was certainly a very early foundation. One of the privileges of this house was that it had the exclusive right to furnish guides to conduct travellers over the treacherous sands across the estuary of the Kent. To the fact that this parish church became the priory church we no doubt owe its preservation, as at the dissolution of the monasteries it did not share the fate of so many fine examples of early Church architecture, but still remains a noble monument of the past. At Coniston, in the extreme north of the county, in 1188 was founded a small hospital for lepers, and it would thus appear that even to that remote district leprosy had spread. This hospital was given in charge of some monks of St. Augustine's Order, who converted it into a priory, at the same time appropriating to themselves the church of Ulverston, over 40 acres of land, and other possessions. It is, however, only fair to add that they took charge of the lepers when there were any. Though never of any considerable size or importance, yet in its early days its establishment consisted of over a dozen canons and a Prior, and the usual number of attendants. After its dissolution in 1536 every trace of it was swept away. Of the Præmonstratensian Order there were two houses in Lonsdale Hundred—one at Cockersand, and the other at Hornby. Amongst this order—which was introduced into England in 1120—a greater strictness of discipline and a less external code of duties prevailed than amongst the Austin canons.

The history of Cockersand is somewhat obscure, but at an early period there was here a hermitage, which was afterwards a hospital, presided over by a Prior, and dependent upon the abbey at Leicester, founded by William of Lancaster; but in 1190 it became an abbey of the Præmonstratensian canons. It was one of the lesser houses which were given to the King in 1536, when it consisted of 22 religious men and 57 laymen, with an annual income of about £200 arising from a rather large rent-roll and customary boons and services.

The establishment at Hornby was scarcely worthy of the name of a priory, but was rather a hospital or cell with a Prior and three canons dependent on the abbey of Croxton, in Leicestershire. It was dedicated to St. Wilfrid, and had a small endowment of £26 a year.

In the hundred of Amounderness the Great Survey only refers to three churches, and these, though not named, were undoubtedly Preston, Kirkham, and St. Michael's-on-Wyre; and in the absence of proof to the contrary we must assume that none others were then in existence, though possibly others may have been erected in Saxon times, but, like the district upon which they stood, were then lying waste (see p. 57). Poulton is dedicated to St. Chad (a Saxon saint), and Garstang may possibly have been the site of a pre-Conquest church, although its proximity to St. Michael's renders it somewhat improbable.

Preston Church was originally dedicated to St. Wilfrid, and was probably built in the tenth century; Kirkham,[1] or the church village, may even be of an earlier foundation than Preston, for from the time that Roger de Poictou granted the church to St. Mary of Lancaster (see p. 187) to the present date its history is clear and fairly complete; no trace of the Saxon building has, however, been discovered.

At St. Michael's, also, all material evidence of the pre-Norman period has long ago disappeared. In Amounderness only two religious houses were established

[1] A compound of "kirk," the Danish or Scandinavian for church, and the Anglo-Saxon "ham," a village or a dwelling.

—one at Preston, the other at Lytham. At Preston was a Franciscan convent of Grey Friars, or Friars Minor, built in 1221 by Edmund, Earl of Lancaster. Within the precincts of this house was buried Sir Robert Holland, who impeached Thomas, Earl of Lancaster of treason. Little is known concerning this friary; in 1379 letters were addressed to the Warden of the order of Preaching Friars there, asking them to pray for the Duke of Lancaster on his going abroad. There was also at Preston a hospital for lepers, which must have been established early in the twelfth century, as Henry II. took it under his protection, as did also King John; there was a chapel attached dedicated to St. Mary Magdalen. The cell at Lytham was dependent upon the Priors of Durham from its foundation in 1190 to 1443, when it became partly independent. They were black monks.

In the hundred of Leyland no churches are mentioned in Domesday Book, but there was almost certainly one at Croston and another at Eccleston, as both these were given to the priory of Lancaster in 1090 (see p. 187), and if not in existence at the taking of the Survey one can scarcely avoid coming to the conclusion that long before that date churches had been erected at Eccleston, Leyland and Standish, the latter being dedicated, like Preston, to St. Wilfrid.

On a site on the opposite side of the river Ribble to Preston stood the priory of Penwortham. Its situation was picturesque, commanding as it did an exclusive view down the valley, through which the river flowed, and not far from it were the parish church and castle. It was founded as a dependent upon the abbey of Evesham, in the county of Worcester, in 1087, by two brothers, Warine and Albert Busset, with the approval of Pope Alexander III., and it was for 400 years regularly supplied with monks from the parent house. The monks were Benedictines, or black monks, and their home in Lancashire was but sparsely endowed, although it included the churches of Penwortham, Leyland and North Meols. At the dissolution it was rated at a little over £100. No great number of churches were erected in this hundred during several succeeding centuries.

In Blackburn Hundred two churches are named in the Survey—St. Mary's at Whalley and St. Mary's at Blackburn—and the only other parish at all likely to have had a church earlier than this period is Ribchester. The present church is dedicated to St. Wilfrid, and tradition adds that its original foundation was laid in Saxon times; it certainly is built close to the walls of the ancient Roman castrum (see p. 27). Another very early foundation was that of Chipping, said to have been built in 1041. St. Mary's of Blackburn is still the parish church, but there is no evidence to prove that its foundation dates back to pre-Norman times.

The church at Whalley is perhaps the most interesting church in Lancashire, not only from its undoubted great antiquity, but from its association with the abbey, which was second only to Furness in importance, but about the history of which much more is known.

John, Constable of Chester, in 15 Henry II. (1163), founded a monastery of the Cistercian Order at Stanlawe, in Cheshire, and having endowed it, he instructed that it should be called *Locus Benedictus*. The situation selected was not a happy one, as not only was the soil barren and unfruitful, but a considerable portion of it was liable to periodical encroachments by the sea, which at spring tide almost surrounded it. After almost a century, the monks — when the monks had become considerably richer by the acquisition of properties, chiefly in Lancashire—decided to remove the abbey to a more convenient site, and ultimately fixed upon Whalley. This translation was, no doubt, hastened by the destruction of

a great part of Stanlawe Abbey by fire in 1289, but it was
not until April 4, 1296, that Gregory, the eighth Abbot of
Stanlawe, and his convent took formal possession of the
parsonage of Whalley, where they continued to live until
the new monastery was erected.   Here they found one
of the oldest church foundations in Lancashire, which
probably dated back to the time when Christianity was
first introduced into the district; it was originally known
as the White Church, and in its churchyard still remain
three very fine specimens of Saxon crosses.   The church
was another of the Northern erections dedicated to St.
Wilfrid, and at the time the monks settled there it had
been rebuilt, and was a good sample of Norman ecclesiastical architecture.

Amongst their other possessions the monks held the
impropriate rectories of Whalley, Blackburn and Rochdale, with the right of presentment to their vicarages and
chapels of ease.   Attached to Whalley were the chapels
of Clitheroe, Colne, Burnley, Altham, Downham, Church
and Haslingden.   Whalley now (to quote the language of
its historian)[1] "became the seat of an establishment
which continued for two centuries and a half to exercise
unbounded hospitality and charity; to adorn the site
which had been chosen with a succession of magnificent
buildings; to protect the tenants of its ample domains in
the enjoyment of independence and plenty; to educate
and provide for their children; to employ, clothe, feed
and pay many labourers, herdsmen and shepherds; to
exercise the arts and cultivate the learning of the times;
yet, unfortunately, at the expense of the secular incumbents, whose endowments they had swallowed up and
whose functions they had degraded into those of pen-
sionary vicars or mendicant chaplains."

Notwithstanding the great abuses that gradually crept
into these and the other monastic houses, and ultimately

[1] Whitaker's " History of Whalley."

brought about their destruction, there is still much truth in the *dictum* of the learned author.

The charters whereby lands were conveyed to Stanlawe and Whalley are very numerous, and have all been printed.[1] They extended over a very large area, and included lands in Rochdale, Blackburn, Whalley, Childwall, and other places in Lancashire and Cheshire. The full complement of monks belonging to this abbey was twenty, exclusive of a Lord Abbot and a Prior; in addition to this there were ninety servants, twenty of whom belonged to the Abbot. That these monks lived well, and probably entertained strangers on a liberal fare, may be inferred from the following table of animal food consumed: for the Abbot's table, 75 oxen, 80 sheep, 40 calves, 20 lambs and 4 pigs; for the refectory tables, 57 oxen, 40 sheep, 20 calves and 10 lambs; whilst 200 quarters of wheat, 150 quarters of malt and 8 pipes of wine were annually consumed.

The dissolution of this house in 1539 was accompanied by a tragic event. John Paslow, the last Abbot, with many of his followers, had taken part in that rebellion known as " the Pilgrimage of Grace," by which this and the county of York were for some time greatly agitated, and on its final suppression Paslow, with others, was lodged in Lancaster Castle, from whence he was taken back to Whalley, and on March 12, 1537, was executed in front of his own monastery along with John Eastgate, one of his monks, who was hung, drawn and quartered, whilst a third brother of his order was on the following day hung on a gallows at Padiham. Of this stately building comparatively little now remains.[2] The whole area of the close contains nearly thirty-seven statute acres, and is defined by the remains of a deep trench which

[1] Chetham Society, Coucher Book of Whalley.
[2] See Whitaker's " History of Whalley," from which this description is taken.

surrounds it.   The abbey was approached through two
strong and stately gateways yet remaining.   These gateways were of the usual plain, substantial character which
was common with the Cistercian brotherhood.   The
central portion of the north-west gateway is almost
entire, and is a fine specimen of the late Decorated architecture, probably of the middle of the fourteenth century.
It is of two stories, the higher being supported on stone
groining springing from wall corbels.   To this upper room,
however, there is now no staircase; access must have been
gained from apartments lying on the north and south of
the existing portions, but no trace of these is left.   The
north-east gateway is of much later date; it has a spiral
staircase in an angle turret which leads to the second
story and roof.   The house itself stood on the bank of
the Calder; it consisted of three quadrangles, besides
stables and offices.   Of these the first and most westerly
was the cloister court, of which the nave of the conventual church formed the north side; the south transept,
sacristy, chapter-house, penitentiary, and part of the
refectory, the east; the kitchens, principal refectory, etc.,
the south; and the guest-house the west.   The roof of
the cloister was supported on wooden posts, the corbels
for bearing the rafters being still visible.   The area
within was the monks' cemetery, and some ancient
gravestones are still remembered to have been there.   In
the south wall of this quadrangle is a wide arched recess,
which was the lavatory.   The groove where the lead pipe
was placed is still conspicuous.

Of the building to the south nothing is now left but a
portion of the north wall of the refectory, etc., but the
eye rests with satisfaction on the beautiful doorway of the
chapter-house, with its numerous pateras and the richly-
moulded and traceried windows on either side, with many
shafts and an amount of carving which serves to illustrate
the peculiar care which was bestowed on the decoration

of the building. The south-west angle of the day-room is ornate and picturesque. The predominating style is that of the transition from the Decorated to the Perpendicular. The guest-house is almost entire, and is now used as a barn and cow-house. To the east is another quadrangle, one side of which is formed by what is believed to have been the Abbot's house. On the southern side of this is a ruin presenting a very beautiful window of the Transitional character, which was probably part of the Abbot's private chapel.

The conventual church would rank amongst the finest of the Cistercian Order in Europe, and exceeded many cathedrals in size. It was almost demolished soon after the suppression, though not entirely, for in the account books of Sir Ralphe Assheton we find in 1661 and 1662 several items such as, " Pd for pulling down the old walls over the inner close, £1 os. 6d. Pulling down the old abbey walls. Pulling down the old part of the steeple and those sides adjoining at 3d. per yard. For taking down the great window or door at the head of stairs in the cloisters."

Near to Ribchester was a small institution belonging to the Hospitallers. Very little is known concerning its early history, but it was founded at a very early date ; it is referred to in the coucher book of Salley as the Hospital sub-Langreg, and Dugdale also calls it the *Hospital sub Langrigh,* and merely mentions two bequests made to it, one by Alan de Syngleton, and the other by Walter, son of Walter de Mutun. There were, however, several other endowments. This religious house was, no doubt, at one time of not inconsiderable size and importance, and was, it is believed, dedicated to our Saviour and the Blessed Virgin Mary.

Alan de Syngleton, son of Richard, gave to God and our Saviour for a hospital four acres of land in Dilewhe (Dilworth), and Walter de Mutun, of Ribelchester,

granted in the time of Henry III. all the lands which his
father, Walter, had bequeathed to the same hospital.   In
a charter of the time of Henry VII. it is called the House
of St. Saviour at Sted.

Nicholas Talbot by will, dated 1501, appointed a priest
to sing for twelve months at Stede, where his father and
mother were buried.

After the dissolution the manor of Stede [Stydd], with
all its rights, in 1544, was granted to Sir Thomas Holt,
of Grizzlehurst.   From this grant it appears that Stydd
was then a house of preceptories, consisting of Knights
Hospitallers dependent on the house of Newland, near
Wakefield.   One of the provisions of this charter was
that out of the revenues of the manor, etc., was reserved
40s. a year for the payment of a curate to perform
divine service at the church at Stydd.

It was, no doubt, at this time that all the buildings
except the small chapel were demolished.   From the
time of the Reformation until quite recently service was
only performed here three or four times a year, although
the church was endowed with the tithes of eleven farms
in the township of Dutton.

The church as it now stands is at once striking and
picturesque; it is composed of gray grit stone, and is
almost covered with ivy.   Small as it is, there were
evidently three entrances to it, one of which, on the north
side, is of very early Norman character.   The principal
entrance is in the west end, and its proportions and
mouldings mark it as of Anglo-Norman date.   The effect
of this doorway is partly destroyed by a rude porch,
which at a comparatively recent date has been added to it.
The east window is of fine proportions; the compartments are lancet-shaped without cuspings, and contain
three lights.   The window on the interior of the mullions
has been ornamented with painting in polychromy, now
hardly visible.   On the south side is a long, narrow

aperture, which was probably used as a hagioscope or
squint. The interior of this interesting little building
looks cold and bare, as it is unseated and almost without
the usual church furniture.[1] It contains several tombstones of great age, one of which is to the memory of
a Lord and Lady of Salesbury Hall, who were living in
the time of Edward III., and another is embellished with
the double cross of the Knights Templars. The head of
this stone is richly ornamented, and is a fine specimen of
its kind. The stone font is a massive octagonal piece of
work, and is probably of the fourteenth century.[2]

In West Derby Hundred, the Domesday Book mentions
five churches: Childwall and Walton-on-the-Hill, Wigan,
Winwick and Warrington; but there had probably been
at some earlier period churches at Kirkby and Ormskirk,
and very soon afterwards others were founded at Prescot, Huyton, Sefton, and North Meols. The church of
Warrington calls for special notice on account of its
dedication to St. Elfin (see p. 55), a saint whose name
does not occur in the Romish calendar, and is unknown
to history. Beamont[3] conjectures that it is the name of
some local benefactor, canonized by the people for the
good deeds which he had done; a cognate name was that
of Elfwin, the brother of Egfrid, and the nephew of King
Oswald, who was slain fighting with Ethelfrid in the
battle on the banks of the Trent in A.D. 679.

At Warrington, probably towards the end of the
thirteenth century, a friary of the Augustine or Hermit
friars was established, but the name of its founder and the
exact date of its foundation are alike unknown; it was
not on a very extensive scale, and was dissolved with the
other lesser houses in 1535. The third house established

[1] Recently forms have been placed in the church.
[2] For detailed drawing of Stydd Church see "The History of Stydd
Chapel and Preceptory," by George Latham; London, 1853.
[3] Warrington Church Notes.

in Lancashire by the Austin canons was the priory of
Burscough, which was founded in honour of St. Nicholas,
by Robert Fitz-Henry, Lord of Lathom, in about 1124.
To this priory was granted a charter in 1286 to hold a
weekly market and a five days' fair in their manor of
Ormskirk; amongst its endowments were the advowsons
of the churches of Ormskirk, Huyton and Flixton, and
lands in many parts of West Derby. At the time of the
dissolution (about the year 1536) it contained a Prior, five
monks, and forty dependents, and its temporalities were
then worth about £1,000 a year, according to the present
value of money. There was here a priory church with
several altars, a chapter-house, and a hospital, into which
Henry de Lacy, Constable of Chester, agreed with the
Prior for a perpetual right to send one of his tenants.
Very little of this ancient priory has been left by the
destroying hand of Time.[1]

A small Benedictine priory, dedicated to St. Thomas of
Canterbury, was founded at Upholland, near Wigan, by
Sir Robert Holland, in 1318, and to it were impropriated
the churches of Childwall in Lancashire and Whitwick
in Leicestershire.

In the great hundred of Salford, the Domesday Book
only names two churches, both of which were in
Manchester, and dedicated to St. Michael and St. Mary,
and it is somewhat remarkable that even the sites of
these buildings are now only a matter of conjecture.
The probability is that one stood in Aldport and the
other in Acres Field, near to the end of the present St.
Mary's Gate. When or why these churches were pulled
down history does not tell us, but for centuries after the
Conquest Manchester was a rural deanery, and probably
was the ecclesiastical centre of the ten parishes comprised
in the county division. Baines says (and others have

[1] For details of remains of Burscough, see *Lanc. and Ches. Hist.
Soc.*, 1889.

repeated) that the church at Bury was named in the Great Survey; this is not the case, but before the end of the twelfth century there were churches not only at Bury, but at Ashton-under-Lyne, Prestwich, Middleton and Flixton, and a little later saw the rise of the churches of Radcliffe, Bolton and Eccles. Rochdale Church was certainly built before 1194, and was almost certainly a Saxon foundation.

In 1421 (August 5) the parish church of Manchester was, at the instigation of Thomas la Warre, twelfth Lord of Manchester, made into a collegiate church, to be governed by one warden and eight fellows, four clerks, and six choristers, and it was ordained that divine service should be celebrated there every day for the good health of the King, of the Bishop, of Thomas la Warre, and for the souls of their ancestors, and for the souls of all the faithful departed for ever. This collegiate church in 1540 obtained the privilege of asylum (as had also Lancaster), whereby any criminal resorting to it for sanctuary should be assured his life, liberty and limbs. At the beginning of the fifteenth century the church of Manchester was a wooden building, on the site where now stands the cathedral.

The only monastic institution in this great division of Lancashire was the priory of Kersal, near Manchester, which consisted of a cell to the Cluniac house of Lenten, near Nottingham. The manor and cell of Kersal was granted by Henry II. (1154—1189) to Lenten, and both passed into the hands of Henry VIII. at the dissolution.

During the two centuries which immediately followed the Norman Conquest, a vast change came over the religious aspect of Lancashire; the commissioners who compiled the Domesday Book found here and there a small church and other evidences of the growth of the Christian faith; but in all directions they found great tracts of country— especially in the northern parts—lying waste, with few or

14

no inhabitants. British settlements had been followed by Roman camps, and these in turn had been destroyed by the Scots, the Saxons and the Danes, in their struggles for supremacy; but, still, it is clear beyond dispute that the teachings of Paulinus, and Bede, and Wilfrid had taken firm hold of the minds of the people, and the time was ripe for a great missionary effort. The opportunity was seized, and in every direction colonies of monks and friars were sent out, and religious houses founded, one effect of this being that gradually a very large number of the existing churches were passed over to and became part of the possessions of the newly-established institutions. There were, of course, exceptions, but as a rule, where the patronage of a church was not held by the King, it was owned by some religious house. One result of this was the appointment of non-resident vicars, many of whom held several livings, the care of which was handed over to others.

One example of this may be cited. In 1289 the patronage of St. Michael's-on-Wyre was vested in the King, and in the December of that year the Pope granted an indulgence to Walter de Languethon, the King's clerk, Rector of St. Michael's, to hold an additional living : in 1290 he held also the Rectory of Croston, and had a dispensation granted to enable him to accept a third, and in the following year he got an indulgence to retain two of these for five years without residing there or *being ordained priest*, whilst he was engaged in the King's service, the churches in the meantime to be served by vicars. Another vicar of this parish in the next century was also acting as receiver for John of Gaunt, Duke of Lancaster; and at Preston, a long series of Rectors probably never were within sight of the church of which they held the living.

The establishment of these religious houses does not appear to have been immediately followed by any considerable increase in the number of churches, though here and there a new one was erected; the number added to those recognised by the valuation of Pope Nicholas in 1291 was very small indeed.

In the fourteenth and fifteenth centuries many chantries were founded by private individuals in the parish churches, very few of the older foundations being without one or more of these altars, nearly all of which were more or less endowed, and there were buried their founders and their successors, to whose memory stately monuments were therein erected. With the birth of the sixteenth century, it was evident that serious abuses had crept into the monastic institutions, which prepared the way for and finally led to their suppression. The change brought about by the violent measure taken by Henry VIII. must have been greatly felt in Lancashire, where then, as now, great difference in opinion must have existed as to its wisdom or otherwise. There are those who now declare that history justifies the course then taken, whilst there are others who maintain that "neither among the friars, with their public ministry and their international character, nor among the Cistercians of Furness and Whalley, with their industries and agriculture, nor among the regular canons, Augustinian and Præmonstratensian, nor among the Benedictines, with their large place in the national history, their local ties, and their varied work, was there found, when the end was at hand, anything to warrant their wholesale suppression."[1] Into this question it is not necessary to enter, but it may be briefly stated that most historians agree that, although many of these houses were well managed and regulated, the abbots and priors were often more concerned about the temporal possessions of their orders than for the spiritual benefit to the community, which alone justified their continued existence. And no one can read the literature of those

[1] Dom. Gilbert Dolan, O.S.B. (*Lanc. and Ches. Hist. Soc.*, vols. vii., viii., p. 231).

times without coming to the conclusion that, at all events in the popular mind, there was then a strong conviction that the lives of the monks were not regulated by the high standard of morality aimed at by the original founders of their institutions.

Acting upon powers given by Parliament, the King took possession of the religious houses in Lancashire, and with no loss of time conveyed all their lands and tenements to willing purchasers, the abbeys, priories, and other buildings being in nearly every instance unroofed and more or less destroyed, and even the silver shrines, the church plate, and the richly embroidered vestments, were all converted into money, which found its way into the royal coffers.

The Reformation was now accomplished, and the Pope was no longer head of the English Church, which was now controlled by Henry VIII., who not only regulated the appointment of its clergy, but to some extent dictated its form of ritual as well as its teaching: images and holy relics were swept away, as well as many forms of worship considered of Popish origin. Edward VI., to make the matter complete, suppressed the private chantries, and converted their endowments to his own use; and soon afterwards (in 1552) inventories of all church goods were taken, and such as were not deemed necessary to carry on divine service according to the reformed method were to be sold. These lists for Lancashire have been preserved;[1] as a sample of the then furniture of a church, the case of Ormskirk may be taken : in it there were found 2 chalices, 1 cope of old green velvet, 2 copes of old blue silk, a vestment of silver velvet, 1 of tawny velvet with yellow crosses, 1 vestment of green satin bridges,[2] with 2 other vestments, 3 albs, 2 altar-cloths, 1 towel, 3 corporases,[3] 5 bells,

[1] Partly printed by Chetham Society, cvii. and cxiii.
[2] Bridge = a kind of thread.   [3] Communion-cloths.

2 cruets,[1] 3 sacring bells, a pair of organs. Organs were now not very common in parish churches; they were, however, found in the churches at Rochdale, Middleton, Preston, and Liverpool; in the latter place the Mayor and Bailiffs in 1588 ordered that there should be a hired clerk who could sing his plain song and prick song and play on the organs. At the time of the suppression of the chantries the number of clergy, including the chantry priests, was considerable in some of the larger parishes; thus we find twenty in Manchester, fourteen in Winwick, fourteen in Blackburn, and eleven in Prescot.

Many of these cantarists, as they were called, were now pensioned off for life. In Lancashire at this time there was a very strong party in favour of the old form of religion; and this wholesale doing away with the institutions which had so long been established in their midst met with almost open rebellion, and thus it was that again progress was arrested in the county.

It has already been stated that during the monkish rule little was done in church-building; indeed, in what is now the Diocese of Manchester,[2] between 1291 and the suppression of the monasteries, there were not a dozen churches erected, whilst during the reign of Henry VIII. seven were built, several of which would perhaps be more properly described as chapels-of-ease; they were Ashworth, Denton, Blakley, Douglas, Hornby, Rivington, and Shaw. On the accession of Mary in 1553, there was a return to the old order of things, and Popery being once again established, the Lancashire Catholics were not slow in taking advantage of the opportunity; thus, we find that in 1558 the Mayor and Bailiffs of Liverpool ordered that the priest of St. John's altar should say Mass

[1] A glass bottle to hold oil.
[2] Created in 1848, and includes all Lancashire, except parts of West Derby which are in Chester Diocese, and the Furness and Cartmel districts, which were added to Carlisle.

daily between the hours of five and six in the morning, that all labourers and well-disposed people might attend. During the troubled times which followed, two of Lancashire's sons became martyrs in the cause of the Protestant religion. John Bradford was a native of Manchester, where he was born in the early part of the century; he became Prebendary of St. Paul's and chaplain to Edward VI., but on his refusal to give up preaching the reformed doctrine he was sent to the Tower, and after an examination before the Lord Chancellor and the Bishop of London, and repeated appeals to conform, he was pronounced to be a heretic, and on June 30, 1554, he was burnt at Smithfield in the presence of a vast concourse of people. On reaching the place of execution he walked firmly up to the stake, and after a short prayer he took up a faggot and kissed it, and took off his coat and delivered it to his servant, and then, turning towards the people, he held up his hands, and exclaimed: "O England, England, repent thee of thy sins! Beware of idolatry, beware of antichrists, lest they deceive thee!" His hands were then tied and the fire lighted, and amidst the flames he was heard to say, "Strait is the way and narrow is the gate which leadeth unto life, and few there be that go in thereat." Fuller describes Bradford as "a most holy man, who, secretly in his closet, would so weep for his sins, one could have thought he would never have smiled again, and then, appearing in public, he would be so harmlessly pleasant, one would think he had never wept before."

During his imprisonment he wrote to his mother, then living in Manchester, and tried to console her by the assurance that he was not going to die "as a thiefe, a murderer, or an adulterer," but as "a witness of Christ, hys gospel and veritye." He left several sermons which, together with his letters and an account of his life, were afterwards published.

George Marsh was a native of Dean, near Bolton, where he was born about the year 1515, and was brought up to follow agricultural pursuits; but having lost his wife when he was about thirty years old, he left his young children with his father, proceeded to Cambridge, and became a student at the University, and being subsequently ordained, was appointed Curate of Allhallows', Bread Street, in London, by the Rev. Mr. Saunders (the martyr), then Rector of that church. In 1555 he appears to have been persecuted for his zeal in the reformed religion, and contemplated leaving the country; but before doing so he paid a visit to his mother and his children, and on this occasion the Earl of Derby sent a letter to Mr. Barton, of Smithell's Hall,[1] near Bolton, to apprehend him and send him to Latham. This order was duly carried out, and after an examination before the Earl, he was imprisoned in what he describes as a " cold windy stone house, where there was very little room," and where he remained for two nights without bed, " save a few great canvas tent-clothes." This was in March, 1555. He remained here for over a fortnight, and on Low Sunday (with some others) was removed to Lancaster Castle. After a time the Bishop of Chester came to Lancaster, and, according to Marsh's statement, he refused to have anything to do "with heretics so hastily," but at the same time he " confirmed all blasphemous idolatry, as holy-water casting, procession gadding, mattins, mumbling, mass-hearing, idols up-setting, with such heathenish rites forbidden by God." Subsequently Marsh was sent to Chester, and brought before the Bishop (Dr. Cotes), and there was charged with having preached at Dean, Eccles,

---

[1] Near the door of the dining-room is a small hole in the flag floor, somewhat like the impress of a human foot, which tradition says marks the place where George Marsh stamped his foot as he protested to the truth of his faith.

Bolton, Bury, and many other places in the diocese, against the Pope's authority, the Catholic Church of Rome, the blessed Mass, the Sacrament of the Altar, and many other articles; whereupon he did not deny the preaching, but asserted that he had only, as occasion served, maintained the truth touching these subjects. Having firmly refused to recant, the Bishop "put his spectacles on his nose," and read out his sentence, after which he added, "Now will I no more pray for thee than I will for a dog." He was then delivered to the sheriffs of the city, and put into prison at the North Gate. On April 24, 1555, he was taken thence to Spittle-Broughton, near the city, being escorted by the sheriffs and their officers, "and a great number of poor simple barbers with rusty bills and poleaxes."

When at the stake he was again asked to recant, but again refused, whereupon he was chained to a post, and "a thing made like a firkin, with pitch and tar" in it, was placed over his head, and the fire lighted.

The religious persecution was now going on all over the kingdom, and many Protestants from Lancashire, in company of thousands from other parts of England, fled for shelter to foreign countries, there to seek that liberty of conscience which was denied them at home. They mostly went to Geneva, Strasburg and Holland. Towards the end of Mary's reign, Pope Paul IV. began to insist on the reinstitution of the abbeys and monasteries in England; but it was found that those who now owned these estates declined to part with them "as long as they were able to wear a sword by their sides."

The war with France following, when the Pope took sides against the Queen, and in which England lost all her dominions in that country, only for a time stayed the persecution of heretics, and in October, 1558, it was again renewed; but the death of the Queen on the

17th of November in the same year closed this dreadful chapter of English history.

The Church was now again freed from the authority of the Pope, and gradually restored to what it was in the time of Henry VIII.; but in order not to hurt the Roman Catholics too much at first, a small number of Catholic ministers were retained in her Majesty's Council. Commissioners were appointed to visit each diocese and to report on the state of things, especially as to the effects of the late persecutions. Amongst those selected for the Northern visitation was the Earl of Derby. The commissioners commenced their work on August 22, 1559, and were directed to minister the oath of recognition; they received many complaints from clergymen who had been ejected from their livings for being married and other causes, and in some cases these were reinstated. In Lancashire the oath of supremacy was ordered to be taken by a proclamation to the Chancellor of the duchy, dated May 23, 1559, both clergy and laity being required to take it. At the same time all the restored chantries were only to be now used . in accordance with the Reformed Church: the Host was not to be elevated, and the Lord's Prayer, the Creed, and the Gospels were to be read in English.

The progress of the Reformation was rapid in the South of England, but in Lancashire the feeling in favour of the old form of religion was so strong that for some years little or no permanent change was effected, as nearly all the oldest and most powerful families in the county were rigid Roman Catholics. It is a remarkable fact that when England, under Elizabeth, again became Protestant, and almost all the bishops gave up their sees, the great majority of the clergy in Lancashire agreed rather to accept the new form of religion than to resign their livings, the result being that in many parishes the vicars or rectors were really Papists in disguise, and had shown themselves but ill qualified shepherds to have the care of such large, scattered, and disunited flocks.   But this exhibition of pliant and accommodating consciences was put in the shade by the rapidity with which the Earl of Derby changed front, and we now find the persecutor of Marsh every whit as keen in running to earth the recusant Roman Catholic.   But in all extreme movements there is gene-rally a reaction; so the harsh measures taken by Queen Mary laid the seeds for the formation of a new body of malcontents, to whom the reform meted out to the Church was not sufficient; and this, at first a mere sect, soon rose into a powerful party, which was recognised under the general title of Puritans.   Queen Elizabeth hated a Puritan only with a less bitter hatred than she did a Catholic; so as both these were represented in Lancashire, this county was at once marked out for persecution; and it was not long before we hear of 600 recusants being presented at one assize at Lancaster, and that all the prisons were full.[1]

Catholics were forbidden to leave the country, and Puritans were not allowed to meet together to worship anywhere except in the church.   In 1567 the Queen addressed a letter to the Bishop of Chester, in which she says : " We think it not unknown how, for the good opinion we conceived of your former service, we admitted you to be bishop of the diocese; but now, upon credible reports of disorder and contempts, especially in the county of Lancaster, we find great lack in you.   In which matter of late we writ to you, and other our commis-sioners joined with you, to cause certain suspected persons to be apprehended, writing at the same time to our right trusty and well-beloved the Earl of Derby, for the aid of you in that behalf.

" Since that time, and before the delivery of the said

[1] State Papers, Dom. Ser., 1547-1565.

letters to the Earl of Derby, we be duly informed that the said earl hath, upon small motions made to him, caused such persons as have been required to be apprehended, and hath shown himself therein according to our assured expectation very faithful and careful of our service."

The letter concludes with instruction to the Bishop to make a personal visitation into the most remote parts of his diocese, especially in Lancashire, and to see for himself how the various church-livings are filled.

Notwithstanding this reproof to the Bishop, he had before this had many times to deal with rebellious clergy and their congregations. Many instances might be quoted. In 1564 the curate of Liverpool was admonished to warn the people " that they use no beades," and that they " abolish and utterly extirpate all manner of idolatrie and superstition out of the Church immediately;" and at the same time the curate of Farnworth was presented " for showing and suffering candles to be burnt in the chapel on Candlemas daye, accordinge to the old super- stitious custom." In the same year complaints were made to the Archbishop of York that in all the livings in Whalley and Blackburn the clergy were neglecting their duty, and very seldom preached to their flocks. The Bishop made a visitation in the summer of 1568, but he has left little record of it, except that he was well entertained by the gentry, the only drawback to his perfect enjoyment being the excessive heat of the weather. The disaffection increased, and there was a determination on the part of a large portion of the com- munity not to attend church nor to hear sermons, but to have Mass celebrated, and otherwise to act against the laws of the land ; indeed, there is not wanting evidence to show that it would at this time not have required much excitement to have resulted in open rebellion.

Many of the Lancashire gentry, hoping to again establish the Catholic religion, openly espoused the cause of Mary, Queen of Scots. The Bishop of Carlisle, writing to the Earl of Essex in 1570, gives an account of the state of Lancashire in that year; he writes: " Before my coming to York, Sir John Atherton arrived there from Lancashire, where he long resided, and not being able to come to my house through infirmities, he sent to my father and declared to him how all things in Lancashire savoured of rebellion; what provision of men, armour, horses and munition was made there; what assemblies of 500 or 600 at a time; what wanton talk of invasion by the Spaniards; and how in most places the people fell from their obedience and utterly refused to attend divine service in the English tongue. How since Felton set up his bull so the greatest there never came to any service, nor suffered any to be said in their houses, but openly entertained Louvainists massers with their bulls."[1] And the same year the Bishop wrote to Sir William Cecil (afterwards Baron Burleigh), that in Lancashire the people were falling from religion altogether, and were returning to " popery and refused to come to church."

Ten years later things seem little improved, as Sir Edmund Trafford writes in 1580 to the Earl of Leicester, informing him that the state of the county was " lamentable to behold, considering the great disorder thereof in matters of religion, masses being said in several places." And he winds up with a request that the Government will cause the offenders to be rigorously dealt with.[2] Possibly in reply to this appeal a Royal Ecclesiastical Commission was now appointed, consisting of the Bishop of Chester, Lord Derby and others, which was to bring the offenders " to more dutiful minds ;"[3] and about the same time an Act was passed by which absentees from church for a month were to be liable to a penalty of £20. A contemporary Roman Catholic writer, commenting upon the

[1] State Papers, Dom. Ser., addenda xix., p. 525.
[2] *Ibid.*, p. 161.   [3] *Ibid.*, cxxxviii., p. 18.

appointment of Sir Edmund Trafford as Sheriff of Lancashire, describes him as a man "so thoroughly imbued with the perfidy of Calvin and the phrensy of Beza, that it might be said he was merely waiting for this very opportunity of in every way pursuing with insult all that professed the Catholic religion, and despoiling them of their property. For the furious hate of this inhuman wretch was all the more fiercely stirred by the fact that he saw offered to him such a prospect of increasing his slender means out of the property of the Catholics, and of adorning his house with the various articles of furniture filched from their houses." He then goes on in the same strain to describe the manner in which the Sheriff's officers took possession of Rossall, and expelled therefrom the widowed mother and sisters of Cardinal Allen.[1] The persecution in Lancashire now became more severe, and very few of the old families adhering to the unreformed religion escaped punishment. Amongst those who were imprisoned were Sir John Southworth, Lady Egerton, James Labourne, John Townley, Sir Thomas Hesketh, Bartholomew Hesketh and Richard Massey.

In 1582 the prisoners, on the ground of recusancy, were ordered to be sent to the New Fleet prison in Manchester, instead of, as heretofore, to Chester Castle. At this time numerous amateur detectives seem to have made out lists of recusants and forwarded the same to the Government officials, so that no man knew who was his accuser; but once his name got down on the list, persecution and fine or imprisonment invariably followed. In 1585 the sanguinary law against Jesuits, seminary priests, and others was enacted, and by it all such were ordered at once to quit the country, and anyone harbouring them was to be adjudged guilty of high-treason. This brought a new crime into existence, and many Lancashire people

[1] See "History of Poulton-le-Fylde" (Fishwick), Chetham Society, viii., new series.

became the victims. Priest-harbouring was soon amongst the most prolific causes of arrest and imprisonment. As samples of the working of this Act in Lancashire, the following are selected from a long list :

NAME OF PRIEST.	WHERE RECEIVED.	BY WHOM PRESENTED.
Sir Evan Banister, an old priest.	Jane Eyves, of Fishwick.	Ralph Serjant, churchwarden of Walton.
" Little Richard."	Mr. Regmaidens, of Weddicor.	Vicar of Garstang.
Robert Woodroof, senr., priest.	Jenet Woodrof, Burnley.	Curate and churchwarden of Burnley.
Divers priests.	Rafe Home, of Chequerbent.	Vicar of Dean.
Jas. Darwen, senr., priest.	Richard Blundell, of Crosby.	Curate of Sefton.
Evan Bannister.	Wm. Charnocke, of Fullwood. (Mass done on our Lady day in Lent last.)	Thos. Sharpell.

The following year (1586-7) no less than 128 gentlemen in various parts of the country were in custody for recusancy, amongst whom were several from this county, who were released on giving bond to yield themselves up on ten days' notice.

In 1591 a report was sent to the Council, from which it appears that the Lancashire commission had made " small reformation," and that, notwithstanding the rigour of the law, the churches were still empty, and there were still " multitudes of bastards and drunkards " ; in fact, the county was in a worse state than ever ; the people, it is added, " lack instruction, for the preachers are few : most of the parsons are unlearned, many of them non-resident, and divers unlearned daily [are] admitted into very good benefices." But even a greater evil is yet added, for the young " are for the most part trained up by such as profess Papistry. The proclamation for apprehension of seminaries, Jesuits and Mass priests, and for calling home children from parts beyond the sea " is not executed, neither are the instructions to the justices to summon before them "all parsons, vicars, churchwardens and sworn men," and to examine them on oath how the statutes of 1 and 25 Elizabeth, as to resorting to churches, are obeyed. It is further reported that some of " the coroners and justices and their families do not frequent church, and many have not communicated at the Lord's Supper since the beginning of her Majesty's reign." Some of the clergy have " refrained from preaching for lack of auditors, and people swarm in the streets and the ale-houses during divine service time," and many churches have only present " the curate and the clerk," and " open markets are kept during service time," and " there are about many lusty vagabonds." Marriages and christenings are celebrated in holes and corners by seminary and other priests. Cock-fights and other games are tolerated on Sundays and holidays during service, at which ofttimes are present justices of the peace, and even some of the ecclesiastical commissioners. The report concludes by stating that Yorkshire and the other adjoining counties cannot " be kept in order so long as Lancashire remains unreformed."

Another report of about the same date, made by several of the Lancashire clergy,[1] confirms this account ; they state that Popish fasts and festivals were everywhere observed, and that " crosses in the streets and waies, devoutly garnished, were plentiful, and that wakes, ale, greenes, May games, rushbearings, bearbaits, doveales, etc.," were all exercised on the Sabbath, and that of the number of those who came to church many do more harm than good by their " crossinge and knockinges of theire breste and sometimes with beads closely handled " (*i.e.*, partly concealed), and that at marriages they brought " the parties to and from churche with piping, and spend the whole Sabbothe in daunsinge," and that the churches

---

[1] *Chetham Society*, xcvi., p. 1.

generally were in a ruinous condition, being "unrepaired and unfurnished," whilst the "churches of ease (which were three times as many as the parish churches)" were many of them without curates, and in consequence were growing into "utter ruin and desolation." This report, which has a strong Puritanical tone about it, was signed by a Fellow of the Manchester Collegiate Church, the rectors of Bury, Wigan, Warrington and Middleton, the vicars of Poulton-in-the-Fylde, Kirkham and Rochdale, and other clergy.

One of the signatories of this document knew well the truth of at all events part of the statement, for in his own parish (Kirkham) was situated the chapel of Singleton, the curate of which in 1578 had been presented because he performed no services, kept no house, did not relieve the poor, nor was he diligent in visiting the sick, he failed to teach the catechism, preached no sermons, churched fornicators without penance, and, to crown his offences, he made "a dunge hill in the chapel yeard and kept a typling hous and a nowty woman in it."[1]

At this date it was customary at most of the Lancashire parish churches to ring the curfew at seven o'clock in the evening from All Hallows' Day (October 31) to Candlemas Day (the Purification of the Virgin), February 2; another duty of the sexton was to whip the dogs out of church. The curfew was tolled in some of the churches up to quite a recent date. Thomas Heneage, Chancellor of the duchy, gave testimony in 1599 that in consequence of the smallness of many of the livings in the county, and the fact that the parsonages were in private hands, there were "few or no incumbents of learning or credit," and the priests were drawing even those from their duty.

The report led to the ordering of salaries to be paid to

---

[1] Chester Presentments at York. See also "History of Kirkham" (Fishwick), *Chetham Society*, xcii. 45.

certain preachers (afterwards called King's preachers), who were to deliver sermons in various parts of the county. In the commencement of the seventeenth century things became somewhat more settled, but still the agents of the Government often met with great opposition in their efforts to carry out their instructions, and this continued to the very end of the reign of Elizabeth, for in 1602-3 the Bishop of London complains that "in Lancashire and those parts, recusants stand not in fear by reason of the great multitude there is of them." Likewise he had heard it "reported publicly that amongst them they of that country had beaten divers pursuivants extremely, and made them vow and swear that they would never meddle with any recusants more. And one pursuivant in particular, to eat his warrant and vow never to trouble them nor any recusants more."[1] On the accession of James to the throne, both the Catholics and Puritans hoped to obtain some redress, or at any rate more freedom from oppression and persecution; but instead of this hope being realized, they soon heard of new penal regulations being issued which in no way encouraged either party. The Puritans in Lancashire were offended by the issue of the "Book of Sports" (see p. 123), and the Catholics were still obliged to resort to all kinds of strategy to avoid arrest and imprisonment or fines. Nor did either of the two great religious factions receivè much better treatment under Charles I., in whose reign two (if not more) Catholics suffered for their religion the extreme penalty of the law at Lancaster. One of these was Edmund Arrowsmith, a priest of the Order of Jesus; he was hung, and afterwards beheaded and dismembered. This was in 1628. At Bryn Hall (lately pulled down), until very recently, was preserved what was said to be the hand of Father Arrowsmith, the tradition being that just before his death he

[1] State Papers, Dom. Ser., Eliz., vol. cclxxix., No. 86.

requested his spiritual attendant to cut off his right hand, which should then have the power to work cures on those who were touched by it and had the necessary amount of faith. Accounts of the miraculous cures worked by this hand were printed as recently as 1737.[1]

It will here be a suitable place to notice briefly a peculiar form of vestry which in the sixteenth century was common in the hundred of Amounderness and recognised as "sworn men." Preston, Kirkham, Goosnargh, Poulton, St. Michael's-on-Wyre, Garstang, Lancaster and Ribchester, each had this executive body, though the number varied; but most of the parishes had twenty-four sworn men. The oath taken by these officers was to the effect that they would keep, observe and maintain all ancient customs as far as they agreed with the law of the realm and were for the benefit of the particular parish or chapelry. Their duties were numerous : they levied the rates, elected the parish clerk in some cases, appointed churchwardens, and even laid claim to nominate the vicar, and in a general way they not only looked after the fabric of the church, but regulated its ceremonies and attended to the welfare of the parish. These men were not re-elected annually, as in the case of churchwardens, but, once appointed, they held office for life, unless they left the parish or were disqualified by becoming Nonconformists or other sufficient reason. The best men in the parish often were included in the list, and in many cases sons succeeded fathers for several generations.[2]

During the years immediately preceding the Civil Wars, Puritanism had gone on increasing, and at the opening of the Long Parliament, in 1640, it was felt that some change in the form of religious worship had become

---

[1] "A True and Exact Relation of the Death of Two Catholics," etc. ; London, 1737.

[2] See "History of Kirkham," *Chetham Society*, xcii., also article in "Bygone Lancashire" ; London, 1892.

an absolute necessity to meet the clamorous demands heard on all sides. Lancashire, just as it had for long been a stronghold of Catholicism, now became a centre of Puritanism; and for many years to come the intolerant spirit of both parties helped to retard the progress of free religious thought.

Parliament distinctly for some time fostered Puritanism, which ultimately led to the adoption of the Presbyterian form of Church government, which was developed between the years 1643 and 1648. A modern writer[1] truly remarks that, " If Puritanism anywhere had scope to live and act, it was here" (in Lancashire); "if anywhere in England it was actually a force, it was in Lancashire. There is no other part of England that can furnish so complete an illustration of the true spirit of this seventeenth-century Puritanism as it was manifested in actual practice, and it is this that gives such a peculiar value to the records of the religious life of the county during the years 1643-60."

The actual change of Church government did not much affect the county, until the Assembly at Westminster replaced the Book of Common Prayer by the Directory; this was effected on January 3, 1645, when it was sanctioned by Parliament : other orders rapidly followed. Altars, raised Communion-tables, images, pictures, organs, and "all superstitious inscriptions" were soon swept away, and the energies of the Presbyterian party became concentrated against the clergy, the churches, and their endowment. In 1646 the titles of archbishops and bishops were abolished, and their possessions placed in the hands of trustees, and not long afterwards the "title, dignity, function, and office" of dean, sub-dean, and dean and chapter were done away with. Under the Act for providing maintenance of preachers, passed in 1649, the issues of Church livings were employed to pay preachers

[1] "Bygone Lancashire" : London, 1892.

appointed by Parliament or the presbytery. The Church
Survey of the Lancashire parochial districts was begun
in June, 1650, and from it we learn the state of each
parish through the evidence brought before the commissioners, who had sixteen sittings in the county; they
met three times at Manchester, six at Wigan, three at
Lancaster, three at Preston, and once at Blackburn.
There were then in the county 64[1] parish churches, 118
chapels-of-ease, of which no less than 38 were without
ministers, chiefly for want of maintenance. All the
churches, with one or two exceptions, had curates,
pastors, or ministers, as they called themselves. The
parishes in many instances were said to be very large,
and subdivision was recommended, whilst some of the
chapels were so far from the mother church that it was
suggested that they should be made into parish churches.

The survey furnishes the names of all the ministers,
and their fitness or otherwise for the office they held; as
most of them were said to be "godly preaching ministers,"
or were " of good lyfe and conversation, but keept not
the fast-days appointed by Parliament," it may safely
be inferred that the old vicars and curates had mostly
either conformed or been superseded by the then holders
of the livings. On September 13, 1646, a petition was
sent to both Houses of Parliament, styled " The humble
petition of many thousand of the well-affected gentlemen,
ministers, freeholders, and other inhabitants of the county
palatine of Lancaster." This petition set forth that,
" through the not settling of Church government, schism,
error, heresy, profaneness, and blasphemy woefully
spread"; separate congregations being " erected and
multiplied, sectaries grew insolent, confidently expecting
a toleration." The petitioners then go on in the true spirit
of those times to pray that some speedy course should
be taken "for suppressing of all separate congregations of

---

[1] Including North Meols, which is omitted in the survey.

Anabaptists, Brownists, heretics, schismatics, blasphemers, and other sectaries" which refused to submit to " discipline and government," and, further, that such " refusers and members of such congregations" should not only be removed from, but kept out of "all places of public trust." Shortly after this (October 2, 1646) the county was divided into nine classical presbyteries, as follows:

1. The parishes of Manchester, Prestwich, Oldham, Flixton, Eccles, and Ashton-under-Lyne. The members nominated consisted of eight ministers and seventeen laymen.[1]

2. The parishes of Bolton, Bury, Middleton, Rochdale, Deane, and Radcliffe. Its members, ten ministers and twenty laymen.

3. The parishes of Whalley, Chipping, and Ribchester. Its members, eight ministers and seventeen laymen.

4. The parishes of Warrington, Winwick, Leigh, Wigan, Holland, and Prescot. Its members, fourteen ministers and twenty-eight laymen.

5. The parishes of Walton, Huyton, Childwall, Sefton, Alcar, North Meols, Halsall, Ormskirk, and Aughton. Its members, fifteen ministers and twenty-three laymen.

6. The parishes of Croston, Leyland, Standish, Ecclestone, Penwortham, Hoole, and Brindle. Its members, six ministers and fourteen laymen.

7. The parishes of Preston, Kirkham, Garstang, and Poulton.[2] Its members, six ministers and thirteen laymen.

8. The parishes of Lancaster, Cockerham, Claughton, Melling, Tatham, Tunstall, Whittington, Warton, Bolton-le-Sands, Halton, and Heysham. Its members, eight ministers and eighteen laymen.

[1] The names were those who were considered "fit to be of the classis."
[2] St. Michael's-on-Wyre and Lytham are left out.

9. The parishes of Aldingham, Urswick, Ulverston, Hawkshead, Colton, Dalton, Cartmel, Kirkby, and Pennington. Its members, five ministers and eleven laymen.

The names of all these members have many times been printed. It does not necessarily follow that all the persons nominated as " fit to be of " each classis absolutely acted in that capacity ; indeed, it is well known that many refused the office.

These classes at once took upon them the management and control of things ecclesiastical. The Manchester classis first met on February 16, 164⅞, when Richard Heyricke, the Warden of the collegiate church, was appointed Moderator, although he had formerly been one of the warmest supporters of the Church and King ; at their second meeting, on March 16, 164⅞, they passed a resolution to the effect that all who preached within the classis who were not members of it were to be called to account, as were also all ministers or others who permitted them so to preach.   A considerable part of the time of the successive meetings was taken up by the inquiry into cases of immoral conduct and social scandals affecting the members of the various congregations: candidates for the ministry were examined by the Presbyters of each classis, and, if approved, were duly ordained ; and it was also part of their work to see that improper persons were not admitted to the Lord's Supper.

From two remarkable papers, signed by a large number of the Lancashire ministers, in 1648 and 1649, we gather something of the spirit of the age.   One of these is "the Harmonious Consent of the Ministers of the Province within the County-Palatine of Lancaster, etc., in their testimony to the truth of Jesus Christ and to our solemn League and Covenant ; as also against the errours, heresies, and blasphemies of these times and the toleration of them ";

the other is, "The Paper called the Agreement of the People taken into consideration, and the lawfulness of Subscription to it examined and resolved in the negative, by Ministers of Christ in the Province of Lancaster, etc." In the "Harmonious Consent"[1] toleration is thus dealt with: "We are here led to express with what astonishment and horrour we are struck when we seriously weigh what endeavours are used for the establishing of an universal toleration of all the pernicious errours, blasphemies, and heretical doctrines broached in these times, as if men would not sin fast enough except they were bidden"; such a toleration, it is urged, would be "a giving Satan full liberty to set up his thresholds by God's thresholds and his posts by God's posts, his Dagon by God's Ark"; and further, "it would be putting a sword in a madman's hand, a cup of poyson into the hand of a child, a letting loose of madmen with firebrands in their hands, an appointing a city of refuge for the devil to fly to, a laying of a stumbling block before the blind, a proclaiming of liberty to the wolves to come into Christ's fold to prey upon his lambs; a toleration of soul-murther (the greatest murther of all others), and for the establishing whereof damned souls in hel would accurse men on earth." The petitioners also dreaded "to think what horrid blasphemies would be belched out against God, what vile abominations would be committed, how the duties of nearest relatives would be violated"; they then express their opinion that "the establishing of a toleration would make us to become the abhorring and loathing of all nations," and after adding the words, "we do detest the forementioned toleration," they conclude by praying that Parliament may be kept from "being guilty of so great a sin" as the granting of it would be.

---

[1] Written by the Rev. Richard Heyricke. Both these tracts are now very scarce.

This petition was signed by eighty-four ministers who had in their charge the principal parishes in the county. The other paper is quite as rabid in its tone, and bears the signature of nearly as many divines as the " Harmonious Consent." It sets forth clearly the points at issue, one of which was that it was proposed that " such as profess faith in God by Jesus Christ (however differing in judgement from the doctrine, worship or discipline publiquely held forth) shall not be restrained from, but shall be protected in their profession of their faith and exercise of religion, according to their consciences." To this proposition the minister of the province of Lancaster exclaims : " Thus all damnable heresies, doctrines of devils, idolatrous, superstitious and abominable religions, that ever have been broached, or practised, or can be devised (if the persons owning them will but profess faith in God by Jesus Christ) are set at liberty in this kingdom; nay, not only granted toleration, but enfranchisement, yea, protection and patronage."

We now find practically all the churches and chapels in the hands of the Presbyterians, and governed by the various classes, which met periodically at central places. These classes sent delegates to attend the provincial synod which met at Preston twice a year. In little less than three years after the formation of these classes difficulties arose in their working, not only because some places, such as Denton, Salford and Oldham, became disaffected, but in other places several members declined to continue their membership. A great cause of division amongst the various congregations was the conduct of the ministers and elders as to the admission of communicants. Oliver Heywood gives an account of the proceedings on this point at Bolton; he says : " There were two ministers, with whom were associated twelve elders, chosen out of the parish. These sat with the ministers, carried their votes into effect, inquired into the conversation of their neighbours, assembled usually with the ministers when they examined communicants, and though the ministers only examined, yet the elders approved or disapproved. These together made an order that every communicant, as often as he was to partake of the Lord's Supper, should come to the ruling elders on the Friday before, and request and receive a ticket which he was to deliver up to the elders immediately before his partaking of that ordinance. The ticket was of lead, with a stamp upon it, and the design was that they might know that none intruded themselves without previous permission. The elders went through the congregation and took the tickets from the people, and they had to fetch them again by the next opportunity, which was every month. But this became the occasion of great dissension in the congregations, for several Christians stumbled at it, and refused to come for tickets ; yet ventured to sit down, so that when the elders came they had no tickets to give in."

This state of things was not confined to a single parish, but was widespread, so that in some churches, rather than administer the Sacrament "promiscuously," the minister declined to administer it at all, and it was in a few places suspended for several years.

Whatever may be said as to the general dogmatical and narrow-minded views of the Lancashire Puritan clergy, they certainly did make great efforts to institute and maintain a high moral tone amongst their flocks. The every-day life of each member was subjected to rigid inquisitorial supervision, and his sins were dealt with in no half-hearted manner, excommunication being a frequent punishment, and even after the offender's death a funeral sermon was preached and the "occasion improved." Lancashire is fortunate in having had preserved several of the diaries of her Puritan divines, and these all bear strong testimony to the almost childlike faith which these men held as to the special interference of Providence in the events of everyday life. If a minister was to be tried at Lancaster, God graciously took away the judge by death; if he journeyed to London, the weather was specially arranged to suit; and if anyone was more than ordinarily rebellious against the Church's discipline and he thereabouts died, it was without the slightest hesitation attributed to a special judgment of God. We have seen with what signs of rejoicing the people of Lancashire (see p. 157) welcomed the restoration of Charles II. The country had got tired of the Commonwealth, and as to the religious feeling, the Episcopalians and Presbyterians were alike glad to have a return to the old form of government; yet the old rancour against Papists was still there, and to it was added a hatred of Anabaptists, Quakers and Independents: against the latter the Puritans were specially exercised.

The passing of the Act of Uniformity in 1662 put the clergy of the county to a severe test, the result being that sixty-seven of them refused to conform, and were summarily ejected from their livings. This act of injustice led to the commencement of Nonconformity in Lancashire, for amongst the ejected were many zealous and pious men, who through honest conviction could not conform to all the conditions required, and were not willing to abandon the views which they held.

Amongst these were Nathaniel Heywood, John Angier, Harry Newcome, Henry Pendlebury, Isaac Ambrose, Robert Bath, Richard Mather, John Harrison, and many others, all of whom soon had around them the nucleus of a future congregation. At first these men preached in private houses with impunity, but the passing of the Conventicle Act and the Five Mile Act, and the presence of large numbers of Roman Catholics, pressed hard upon them, and the amount of persecution and suffering which followed was extreme. For the next few years Nonconformists were persecuted with a vindictiveness worthy of the Dark Ages. Surrounded with spies on every hand, they were driven to hold secret meetings in out-of-the-way places, where they often met in the night-time. Those who were most zealous, or the most careless of discovery, were often apprehended at once, marched off to Lancaster, and sometimes, as in the case of Thomas Jolley (ejected from Altham), detained nearly twelve months in prison.

Perhaps no sect suffered more severely in Lancashire than the Quakers, who took no care to hide their meetings, and from them not only were fines enforced and goods sold, but many of them were for long periods locked up in gaol with felons and other criminal prisoners. Dr. Halley[1] says that although " their sufferings were cruelly severe, it must be acknowledged that they provoked much of the persecution which they so patiently endured, and repelled the assistance which good men of other parties would have been ready to afford them. A modern Friend, mild, pleasant, neatly dressed, carefully educated, perfected in proprieties, is as unlike as possible, except in a few principles, to the obtrusive, intolerant, rude, coarse, disputatious Quaker of the early days of their sect." The Society of Friends may almost be said to have arisen in Lancashire, so great was the support which it received here in the days of its infancy. In 1652 George Fox made a visit to Swarthmore Hall, near Ulverston, when he made a convert of the young wife of Judge Fell, and by their united efforts they soon obtained a considerable number of followers in the district of Furness and Cartmel, whose sympathies were no doubt quickened by the knowledge of the cruel persecutions of these " children of the light " (as they were sometimes called) constantly being enacted in Lancaster Castle. Margaret Fell, after the judge's death, became the wife of George Fox, and

[1] "Lancashire : its Puritanism, etc.," i. 465.

she was subsequently the writer of several treatises, and journeyed to London to deliver a copy of one of them to the King. The Lancashire Quaker literature of the seventeenth century is remarkable not only for the quantity of it, but for the light it throws on the religious thought of those writers for and against the teachings of the early pioneers of the sect.[1]

Of the cruel persecutions to which many of this sect in Lancashire were subjected, many examples might be cited; indeed, at one time the castle at Lancaster was said to be almost full of them, that town being one of their centres. In November, 1660, the Quakers of Lancaster, being assembled at one of their meetings, were surprised by a party of soldiers, who entered the room where they were with " drawn swords and pistols cockt," and took the whole of them prisoners. A Lancaster Quaker called John Lawson, in 1652, was seized at Malpas (in Cheshire), where he had been preaching in what he called " the Steeple House[2] Yard." He was set in the stocks for four hours, and afterwards imprisoned for twenty-three weeks; but shortly after his release he repeated the offence in the Lancaster church-yard, for which at the assizes he was fined £20 or in default one year's imprisonment; and again in 1660 he was sent a prisoner to the castle for refusing to take the oath tendered to him in court. Another example of the treatment which the early converts in Lancashire to this sect met with is found in the case of John Fielden, of Inchfield, near Todmorden, who in 1664 was fined £5 for attending a Quakers' meeting, and his goods were seized by the churchwarden and sold to pay the church-rate. In 1668 he was kept in prison thirty-one weeks for being absent from church, and this kind of persecution continued

---

[1] "Lancashire Quaker Literature" (Fishwick), *Trans. of Lanc. and Ches. Ant. Soc.*, 1887.

[2] They so designated the church.

until he was quite an old man, as seventeen years later we find him in Preston House of Correction, where he was retained for eight weeks, the offence being his having attended a meeting of the Society of Friends at Padiham. Very many similar cases might be quoted.

In 1689 the Toleration Act was passed, which recognised all the various forms of Dissent, which now became entitled to a place amongst the religious institutions of the county.

No time was now lost in establishing meeting-houses all over the county, and in almost every parish there soon arose Presbyterian or Independent chapels; many of the former ultimately passed to the Unitarians.

From a list prepared for Dr. Evans in 1715, it would appear that there were then in Lancashire forty-three Presbyterian and Independent congregations, consisting of 18,310 regular hearers; and that in Manchester there were 1,515 Dissenters, in Liverpool 1,158, in Bolton 1,094, and in Chowbent 1,064. Bishop Gastrell,[1] writing a little later, reports that in Rochdale there were no Papists, but about 200 Dissenters, who had a meeting-house; Bolton he puts down as having only 400 Dissenters, and to Manchester he gives 233 Dissenting families.

Many of these early chapels have interesting histories, which cannot be dealt with here.[2] Amongst the oldest ones may be named the following : Elswick Chapel, in the parish of St. Michael's-on-Wyre, was built as a sort of chapel-of-ease to the parish-church, by a party of Presbyterians a little before 1650, and a minister appointed by the classis. At the Restoration it was probably vacated ; but in 1671-72 it was duly licensed as a place to be used for such as did not

---

[1] "Notitia Cestriensis," *Chetham Society*, xix.

[2] See "Lancashire Nonconformity," by the Rev. B. Nightingale also Dr. Halley's "Lancashire Puritanism," etc.

conform to the Church of England, who were "of the persuasion commonly called Congregational. Shortly after this an Act was passed repealing this and similar licenses, whereupon the meeting at Elswick became illegal, and the chapel was closed until the passing of the Act of Toleration in 1689, since which time it has been regularly used as a Nonconformist chapel. At Wymondhouses a small chapel was built by the Rev. Thomas Jolley (who was ejected from Altham) in 1689. The chapel of the Presbyterians at Cockey Moor was one which obtained a license in 1672. The first Dissenting chapel in Manchester was in Cross Street; it was built in 1672 for the congregation of the Rev. Henry Newcome. This chapel was destroyed in 1714 (see p. 242). The Independents had no chapel in Manchester until 1761, when the one in Cannon Street was erected.

Toxteth Park or Dingle Chapel, near Liverpool, existed certainly in the early part of the seventeenth century, and is believed to have been built by the Puritans living in the district. Richard Mather (the grandfather of Dr. Cotton Mather) was for some time minister here, but was silenced by the Archbishop of York in 1633, and his successor was a Conformist, who was probably removed by the Presbyterian classis, 1646; in 1671-72 it was licensed under the Indulgence Act. From this congregation arose the Renshaw Street Unitarian Chapel in Liverpool[1] about the year 1687. Meeting-houses, as they were called, were established in almost every town under the Indulgence Act, and in most cases before the close of the century regular chapels were erected.

The Society of Friends, notwithstanding the persecution to which they were subjected, began to build meeting-houses even before the indulgences were granted. At Lancaster a Quakers' meeting-house was erected in

[1] The original meeting-house was at Castle Hey.

1677, at which time there was no other Nonconformist place of worship in the town.

A few years later the Mayor found it necessary to place a guard at the door of the house to prevent a meeting being held. In 1708 this meeting-house was found to be small, and a much larger one was erected. The meeting-house at Swarthmoor was built in 1686 upon land given by George Fox, who also endowed it with land free from tithes, so that (to quote his letter) " Friends may be sure of a meeting-house for ever that is free and will maintain itself, and which is the Lord's." In this meeting-house is still preserved George Fox's folio Bible, to which is attached the chain with which it was formerly fastened to the pulpit. The number of meeting-houses of the Society of Friends was never very great in Lancashire, and in the larger towns there were very few built before the early part of the eighteenth century. Most of them had graveyards attached, and in some cases (as in Manchester) these remain, whilst the meeting-houses have been pulled down.

Wesley made many visits to all parts of Lancashire; but the growth of Methodism was at first slow in the county, as it met with much opposition from many quarters, and in several towns the appearance of its founder led to disorder and riots. Methodism began in a very humble way in Lancashire, the handful of converts forming themselves into "classes," and often meeting in small cottages. In Manchester the first gatherings were held in a small room in a house near the Irwell, where a woman lived, having in the room her spinning-wheel, her coals, her bed, chair and table. Some of the earlier societies (about the year 1744) were called " William Darney's societies." Another man who assisted Wesley in Lancashire was John Bennet of Derbyshire, who introduced Wesleyanism into Rochdale a little before 1746.

Methodism was not introduced into Preston until 1750, and in some districts it did not obtain a footing until a much later period; but long before the close of the century its chapels were found in almost every large town as well as in isolated rural districts.

Early in the seventeenth century Baptist chapels were erected in several parts of the county. Of the many sects which have arisen within the last hundred years, it is not our province to record either the origin or progress, as Lancashire, in common with all the country, has now inhabitants who worship under many forms; but there no longer exists that bitter, antagonistic feeling between one denomination and another which has for so many centuries been a blot upon the pages of England's history.

In 1819 there were in Lancashire 77 Roman Catholic chapels, and in 1823 the Dissenting chapels included: 68 Independent, 27 Baptist, 32 Unitarian, 4 Scotch Kirk, 3 Scotch Presbyterian, and 180 Wesleyan.

CHAPTER X.

THE REBELLIONS.

THE most striking event in Lancashire in the beginning of the eighteenth century was the rebellion of 1715, which arose out of the Highland feeling in favour of the elder Stuart line, and the discontent of the lairds with the recent Parliamentary union. Those who planned the insurrection were in hopes of obtaining the support of the Roman Catholics in the North of England, who still owned the Pope as the supreme head of their Church. In September, 1715, the Earl of Mar raised the royal standard of "James VIII. and III." at Braemar, and was shortly afterwards at Perth with an army of 12,000. In the rising, of which this was the prelude, the Presbyterians in Lancashire attached themselves to the Whig party, whilst the Roman Catholics took the side of the Tories. A writer on this subject[1] says: "That the Roman Catholics in Lancashire should have appeared in arms during the movement of 1715 can excite no surprise whatever. They were stimulated by a deep recollection of long bygone persecutions, to which, as a cause, they referred their existing political and religious grievances. This historical retrospect comprises in its earliest date

[1] S. Hibbert Ware, M.D. See *Chetham Society*, v. (old series), from which many of the facts concerning this rebellion are taken.

the persecutions and degradations which they underwent in the reign of Elizabeth, and the sympathy which they subsequently met with from the unfortunate Charles, who was the first to show concern for their sufferings and civil disabilities."

The Roman Catholics who joined the Jacobite party in 1715 were strongly opposed, not only to the Whigs, but also to the Presbyterians, as they no doubt considered that to one or other of these factions they owed much of the persecution of past years. In Lancashire there were still many Roman Catholics, and it is not a matter of surprise that they should be ready to welcome any attempt to restore the succession of the Stuarts, in whose cause they had, during the Civil Wars, shed their blood and sacrificed many of their ancestral estates, especially as they were indignant at the attempts made by King William to meet the wishes of the Nonconformists. But perhaps the greatest excitement amongst the Tories was caused by King George's determination to continue the Toleration Act. In Manchester the feeling was very strong, and there, on June 13, 1715, a considerable mob assembled, which was led by Thomas Syddal, a peruke-maker, and continued daily to meet " with beat of drum " for several days, during which they ravaged many of the houses of those favourable to the Government, and ended by almost destroying the Presbyterian chapel in Acres Field (now Cross Street), which was at that time the only Dissenting place of worship in Manchester, and which in derision was called " St. Plungeons."

The Manchester mob having been joined by men from Warrington and the surrounding towns, they marched into Yorkshire, demolishing several meeting-houses which they passed on their way. Similar mobs were doing the same thing in several other parts of England at or near this date. Strong measures being taken by Parliament, by the end of July these riots for the time were suppressed.

Syddal and a man known as the colonel of the mob at Manchester were captured; they were tried at Lancaster in the August following, and were sentenced to imprisonment and to stand in the pillory.

The breaking out of the rebellion in Scotland and the rising in Northumberland were soon followed by a threatening attitude assumed by the people of Manchester, which was the chief centre of High Church Toryism; to foster this feeling and to obtain active assistance, Lord Widdrington and other Catholics visited the town; they were not only received with enthusiasm, but were promised at least 20,000 men, when once the Scottish force had entered Lancashire. In the north of the county there were a considerable number of adherents to the cause of the Chevalier de St. George, amongst them being many members of some of the oldest and most powerful families in the district.

On November 6, 1715,[1] the insurgents were at Kirkby Lonsdale, and being told that the town of Lancaster had ceased to make preparations for defence, they decided to march on to that place, outside of which they arrived the day following, being met by Lord Widdrington and others, who roused their drooping spirits with the intelligence that the Lancashire gentlemen were willing to join them, and that Manchester (as an instalment towards the 20,000 promised) had got arms for 50 men besides other volunteers. The Lancaster people were, it appears, waiting for some dragoons from Preston which did not arrive, so that although Sir Henry Hoghton was prepared to defend the town, he was powerless to do so; and on November 7 the Scottish army entered Lancaster with swords drawn, drums beating, colours

---

[1] Works consulted: Patten's "History of the Rebellion," Rae's "History of the Rebellion," "Lancashire Memorials of 1715" (*Chetham Soc.*, v.), "Manchester Collectanea" (*Chetham Soc.*, lxviii.), "History of Garstang," etc.

flying, and bagpipes playing; at the head of the troops
rode Lord Wintoun. At the market cross the Pretender
was proclaimed King. The next thing they did was to
release all the prisoners on the Crown side in the castle,
amongst whom were Thomas Syddal, the Manchester mob
leader, and his "colonel," both of whom joined the rebels.
Besides these, John Dalton[1] of Thurnham Hall, John
Tyldesley of the Lodge, Richard Butler of Rawcliffe, and
a few others of the Roman Catholic gentry, were added to
their ranks. The only inhabitants of the town who
volunteered were a barber and a joiner. On November 8
service was held in the church, when, the Vicar declining
to pray for the Pretender, the Rev. William Paul,[2] who
was with the insurgents, read the prayer.

A writer, friendly to the rebels, narrates how the
gentlemen of the army, "trimed in their best cloathes,"
went to take "a dish of tea with the ladyes" of Lancaster, who "apeared in their best riging" in honour of
the occasion.

On November 9 the forces set off for Preston. The
day proved wet, and as the ways were deep and heavy, one
may easily realize that the march was disagreeable and
dispiriting, so much so that at Garstang the foot were
allowed to stay all night, with instructions to follow the
horse troops on to Preston the following day. Here, no
doubt through the influence of Thomas Tyldesley, Roger
Moncaster, an attorney and Town Clerk of the Corporation, joined the standard of the Chevalier; with him also
went some half dozen more from the same district.

At Preston on November 10 the Pretender was proclaimed at the cross, and all authorities agree that here
the army was joined by a considerable number of gentlemen, with their tenants and servants; but they were all
Roman Catholics, the High Church party being still

[1] His real name was Hoghton.
[2] A clergyman of the Church of England.

conspicuous by their absence. Amongst the volunteers were Richard Townley, Sir Francis Anderton of Lostock. Richard Chorley of Chorley, Gabriel Hesketh of White-hill (in Goosnargh), Ralph Standish of Standish, John Leybourn of Nateby, and many other men of high position in the county. The total strength of the rebel force has been estimated at 4,000 men. What had the Government been doing all this time? News then travelled slowly, and it appears that while the rebels were at Lancaster General Carpenter was with his soldiers at Newcastle. He afterwards set off towards Lancashire.

The insurgents knew of this, but they appeared to have been ignorant of the movements of General Wills, the commandant of the Chester garrison, who was sending out forces to Wigan. On November 8 Wills was at Manchester, where he found it would require a regiment to prevent a rising, and having provided against this emergency by sending to Chester for the militia, he set off with his troops to Preston. On November 10 Pitt's horse and Stanhope's dragoons reached Wigan, where they were quickly followed by other regiments, who were arranged in readiness to advance to Preston. The rebels in the interior were having a fine time of it in " proud Preston," where they found the " ladys so very beautifull and so richly atired " that they minded " nothing but courting and feasting." Whilst General Wills was at Wigan he appealed to Sir Henry Hoghton to raise some recruits, who, it appears, considered that the most likely party to find them was the Presbyterians; and with this in view he wrote to the Rev. James Woods, pastor of Chowbent, in the following terms:

" The officers here design to march at break of day to Preston; they have desired me to raise what men I can to meet us at Preston to-morrow, so desire you to raise all the force you can—I mean lusty young fellows, to draw up on Cuerden Green, to be there by ten o'clock, to bring with them what arms they have fit for service, and scythes put in streight polls, and such as have not to bring spades and billhooks for pioneering with. Pray go immediately all amongst your neighbours, and give this notice.

" I am your very faithful servant,

" W. Hoghton."

"Wigan, November 11, 1715."

This James Woods was the son of the Rev. James Woods, who, as the Nonconformist minister of Chowbent, was imprisoned in 1670. To the appeal of Hoghton, Woods hastily responded, and in' his efforts met with ready assistance from two neighbouring pastors, John Walton of Horwich and John Turner of Preston, and they and their volunteers are reported to have done good service to the Hanoverian cause. So enthusiastic was the pastor of Chowbent that he obtained the sobriquet of " General Woods." It seems almost incredible that all this time the commanders of the forces at Preston were unaware of the approaching enemy; yet if they did know of it, they at all events very considerably underrated the strength of General Wills's army.

On Saturday, November 12, at daybreak, the vanguard of General Wills's forces arrived at Walton-le-Dale, where the river only separated them from Preston.

On this being discovered, Lieutenant-Colonel Farquharson was sent with a detachment of 100 men to defend the Ribble Bridge, but afterwards it was deemed advisable to abandon this position in order that an advantage might be given to the Scotch troops in forcing the invaders to meet them in or near the town instead of near the open plain, where their want of sufficient horse and artillery would, it was thought, tell heavily against them; beside which, they would be able to fight under cover of the barricades which they had hastily thrown up near the centre of the town. Notwithstanding that the Government troops got possession of the houses of Sir Henry Hoghton and Mr. Ayres, the rebels held their position during the whole of the Saturday; but on the following day General Carpenter's troops came up and encamped round the town. The insurgents having discovered that Carpenter and Wills had now made a simple cordon round Preston, and that every avenue of escape was closed, made overtures for surrender. The reply of General Wills was: "I will not treat with rebels! They have killed several of the King's subjects, and they must expect the same fate. All that I can do for you is, that if you lay down your arms and submit yourselves prisoners at discretion, I will prevent the soldiers from cutting you to pieces, and give you your lives until I have further orders; and I will allow you but one hour to consider these terms."

To this proposal some of the English were inclined to submit, but the Scotch troops would not listen to it; and there arose a strong division amongst the insurgents, which led to something like a fight between the two parties.

After some parley, however, on November 13 Preston was surrendered, and the swords of the insurgent officers were given up, some in the churchyard and others at the Mitre Inn. Afterwards the lords, officers and the gentlemen volunteers were taken prisoners, and placed under guards in the inns known as the Mitre, the White Bull, and the Windmill; the Highlanders and other troops, having laid down their arms, were marched into the church, and placed under a strong guard. The total number thus taken prisoners is stated as 1,550, of which over 1,000 were Scotch. During the whole engagement the number killed probably did not reach 200. As far as Lancashire is concerned, this closed the rebellion.

Amongst the prisoners taken at Preston were the Earl of Nithsdale, the Earl of Cornwall, the Earl of Winton, and the Viscount of Kenmure, and over 200 other Scots noblemen and gentlemen; of the English there were the Earl of Derwentwater, Lord Widdrington, and over 70 gentlemen. After some little delay (awaiting instructions), about 400 rebels were sent to Lancaster Castle, where they slept on straw and were allowed for maintenance per man each day 2d. (for bread and cheese 1d., and 1d. for small beer); other of the prisoners were removed to Chester, Liverpool, and Wigan. Some of the officers of the royal army were tried by court-martial at Preston for desertion, and taking arms against the King; four of their number were convicted and shot, viz., Major Nairn, Captain Philip Lockhart, Ensign Erskine, and Captain John Shaftoe. Lord Charles Murray, though convicted, was ultimately reprieved. Towards the end of the month some of the prisoners at Wigan were sent off to London.

Nothing now remains to be told except to briefly state the fate of some of the rebel prisoners. The Earl of Derwentwater and Lord Kenmure were beheaded on Tower Hill, February 24, 1716; and of the prisoners condemned in Lancashire, sixteen were hanged at Preston, five at Wigan, five at Manchester, four at Garstang, four at Liverpool, and nine at Lancaster. Amongst the Lancashire victims were: Richard Shuttleworth, of Preston, gentleman; Roger Muncaster, Town Clerk of Garstang; Thomas Goose, who tradition says was arrested at Garstang for calling out as the rebel army passed, " Hev ye on, me lads, and you'll take the crown with a distaff"; William Butler, of Myerscough, gentleman; John Wadsworth, of Catterall, gentleman; Thomas Syddal, the Manchester peruke-maker; William Harris, of Burnley; and Richard Butler, of Rawcliffe.

The rebellion was followed by strong measures being

taken against Roman Catholics, as it gave another pretext for the seizing of their estates by the Commissioners, more particularly the properties of those who had died just before the events of 1715; and there is no doubt but that many of their descendants were harshly and unjustly dealt with. The oaths of supremacy and allegiance were now urged upon both clergy and laity, and all Roman Catholics and Nonjurors were compelled to register the value of their estates. The returns made by the Commissioners showed that in Amounderness there were 73 estates, worth per annum £2,260; in Lonsdale, 25, yielding £1,432; in Blackburn, 29, yielding £972; in Leyland, 54, yielding £1,463; in Salford, 17, yielding £721; in West Derby, 122, yielding £5,901. From this return it appears that the yearly value of the Nonjurors' estates (chiefly Roman Catholics) in Derby and Amounderness was nearly twice as much as all the rest of the county put together; and the numbers of estates in these two hundreds, though not quite in the same proportion, was very much greater than that in the other parts of Lancashire.

Shortly after the events just narrated, a strong controversy arose in Lancashire and other parts of the kingdom as to what was spoken of as the *Divine right of kings*, the Nonjurors maintaining that no circumstances whatever could justify an insurrection against the King, and therefore no one but a descendant of James II. could claim from them an oath of allegiance. The holders of this doctrine were plentiful in Lancashire, and in Manchester particularly, and there were many who at once espoused the cause of Prince Charles Edward (the son of the Pretender), when in August, 1745, he landed in the Hebrides on his way, as he fondly hoped, to the throne. On November 16 following, the Young Chevalier, with a small army, got possession of Carlisle, and was proclaimed King of Great Britain.

Leaving Carlisle, the Young Pretender marched through
Penrith to Lancaster, where he arrived on November 24,
at the head of about 5,000 men, chiefly Highlanders;
from thence they passed on to Preston, which was
reached on November 27, and by a forced march they
arrived at Manchester the following day. Here for the
first time during their passage through Lancashire they
obtained some substantial assistance, by the addition to
their forces of some 200 men, which were placed under
the command of Colonel Francis Townley, and were
designated the Manchester Regiment. The Jacobites
of Manchester received the Prince with public demon-
strations of joy. From Manchester the insurgents went
to Derby, where they ascertained that they were in
danger of being hemmed in by two armies of the Government, and therefore they wisely at once began to retreat,
passing again through Manchester, Preston, and Lancaster, and crossed the Scottish Border on the 20th,
having marched 200 miles in fourteen days.

The arrival of the Duke of Cumberland and his forces
in Lancashire soon re-established public peace and
confidence. The rebellion terminated at the battle of
Culloden, on April 16 following. The Prince ultimately
escaped to France. Amongst those taken as prisoners-
of-war there were several Lancashire men, who had
mostly been part of the unfortunate so-called Manchester Regiment, although, according to one account,
it was by no means composed solely of men from that
town.

Francis Townley was a Roman Catholic, and a son of
one of the Townleys of Townley, but, owing to some
family circumstance, he had for a time before the rebellion been living in France. On coming to Manchester
he made friends with some of the leading Jacobites,
amongst whom was Dr. Byrom. He appears to have
joined the Prince at Carlisle, and accompanied him

through England. In the rapid retreat which followed, he went as far as Carlisle, and was there left with some 400 men, while the Prince and the main body of Highlanders went over the Border. By this time nearly two-thirds of the Manchester Regiment had deserted. Thomas Syddal (the son of the Syddal executed after the 1715 rebellion (see p. 248), was also left in Carlisle, and acted as adjutant, for which post, being like his father a peruke-maker by trade, he could scarcely be qualified, neither could Captain George Fletcher, who heretofore had managed his mother's drapery shop in Salford.

Another Manchester man was Thomas Cappoch (the son of a well-to-do tailor), who joined the Pretender as chaplain, and during the occupation of the capital of Cumberland by the rebels was appointed as " Bishop of Carlisle."[1] There were also three sons of the nonjuring Dr. Thomas Deacon. On the surrender of Carlisle, the officers of the Manchester Regiment, twenty in number, and ninety-three non-commissioned officers and privates, were all taken prisoners and conveyed in waggons to London,[2] and placed in Newgate.

On the trial, which began July 16, 1746, all the prisoners were found guilty, and nine were ordered to be executed, which sentence was duly carried out on Kennington Common on July 20. The heads of Townley and George Fletcher were placed on Temple Bar, but the heads of Syddal and Thomas Deacon were sent to Manchester, and there fixed on spikes on the top of the Exchange; and it is said that one of the first who came to look at them was Dr. Deacon himself, who, taking off his hat, expressed his satisfaction that his son had died a martyr.

[1] " The Authentic History of the Life and Character of Thomas Cappoch (the rebel Bishop of Carlisle), etc." ; London, 1739.
[2] One of Dr. Deacon's sons died on the road.

After this no Jacobite passed the Exchange (so long as the heads remained there) without reverently removing his hat.

Thomas Cappoch and eight others were hung, drawn and quartered at Carlisle on October 18, 1746.

Many of the other Lancashire men, though convicted of high-treason, were afterwards pardoned.

CHAPTER XI.

PROGRESS IN THE EIGHTEENTH CENTURY.

THE general appearance of the chief Lancashire towns in the early part of the eighteenth century has been graphically described by a lady who rode through England on horseback;[1] and from this source we take our descriptions of Manchester, Liverpool, Lancaster, Wigan, Preston, and Rochdale.

Manchester consisted of not very lofty, but substantially built houses, mostly of brick and stone, the older houses being of wood ; from the churchyard you could see the whole of the town. The market-place was large, and took up the length of two streets, when it was kept for the sale of the " linnen-cloth and cottontickens," which were the chief manufactures of the place.

Liverpool was also mostly of brick and stone, but the houses were " high and even that a streete quite through looked very handsome"; in fact, the fair eques-trienne describes it as " London in miniature," and was much struck with its Exchange, standing on eight pillars, and over it " a very handsome Town-hall," from the

---

[1] " Through England on a Side-saddle," by Celia Fiennes ; London, 1888. The date ascribed to this journey is the time of William and Mary. This, strictly speaking, is in the last decade of the seventeenth century, but it is near enough to the eighteenth century to serve as an illustration.

tower of which you could see the whole country round. Lancaster was "old and much decayed," and some of the carved stones and figures belonging to the dissolved priory were still to be seen. The town was not much given to trade, though within it various trades were carried on; some of the streets were "well pitch'd and of good size." Preston was a very good market-town, leather, corn, coals, butter, cheese, and garden produce being exposed for sale. At the entrance to the town was a lawyer's house, all of stone, with fine windows in the front, and "high built, according to ye eastern buildings near London; on each side of it were neatly kept gardens. There were in some parts of the town some more of these handsome houses, and the streets were spacious and well pitch'd." Wigan is described as another "pretty market town, built of stone and brick," and as being the place where the "fine channell coales" are in perfection, and the writer adds, "Set the coales together with some fire, and it shall give a snap and burn up light." The Wigan people at this time were in the habit of making salt-cellars, stand-dishes, and small boxes out of cannel, and these were sent to London as curiosities.

Rochdale is described as a "pretty neate towne, built all of stone." The ride over Blackstone Edge is well described; the author mentions it as "noted all over England," and, after referring to the ascent from the Yorkshire side, says, "Here I entred Lancashire; the mist began to lessen, and as I descended on this side ye fogg more and more went off, and a little raine fell, though at a little distance in our view the sun shone on ye vale, wch indeed is of a large extent here, and ye advantage of soe high a hill, wch is at least 2 mile up, discovers the grounds beneath as a fruitfull valley full of inclosures and cut hedges and trees. That wch adds to the formidableness of Blackstone Edge is that on ye one hand you have a vast precipice almost the whole way one ascends and descends, and in some places ye precipice is on either hand."

Of the state of the roads in Lancashire this writer has somewhat to say; her ride from Wigan to Preston, though only twelve miles, took her four hours; and she adds, "I could have gone 20 miles in most countrys" in the same time; but she found one good thing in the county roads, which was, that at cross-roads there were posts with " hands pointing to each road, wth ye names of ye great towns on." Daniel Defoe, passing over Blackstone Edge in 1724, complains that the road was " very frightful narrow and deep, with a hollow precipice on the right," and that after he had gone a short distance this hollow got deeper and deeper, and, though they led the horses, they found it " very troublesome and dangerous." Yet this was the direct and only road to Yorkshire from the Rochdale valley. The turnpike system,[1] before the advent of the nineteenth century, had not been adopted in any part of Lancashire, but, with the commencement of the new industries and commercial enterprises of the period, it soon became apparent that the old " pack and prime "[2] ways were no longer adequate to carry on the business which had now to be done. Some of these old roads were little better than footpaths, which the repeated tread of long strings of pack-horses had worn deep into the soil, so that in rainy weather they served at once as roads and watercourses, and these were often crossed by rivers, which at flood-times were both deep and rapid, and a constant source of danger to travellers and their goods.

[1] See article by Mr. W. Harrison in the *Lanc. and Ches. Hist. Soc.*, vol. iv.

[2] These roads were not cart-roads, but intended for horse and foot passengers, and in Lancashire were paved with narrow blocks of millstone grit, which are still in places to be seen, the] centre deeply worn by the tread of the horses.

In 1753 all the roads in the county were infested with highway robbers, and to guard against them travellers went in groups. Thus, every Tuesday a gang of horsemen set off from London, and arrived at Liverpool on the Monday following. Goods were carried on stage-waggons, and were usually from ten days to a fortnight in coming to Lancashire from the Metropolis.

As late as 1770 Arthur Young passed along the road for Preston and Wigan, and thus refers to it: " I know not in the whole range of language terms sufficiently expressive to describe the infernal highway. Let me most seriously caution all travellers who may accidentally propose to travel this terrible country to avoid it as they would the devil, for a thousand to one but they break their necks or their limbs by overthrows or breakings down. They will here meet with ruts which I actually measured four feet deep and floating with mud only from a wet summer! What must it, therefore, be in winter!"

The earliest Turnpike Act was passed in 1663, and referred to the great north road through the counties of Hertford, Cambridge, and Huntingdon, and near the end of the century similar Acts were adopted for other districts, but none of them applied to Lancashire. Of the main roads through Lancashire at this period we have little information, but there was one from Chester which passed through Warrington, Manchester, Rochdale, and over Blackstone Edge to York; another from Manchester to Buxton and on to London; and a third from Lancaster to Skipton in Yorkshire. There was also one from Warrington, through Wigan, Preston, and Lancaster, to Kendal. Of course there were several other cross-roads, but these were the main trunks. The great Northern centre of these roads was Chester; between there [and Liverpool was all but impassable at this time with[anything like a waggon.

The first Turnpike Act for Lancashire was passed in

1724, and applied to the road from Buxton to Manchester, which is described as the nearest road from London to Manchester. Other districts soon followed this example, and Acts were obtained for turnpiking the road from Liverpool to Prescot in 1725 ; Wigan to Warrington and Preston in 1726; Rochdale to Elland (over Blackstone Edge) in 1734 ;[1] Preston to Lancaster, 1750 ; Salford to Warrington and Bolton, 1752 ; Rochdale to Burnley, 1754; Manchester to Rochdale, 1754; Liverpool to Preston, 1771 ; Clitheroe to Blackburn, 1776 ; Bury, and Haslingden to Blackburn, 1789 ; Rochdale to Edenfield, 1794; Rochdale to Bury, 1797; and other lines of route. So that before the century closed the county was intersected[2] in all directions by turnpike roads, which were maintained and formed under the regulations of their several Acts, and no longer dependent upon the uncertain measure of repair formerly reluctantly furnished by the local rates, which had often to be paid by those who used the road the least. Some of the preambles to these local Turnpike Acts furnish curious particulars as to the then state of the roads. For example, in 1750 the road from Crosford Bridge (near Sale), which passed through Stretford and Hulme to Manchester, is described as being "a common High road and part of the Post road from London to Manchester ; and by reason of the nature of the soil and the many and heavy carriages passing the same, the said road is become so exceedingly deep and ruinous that in the winter season and frequently in summer it is very difficult and dangerous to pass through the greatest part thereof with waggons, carts, and other wheel carriages ; and travellers cannot pass without danger and loss of time. And whereas some part of the said road lying

[1] Another, A.D. 1766.
[2] See Mr. Harrison's List of Turnpike Roads (*Lanc. and Ches. Ant. Soc.*, x.).

next to Crosford Bridge is many times overflowed with water and impassable; whereby the Post is delayed, and severall persons in attempting to pass through the same have lost their lives."

Towards the end of the century many parts of the old roads were abandoned, and shorter routes adopted, thus materially contributing to that ready access between town and town and the county with the Metropolis which was now becoming an absolute necessity. In places where the Turnpike Act had not been adopted it was now often found necessary to enforce the law as to repairs by indicting the parish at quarter sessions, where the justices ordered a fixed sum to be paid, which had to be levied by rates. The vast improvements made in the highways led to a very rapid development of the stage-coaches and stage-waggons.

An adventurous Manchester man advertised in 1754 that his flying coach, " however incredible it may appear, will actually (barring accidents) arrive in London in four days and a half after leaving Manchester."

In 1756 the " Flying Stage " coach left Warrington on Mondays, and got to London on Wednesdays, the inside fare being two guineas, with an allowance of fourteen pounds of luggage.

It was not until 1760 that a stage-coach began to run between Liverpool and London direct.

Between Manchester and Liverpool a stage-coach was established in 1770, which ran twice a week.

But along with the improvement of roads other schemes were being developed which ultimately led to the formation of the navigable canals which now intersect the county. The first of these is the one known as the Bridgewater Canal, which was commenced in 1758, when the Duke of Bridgewater obtained power to construct a water way from Worsley to Salford and to Hollinfare (or Hollin Ferry), on the river Irwell, and also to carry his canal across that river through Stretford into the town of Manchester. This work, which was then considered a masterpiece of engineering, was carried out under the direction of James Brindley. In addition to the aqueduct over the river, which is upwards of 200 yards long, there were other difficulties to be overcome, amongst them a tunnel of three-quarters of a mile in length. The bridge over the Irwell consists of three arches, the centre one 63 feet wide and 38 feet high, thus admitting barges to go through with masts standing, and, as Baines put it (writing in 1836), affording the spectator the "extraordinary sight, never before witnessed in this country, of one vessel sailing over the top of another." In 1761 a much bolder scheme was commenced by the Duke, which, when completed, formed a canal nearly 30 miles long, from Stretford to Runcorn on the Mersey. This took five years to construct, and it had the effect of at once lessening the cost of carriage by water between Manchester and Liverpool by at least fifty per cent. But this first Lancashire canal was not used only for the conveyance of goods; boats on the model of the Dutch *trekschuyt* were used daily to take passengers from Manchester to the places on the line of route. A branch from Worsley to Leigh was cut in 1795. Before the establishment of canals powers had been obtained in 1720 to render navigable the Irwell and Mersey from Liverpool to Manchester, and in 1726 the river Douglas (*alias* Asland), from Wigan to the Mersey. These river improvements were made at great cost, and at the best were not found to work in a very satisfactory manner, and were soon superseded by the ordinary canals. One of the first Lancashire canals was the Leeds and Liverpool, which was begun in 1770, when it was considered one of the boldest schemes which had ever been undertaken in England. Its length from Leeds to Liverpool is 107 miles. Dr. Aiken, writing near the close of the century, says of this canal : " On a cursory survey, the tract of country through which it passes will probably appear not extremely inviting to such an undertaking. It is but lightly peopled, and though the great towns at the opposite extremities abound in objects of commercial importance, yet their connection with each other is not very intimate, nor does it seem likely to be much promoted by such a circuitous communication. Coal and limestone are the chief natural products of the intermediate country ; and as the districts abounding in the one often want the other, a considerable transport of these articles on the canal may be expected, as well as other useful kinds of stone found in quarries near its course."

After the American War, which ended in 1783, Manchester showed great activity in pushing forward various schemes for the extension of the water-communication with the surrounding districts. Amongst the canals made before the end of the century were those to Bolton and Bury, Ashton-under-Lyne and Oldham ; Manchester to Rochdale and Yorkshire ; Kendal to Lancaster, Garstang, Preston, and West Houghton. On the latter packet boats conveying passengers to Preston went daily for many years.

The only place in the county where the maritime trade was increasing was Liverpool, where in the last decade of the century some 4,500 vessels arrived annually, their tonnage being about one-fifth that of the ships which reached London each year. The chief trade was with Africa and the West Indies, at least one-fourth of the Liverpool vessels being employed in the slave trade. From Lancaster, before the stagnation of trade set in, about forty-seven vessels were trading with foreign ports, their chief cargoes being mahogany furniture and goods made in Manchester and Glasgow. The Ribble was not much used by boats of any considerable burden.

To the cotton trade and all its developments must we look for the vast increase in the commercial prosperity of Lancashire which so strongly marked the last fifty years of the eighteenth century. The first invention which led to the present mode of spinning wool was the patent taken out in 1738 by Lewis Paul,[1] of Birmingham, for spinning of wool or cotton by machinery. The preamble to this grant sets forth that the machine was "capable of being set so as instantaneously to spin wool, cotton waste and wick-yarn to any degree, size, or twist with the greatest exactness, and is to be worked without handling or fingering the matter to be wrought, after the same be once placed in the machine, and requires so little skill that anyone, after a few minutes' teaching, will be capable of spinning therewith; and even children of five or six years of age may spin with the same, by which means the poorest of the clothiers will be enabled to supply their customers without suffering under the encumbrance of a dead stock of yarn, and the weavers may be supplied with such yarn as they shall want for their several occasions without that loss of time which often happens to them."

The principle of this and a later patent taken out by Paul covered the invention of what is technically known as roller-spinning, but which required further improvement before it could be profitably used. John Kay, a native of Walmersly, near Bury, where he was born July 16, 1704, was the undoubted inventor of the fly-shuttle which was patented in 1733, and of several other important machines connected with the trade. His melancholy history cannot here be repeated, but his life was one long struggle against ignorance and ingratitude. The people who were most to be benefited by his invention broke up his machines and drove him homeless to France.

[1] This invention is by some attributed to John Wyatt, of Birmingham, but recent research gives the credit to Lewis Paul. (See Espinasse's "Lancashire Worthies.")

His appeal to Government was in vain, and even those who adopted the fly-shuttle refused to pay for its use. He died an exile from his country in obscurity and poverty.

Let us take a glance at the daily work carried on by the cottagers and small farmers in Lancashire at the time when Kay made known his great invention. Samuel Bamford, of Middleton, who was well able to give testimony on this subject, writes: "The farming was generally of that kind which was soonest and most easily performed, and it was done by the husband and other males of the family, whilst the wife and daughters and maid-servants, if there were any of the latter, attended to the churning, cheese-making, and household work; and when that was finished, they busied themselves in carding, slubbing and spinning wool or cotton, as well as forming it into warps for the looms. The husband and sons would next, at times when farm labour did not call them abroad, size the warp, dry it, and beam it in the loom, and either they or the females, whichever happened to be least employed, would weave the warp down. A farmer would generally have three or four looms in his house, and then—what with the farming, easily and leisurely though it was performed, what with the housework, and what with the carding, spinning and weaving— there was ample employment for the family. If the rent was raised from the farm, so much the better; if not, the deficiency was made up from the manufacturing profits." William Radcliffe, himself an improver of the power loom, gives another account of the life of the hand loom weaver. In 1770, he says, "the land [in Mellor, near Manchester] was occupied by between fifty and sixty farmers . . . and out of these there were only six or seven who raised their rents directly from the produce of the farms; all the rest got their rents partly in some branch of trade, such as spinning and weaving woollen, linen or cotton. The cottagers were employed entirely in this manner, except for a few weeks in harvest. Being one of those cottagers, and intimately acquainted with all the rest, as well as every farmer, I am better able to relate particularly how the change from the old system of hand labour to the new one of machinery operated in raising the price of land. Cottage rents at that time, with convenient loom-shop and a small garden attached, were from one and a half to two guineas per annum. The father would earn from 8s. to half a guinea, and his sons, if he had one, two, or three alongside of him, 6s. or 8s. a week; but the great sheet-anchor of all cottagers and small farms was the labour attached to the hand-wheel; and when it is considered that it required six or eight hands to prepare and spin yarn, of any of the three materials I have mentioned, sufficient for the consumption of one weaver, this shows clearly the inexhaustible source there was for labour for every person, from the age of seven to eighty years (who retained their sight and could move their hands), to earn their bread, say from 1s. to 3s. per week, without going to the parish."

A weaver at this date had frequently to walk many miles to collect from various spinners the quantity of weft required to keep his hand-loom going, but the invention of the fly-shuttle made matters no better for him, as, although he could now turn out with the same labour as heretofore double the amount of pieces, he found no material increase in the product of the spinning-wheel. Here, then, was a block, to get over which there was only one way, and that was a corresponding increase in the production of the weft.

Many attempts were made to bring the old spinning-wheel up to the requirements of the day, but not one of them proved efficacious.

It may be noted here *en passant* that, whilst most of the patents taken out at this period were intended to improve the processes in cotton manufacture, Kay's fly-shuttle was first applied in the weaving of woollen, but was afterwards made adaptable for cotton. Another great improvement was what was known as the " drop box," which was invented by Robert Kay (a son of John Kay) in 1769.

This difficulty in keeping the woollen and cotton looms at work was brought before the Society of Arts in 1763, when its members, fully recognising the importance of the crisis, offered a prize of £50 for " the best invention of a machine that would spin six threads of wool, flax, hemp or cotton at one time, and require but one person to work and attend to it." This incentive caused many model spinning-wheels to be submitted for approval, none of which furnished what was required.

The solution of the difficulty was reserved for James Hargreaves, a weaver of Stanhill, near Blackburn, a town which had then about 5,000 inhabitants, many of whom were employed in making a kind of cloth known as " Blackburn gray." Hargreaves for several years was engaged in making improvements in the carding machines, which displaced the hand-cards then in use for clearing and straightening the cotton fibres preparatory to their being spun ; but in 1765 he turned his attention to the mechanical operation for spinning yarn, and having matured his ideas, he had a machine secretly made in his house, where he afterwards used it to great advantage. The machine was subsequently called the spinning-jenny, and did for the spinner even more than the fly-shuttle did for the weaver. Several of these machines were soon privately sold to some of his neighbours, who were not slow to discover the immense advantages which they furnished. Of course, an invention like this could not long be kept secret, and when it became known that here was a machine by which one spinner, instead of working with one thread, could, with equal ease, work with sixteen or even twenty threads, and that henceforth much of the female labour at the spinning-wheel would no longer be wanted, the unreasoning and ignorant populace began to rise against it and its inventor. The result was that, on a fixed day, weavers from Darwen, Mellor, Tockholes and Oswaldtwistle met in Blackburn (where their numbers were greatly augmented), and from thence made their way to Hargreaves' house; but not finding the inventor at home, they broke to pieces the spinning-jenny, and totally destroyed the household goods and furniture. They then proceeded to a mill of Robert Peel's, where the jenny was used, and reduced the place to ruins. After this, Hargreaves fled to Nottingham, and in 1770 took out his first patent for the machine which may almost be said to be the foundation of the cotton trade.

Like most other great inventors, Hargreaves did not make much money from his invention; but after a vain attempt to protect his patent, he settled down at Nottingham, and, in partnership with Thomas James, a joiner of the town, erected a small building which they ultimately used as a cotton factory, and which is believed to have been the first cotton mill in the world;[1] it was originally 40 feet long and 20 wide, and consisted of three stories. Hargreaves died at Nottingham in the spring of 1778.[2]

Notwithstanding the working-man's opposition to the spinning-jenny, before 1771 it had been adopted by nearly every spinner in Lancashire. Riots against the "jenny" continued, however, for a time to break out in the neighbourhood of Blackburn for several years after Hargreaves' death.

Another Lancashire inventor was Richard Arkwright, a barber, who was born at Preston, December 23, 1732, and was said to have been the youngest of thirteen

---

[1] Some authorities assert that Arkwright's mill in Nottingham was built prior to Hargreaves'.

[2] He did not, as has been frequently stated, die in poverty. He left property worth £4,000.

children.   About the year 1750 he, having married a
daughter of Robert Holt, of Bolton, removed to that
town, where, in 1769, he so far improved upon the
invention of Lewis Paul (see p. 261) for spinning cotton
by rollers, as to make it not only practicable but profitable, and thus at once opened a new era in cotton
manufacture.   Taking warning from the treatment which
Hargreaves had received, he removed to Nottingham,
where he had a small mill worked by horses, which was
subsequently abandoned and a new factory built at
Cromford, in Derbyshire, where the river Derwent supplied the water-power.   The dispute and connection
between Kay and Arkwright need not here be detailed.[1]
Arkwright was also the inventor of other mechanical
improvements in the manufacture of cotton.

Amongst other mills built by Arkwright was one at
Chorley, and this was one of those selected for destruction
by the mobs in 1779, of the doings of which the *Annual
Register* for October 9 in that year records : " During the
week, several mobs have assembled in different parts of
the neighbourhood, and have done much mischief by
destroying engines for carding and spinning cotton wool
(without which the trade of this country could never be
carried on to any great extent).   In the neighbourhood of
Chorley the mob destroyed and burned the engines and
buildings erected by Mr. Arkwright at a very great
expense.   Two thousand or upwards attacked a large
building near the same place on Sunday, from which
they were repulsed, two rioters killed, and eight wounded
taken prisoners.   They returned strongly reinforced on
Monday, and destroyed a great number of buildings, with
a vast quantity of machines for spinning cotton, etc.   Sir
George Saville arrived (with three companies of the York
Militia) whilst the buildings were in flames.   The report

---

[1] See Guest's " Compendious History"; Baines's " History of Cotton
Manufacture" ; Espinasse's " Lancashire Worthies," etc.

of their intention to destroy the works in this town—Manchester—brought him here yesterday noon.

"At one o'clock this morning two expresses arrived—one from Wigan and another from Blackburn—entreating immediate assistance, both declaring the violence of the insurgents, and the shocking depredations yesterday at Bolton. It is thought they will be at Blackburn this morning, and at Preston by four this afternoon. Sir George ordered the drums to beat to arms at half after one, when he consulted with the military and magistrates in town, and set off at the head of three companies soon after two o'clock for Chorley, that being centrical to this place, Blackburn and Wigan. Captain Brown, of the 24th Regiment, with 70 invalids—pensioners, presumably—and Captain Thorburn, of Colonel White's Regiment, with about 100 recruits, remained at Preston; and for its further security, Sir George Saville offered the justices to arm 300 of the respectable house-keepers, if they would turn out to defend the town, which was immediately accepted. In consequence of these proceedings, the mob did not think it prudent to proceed to any further violence."

These riots, which were pretty general in the district where machinery was used, arose from a temporary depression of trade, which the spinners mistook for the effects of the introduction of the recent inventions.

At Bolton £10,000 worth of mill property was destroyed. This dread of machinery was not entirely confined to the operatives, for some of the middle and upper classes connived at these appeals to brute force, if they did not actually encourage them.[1] Arkwright for many years suffered from attempts to infringe upon his patents, and his name often appeared in the law courts as plaintiff or defendant; but the details are of too complicated and technical a character to find a place in these pages,

[1] *Quarterly Review*, No. 213, p. 64.

beyond stating that, notwithstanding that in 1785 his patents were declared by the Court of King's Bench to be null and void, he amassed a large fortune, in the year following was knighted, and in 1787 was made High Sheriff of Derbyshire. He died on August 3, 1792, leaving property estimated at half a million sterling.

One other of the pioneers of the Lancashire staple trade remains to be noticed. Samuel Crompton was the son of a farmer living at Firwood, near Bolton, where he was born on December 3, 1753. Soon after the birth of his son, the elder Crompton removed to a house near Bolton, known as " Hall-in-the-Wood," which has since become famous as the birthplace of the "mule," which was to enable the spinner to produce a yarn out of which delicate fabrics could be woven such as heretofore had defied the skill of the English manufacturer. Crompton is said to have been five years in bringing his cherished scheme to perfection, during which time he worked secretly at his machine, and often prolonged his labour far into the night. In the memorable year when the rioters were busy destroying all the spinning-jennies they could find, Crompton completed his model, and, to hide it from the sight of doubtful visitors, he contrived to cut a hole through the ceiling of the room where he worked as well as a corresponding part of the clay floor of the room above, and had thus always ready a place in which he could hide the evidence of his patient industry. Part of Crompton's model had been in a measure anticipated by Arkwright; but "the great and important invention of Crompton was his spindle-carriage and the principle of the thread having no strain upon it until it was completed. The carriage with the spindles could, by a movement of the hand and knee, recede just as the rollers delivered out the elongated thread in a soft state, so that it would allow of a considerable stretch before the thread had to encounter the stress of winding on the spindle. This was the corner-stone of the merits of his invention."[1]

Crompton's " mule " was at once a success ; but instead of securing himself by a patent, he vainly endeavoured to work with it in secret, but was at length reduced, he tells us, " to the cruel necessity either of destroying my machine altogether or giving it to the public. To destroy it I could not think of ; to give up that for which I had laboured so long was cruel. I had no patent, nor the means of purchasing one. In preference to destroying I gave it to the public." In taking this step he was acting under the advice of a large manufacturer of Bolton, who was doubtless fully aware of the merits of the machine, and, in order to induce Crompton to make this valuable concession, some eighty firms and individuals of that town promised each to pay to him one guinea ; but, as a matter of fact, the total sum received did not much exceed £60, or scarcely enough to cover the cost of the construction of the model, which he also gave up.

Leaving Crompton for the moment, we must note that in 1784 the Rev. Edmund Cartwright took out his first patent for the invention of a power-loom, for which he obtained a grant from Parliament of £10,000. This loom never came into general use. It was not until some years later, and after several futile attempts, that a power-loom was made adaptable. Crompton, after much trouble and anxiety, did ultimately get from the House of Commons £5,000, which he afterwards lost in the bleaching trade, which was at that time making considerable progress. When he had reached his seventy-second year, some friends raised for him an annuity of £65, which he only enjoyed for a short time, as he died

[1] Kennedy's " Brief Memoir of Crompton " ; see also French's "The Life and Times of Samuel Crompton," and Espinasse's " Lancashire Worthies."

in Bolton on June 26, 1827, aged seventy-four years. Thus was treated another of Lancashire's greatest benefactors, who, whilst he lived, was left to feel that "chill penury" which "froze the genial current of his soul," but who after his death was thought worthy of a statue in copper-bronze, which cost nearly £2,000, and now forms one of the chief monuments of the town of Bolton.

So rapid was the result of these various means of developing the manufacture of cotton that in 1787 there were over forty cotton-mills in Lancashire, and seventeen in Yorkshire; those in other parts of England increased the aggregate to 119, whilst the value of cotton goods manufactured rose from £600,000 in 1766 to £3,304,371 in 1787, showing the increase in twenty-one years to be five and a half fold.

In the last decade of the century a stop to further progress appeared imminent, as nearly all the sites where water-power was available had been utilized to the utmost; but fortunately, while Arkwright and Crompton had been perfecting the machinery for cotton manufacture, Watts was completing his labours to render steam-power available for rotative motion.

Before 1782 steam-engines had been used exclusively for pumping water out of mines, but in 1785 Boulton and Wall erected a steam-engine to work the cotton mill of Messrs. Robinson, at Papplewick, in Nottinghamshire, and four years later Manchester had its first steam-engine applied to cotton manufacture. In 1790 in Bolton a cotton mill was turned by steam, and before the end of the century this motive power was adopted in a few other places in the county. Cotton-mills worked by horse and water power were now common enough in all the large towns where textile manufacture formed part of the trade carried on. This enormous increase in local textile manufacture led at once to a similar development of the manufacturing of machinery, the raising of coals, and of all other industries required to carry on the now staple trades.

Before closing the account of Lancashire in the eighteenth century, some reference must be made to its press, and this must always afford some clue to the character of the people. In the time of Elizabeth there was in Lancashire a secret press from which were issued a few Roman Catholic books; this was probably located at Lostock Hall, near Bolton. There was also the wandering press from which came the Martin Marprelate tracts; this press was seized by the Earl of Derby at Newton Lane, near Manchester.[1] In 1719 Roger Adams was established in Manchester as a printer; from his press came "Mathematical Lectures : being the first and second that were read to the Mathematical Society at Manchester." Adams also, in that same year, printed and published the *Manchester Weekly Journal*, which in 1737 became *Whitworth's Magazine;* this periodical enjoyed a run of twenty years. Whitworth published a considerable number of books, some of which were of more than local interest. In 1738 a second Manchester periodical was published entitled *The Lancashire Journal*, of which only about sixty numbers were printed. After this date, Manchester-printed books were pretty numerous.

A newspaper called *Orion Adams' Weekly Journal* was started here in 1752; it was followed by Harrop's *Manchester Mercury* and Whitworth's *Manchester Advertiser*. Liverpool probably began to print a year or two before Manchester; the first book known to have been issued there is a volume of "Hymns sacred to the Lord's Table," by Charles Owen—"Leverpoole, printed by S. Terry, for Daniel Birchall, 1712." After this very few books can with certainty be placed to the credit of the Liverpool press, but in 1736 appeared Seacome's "Memoirs of the House of Stanley," and subsequently many other works

[1] Article by Mr. W. E. A. Axon, *Lanc. and Ches. Ant. Soc.*, vol. iv.

bearing the imprint of Liverpool. Terry in 1712 published the *Leverpoole Courant,* and in 1756 appeared
Williamson's Liverpool Advertiser. Its price was originally
2d., the stamp being one halfpenny. It appears to have
had a considerable circulation; on the first page of the
issue for October 17, 1760, is the following announcement:
" The publisher of this paper begs leave to return his
grateful thanks to his friends and readers in the northern
parts of Lancashire for their kind indulgence in promoting
and encouraging this paper; and, as he has been at the
continued expense of expresses to meet the London post,
in order to be as early with the news as possible, and
messengers to distribute the paper, which have entirely
taken away all profits arising from the sale, he presumes
that his customers in Ormskirk, Preston, Lancaster and
adjacent neighbourhoods, will further indulge him by
advancing the price of the paper to 2½d., as no other
newspaper in England of the same size and make is sold
under that price." Its size was small folio, and it consisted of four pages; it contained no leading article, and
did not report the meetings of Parliament.

In 1799 Liverpool had three weekly newspapers. The
smaller towns were somewhat later in setting up the
printing presses, but the following names of places, with
the dates of the first issue of books with their imprint,
will give some idea of the respective rate of progress in
this direction: Warrington, 1731; Preston, 1740 (and
probably a little earlier) ; Wigan about 1760; Bolton about
1761 ; Prescot, 1779; Lancaster, 1783; Kirkham, 1790;
Blackley, 1791; Blackburn, 1792; Bury, 1793; Haslingden,
1793; Rochdale, 1796, and Burnley, 1798. At Preston
several attempts were made to establish newspapers in the
eighteenth century, but neither the *Preston Journal,* in
1744, nor the *Preston Review,* in 1791, proved successful.

From the literature of Lancashire we may turn to its
amusements. In Liverpool, a theatre was opened in

1772. Manchester's first theatre was built of wood, which was afterwards, in 1753, superseded by a regular theatre, which stood somewhere near the top of King Street; but this proving too small, forty gentlemen subscribed £50 each, and, having obtained an Act of Parliament, erected a larger playhouse in 1775 in Spring Gardens, which was burnt down in 1789, but was rebuilt and again opened in 1790.

Towards the close of the century Rochdale had its theatre, and probably several other towns; and where such buildings did not exist, the strolling players, during the season, acted their parts in assembly or other convenient rooms. Horse-races were now very popular, and meetings were regularly held at Manchester, Preston and Liverpool. Kersal Moor Races, near Manchester, were begun in 1730. Cock-pits were also found in nearly all our large towns, and bull-baiting was a common amusement. But there was not wanting evidence of a higher taste. Subscription libraries were being established, and few towns were without regular organized musical, literary or scientific societies.

On all sides the growth of trade was calling into existence new villages and towns, and the rapidly increasing number of wealthy families led to the formation of that now world-renowned place of resort—Blackpool. Here, in 1750, there were a few scattered clay-built cottages with thatched roofs, which could by no effort of imagination be called a village, when one Ethart Whiteside ventured to open a house of entertainment, which consisted of a long thatched building, which he subsequently converted into an inn. Nineteen years afterwards there were only in its neighbourhood twenty or thirty cottages, but not a single shop. In 1788 W. Hutton records that "about sixty houses grace the sea; it does not merit the name of a village, because they are scattered to the extent of a mile"; yet in August of that year there were 400 visitors; and for their entertainment there were bowling-greens, "butts for bow-shooting," and many of the company "amused themselves with fine ale at number three"; and for the evening the threshing-floor of a barn was turned into a theatre, which when full held six pounds. Of bathing-machines there were but few; a bell was rung when ladies went to bathe, and if, during the time set apart for them, a gentleman was seen on the beach, he was fined a bottle of wine. The price charged for boarding at one of the hotels was 3s. 4d. a day.

From this date the progress of this town was very rapid, and it soon became the great fashionable resort (during the season) of not only Lancashire, but all the North of England.

From this period many of the towns in Lancashire date their rise from the obscurity of small villages. Oldham, in 1794, had only a population of some 10,000, and within its area were at most a dozen small mills. Middleton did not get a right to hold its market and fair until 1791, whilst Bury at that date had not more than 3,000 inhabitants. The population of the municipal borough of Blackburn in 1783 was 8,000; the four townships, on the corners of which now stands St. Helens, in 1799 did not contain more than 7,000 souls. Over Darwen had in 1790 about 3,000 inhabitants, and Lower Darwen not more than half that number. The now prosperous town of Burnley had in 1790 certainly not above 2,000 inhabitants, whilst its neighbouring towns of Colne and Accrington had even a less number. Haslingdon, Newchurch, Bacup, and other towns in the Forest of Rossendale, were at this time mere villages; indeed, the entire population of the Forest did not, in 1790, exceed 10,000.

As a guide to the varied extent of business transacted in Manchester at the end of the century, much information may be gleaned from the local directories which were published from time to time, between 1772 and 1800. The first directory, prepared by Mrs. Elizabeth Raffald, appeared in 1772, and contained a list of all the merchants, tradesmen, and principal inhabitants, "with the situation of their respective warehouses"; also a list of stage-coaches, waggons, carriers, and vessels to Liverpool "upon the old navigation and Duke of Bridgewater's Canal."

There were 119 country manufacturers having warehouses in Manchester. The coaches went to London in two days during the summer, but in winter they required one day more. Coaches also went to all the surrounding districts; in some cases once a week, in others thrice.

Twenty-one vessels went to Liverpool by the Mersey and Irwell navigation ("the old navigation"), and eleven by the Duke of Bridgewater's Canal. Manchester had then one bank and one insurance office. Passing over a quarter of a century to 1797, the directory of that year gives about 5,600 names, many of whom are engaged in trades not mentioned in the earlier list, such as twist manufacturers, cotton-spinners, cotton-merchants, bleachers, and printers. The list of country manufacturers and others who attended the Manchester market gives the names of 332 individuals or firms. The names of the officers of the Infirmary and the magistrates acting in the Manchester, Rochdale, Middleton, and Bolton divisions of Salford Hundred are also furnished. The coach-service had considerably improved, as we now find that the Royal Mail, "with a guard all the way," left Manchester every morning, and reached London in twenty-eight hours, the fare being £3 13s. 6d.

One other trait in the eighteenth-century character of the Manchester men deserves a passing notice, that is, their patriotism. In 1777, on the breaking out of the American War, they raised a fine body of volunteers, which was enrolled as "The 72nd, or Manchester Regi-

ment," and did some service at Gibraltar under General
Elliott; they were disbanded on their return home in
August, 1783, their colours being deposited with much
ceremony in the collegiate church. The year following,
Sir Thomas Egerton, of Heaton Park, raised "The
Royal Lancashire Volunteers," and in 1782 the inhabitants of Manchester raised another volunteer corps of
150 men to serve in the American War. Several other
corps were afterwards raised in the locality and incorporated with the regular army. On August 25, 1796,
there was a review on Kersal Moor of volunteers from
Rochdale, Stockport, and Bolton. The end of the
eighteenth century gives us a remarkable standpoint
from which to glance at the then position of the
county. The rebellion had passed through its midst
and excited its people to a greater degree than was
probably the case in any other county. The prolonged
struggles between Puritan, Presbyterian, Episcopalian
and Romanist had at length died out; and although
war and rumours of war, ever and anon, obscured
the political atmosphere, and good times and bad
times followed each other in trade and commerce, yet
there was an ever-increasing feeling that the days had
for ever gone when tyranny and oppression could
flourish in the land. New industries on every hand were
being developed, and one invention followed another in
rapid succession; no sooner was a want declared than
someone was ready to supply the requirement, thus opening out bright prospects for the future. The highways
had been vastly improved, canals cut from north to south
and from east to west in the county; machinery was at
work which far more than realized the hopes of its
inventors, and everywhere there were signs of coming
prosperity. During this century Manchester and Liverpool had enormously increased in population and in
commercial importance; and some other of our towns

had to a considerable extent followed in the same direction, whilst here and there little quiet villages had seen
rise in their midst the one small mill which was destined
to be the forerunner of many others which would in no
very long period make the insignificant village into a
large and prosperous town.

Religion had widened out her views, and now denomina-
tions heretofore unheard of had arisen, and churches and
chapels were multiplying in every community. Some
feeble attempts were being made for popular education ;
but the press was almost the only means then at command, and that, whilst so many of the poorer classes
could neither read nor write, was at best but of small
avail. But there was a future opening out when much of
the intellectual darkness—which had so long prevailed,
not only in Lancashire, but all over the land—should
become a thing of the past, and the workman should
cease from being a mere machine and become an educated and enlightened citizen. Nothing but the utter
want of knowledge of the simplest elements of political
economy could justify or account for the manner in
which each of the great inventions which were to bring
about such gigantic results were received ; there was
scarcely one of the great improvements of the age which
was not, on its introduction, opposed by disorder and
riot by the very people who were in the long-run to be
most benefited by its adoption.

Nevertheless, the close of this century witnessed a
tremendous progress in the direction which led to the
results which placed the trade of Lancashire in the
position which it ultimately attained.

CHAPTER XII.

THE DAWN OF THE NINETEENTH CENTURY.

THE cotton trade of Lancashire was now fairly established; steam was just beginning to be commonly used as the motive power instead of the old water-wheel, and consequently the sites suitable for factories were no longer limited, and this at once led to a further very great development of textile manufactures. This rapid growth was not unattended with intermittent periods of depression, which the working men of the day were not always prepared to attribute to the right cause, and thus riots and disturbances were of frequent occurrence in the manufacturing districts. One of the most serious of these terminated in what has ever since been known as "the Peterloo." In 1816 the staple trades of Lancashire were in a very depressed state, and this led to the formation of political union societies, one of the chief objects of which was to obtain annual parliaments and universal suffrage. These societies met in St. Peter's Fields, Manchester, in October, 1816, when all passed off quietly and orderly, but on March 10 following a larger meeting was held at the same place, at which about 1,000 men appeared with blankets over their shoulders, and with the avowed intention of marching to London to lay their grievances before the Prince

Regent. This meeting was dispersed by the military, and several of the *Blanketeers* (as they were called) were taken to prison. The popular feeling was, however, not appeased, and the turn-out for an advance of wages of the spinners, weavers and colliers, towards the end of 1818, added fuel to the fire. Led on by Henry Hunt of London and others, it was decided to hold a mass meeting in St. Peter's Fields on January 18, 1819, which meeting was held, and a resolution passed calling for the immediate repeal of the Corn Law. In the August following, the borough reeve and constables of Manchester refused to call a public meeting to consider the best means of obtaining a reform of the House of Commons, although 700 householders had signed the requisition. The result was that the requisitors themselves summoned the meeting, which was held near St. Peter's Church on August 16, Henry Hunt being called upon to preside.

This meeting was attended by members of the societies from Oldham, Rochdale, Middleton, Ashton, Stockport, and all the surrounding villages, each contingent being accompanied by its band of music. The magistrates, being determined to disperse the vast assembly, called to their aid 200 special constables, the Manchester and Cheshire Yeomanry Cavalry, the 15th Hussars, and a detachment of the 88th Regiment of Foot, some pieces of artillery also being ready if required.

The mob was unarmed, but carried a plentiful display of banners with inscriptions more or less revolutionary. Acting under the orders of the magistrates, the Manchester Yeomanry and the hussars, with drawn swords, dashed through the crowd in the direction of the temporary platform, where they captured Henry Hunt and others. The would-be reformers fled in every direction, and the arrival of the Cheshire Yeomanry assisted rapidly to clear the field. After this onslaught—for it could not be called a fight—three or four people were found to have been killed, and twenty-two men and eight women were carried off to the infirmary; but it subsequently transpired that eight persons were killed and several hundreds were wounded. Henry Hunt was tried for sedition, and sentenced to two years' imprisonment, but some of his friends got off with a lesser penalty.

When the times again became settled, there was a vast increase in the population of the towns and villages where factories and workshops were established, and this increase came from all the surrounding districts and from other counties, whose sons, hearing of the rise of new trades and industries, came with their families and settled in Lancashire.

A careful study of the surnames of any of our manu-facturing towns will show that about this time a very large number of names now for the first time appeared in these districts, a small percentage of which were of foreign origin, but the greater proportion were English. The ten-dency was, therefore, to concentrate the scattered popula-tion around certain centres; thus it came about that in some parishes which remained purely agricultural, the population for years remained stationary, or even de-creased. Thus we find, in the extensive parish of St. Michael's-on-Wyre, the population between 1801 and 1871 had only risen from 1,197 to 1,290, whilst that of Goosnargh shows an actual decrease of 545 inhabitants between 1821 and 1861. The railway system was first introduced into Lancashire in 1830, when the line between Manchester and Liverpool was opened, which ceremony was marred by the fatal accident to William Huskisson, which happened at Parkside, near Newton-le-Willows. The cost of this rail-way up to June 30 previous to its being opened for traffic was £820,000, but before the end of 1838 the total ex-penditure had reached £1,443,897; other railways soon followed, and before a generation had passed away the county was intersected in every direction by these iron roads. Steam packets were in use before the railways were started; they first plied on the canals in 1812.

The sudden progress in commercial affairs could not be accomplished without some inconveniences and evils following in its course. The overcrowding of towns brought a condition of social life which took all the powers of the local authorities to grapple with. Some of the sleepy old towns with ill-lighted and worse-paved streets, with their old tumble-down dwellings and their utter want of anything like sanitary arrangements, were ill adapted to receive suddenly large additions to their population. Then, again, the time-honoured grammar schools and the few sparsely endowed free schools were all inadequate to meet the educational requirements.

Very early in the century a few schools were started on Dr. Bell's system, and subsequently what were called national schools became common in large towns, and to supplement them the Sunday-schools (which were first started about the year 1782) were giving an elementary education to many who did not or could not give regular attendance on the week-day. Another great evil rising out of the increase in manufactories was that men, women, and especially children, all worked too many hours a day, which, had not a wise Legislature stepped in to arrest, would soon have told dreadfully on the physical, moral, and mental condition of the labouring classes. With the necessary improvements of the sanitary condition of our towns came the introduction of the use of gas for illuminating purposes, and our streets became safe by night as well as by day.

To trace the growth of the various towns and villages of Lancashire during the present century is outside the scope of the present volume, and if it were not so, it would be quite impossible to do anything like justice to the subject within the limits assigned to this series of "Popular Histories." It must therefore suffice to say that in all the grand movements achieved by Great Britain in the nineteenth century, Lancashire has done its share, and that in trade, commerce, education, and every modern advance in moral, religious, or social life, the county has been in the van. Before closing this very brief notice of the present century, a few statistics may with advantage be given which will serve to illustrate the enormous growth of material progress and the ever-increasing numbers of its teeming population. Preston, in the first twenty years of this century, doubled its population, and between 1821 and 1868 it rose from 24,000 to 90,000, and in the latter year there were in the town seventy-seven cotton-mills, which gave employment to 26,000 persons. Through this important centre—just before the railways were opened—there passed daily seventy-two stage coaches. In Bolton the population rose from 11,000 in 1791 to 105,414 in 1881. Wigan, through the large coal-fields in the neighbourhood, advanced from 25,500 in 1801 to 78,160 in 1861, and about the year 1831 6,000,000 tons of coal were annually raised in the parish; other of the now large towns increased in the same proportion. But Liverpool and Manchester were the two centres in the county.

Liverpool, very early in the century, began to exhibit that spirit of enterprise which soon placed that city in the foremost rank in the maritime world. It was only in 1815 that the first steamer appeared on the Mersey, yet in 1835 there had been constructed docks which extended for two miles along the shore, with a water area of 90 acres; these docks have now a frontage of considerably over six miles.

In 1834 the total number of bales of cotton imported into this country and landed in London was 40,400, whilst at Liverpool the number was 839,370; in 1868 at the latter were landed 3,326,543 bales, and it has been estimated that in 1834 the value of the export trade of

Liverpool reached £20,000,000, the goods mostly consisting of woollens, linens, and cotton goods; the imports in the same year were put down as being worth £15,000,000. The dock dues paid in 1812 amounted to £44,403, and in 1862 to £379,528. The number of vessels which entered the port in 1802 was 4,781, with a tonnage of 510,691; in 1832 there were 12,928 vessels, with 1,540,057 tonnage; and in 1862 the vessels numbered 20,289, their tonnage being 4,630,183. The population of Liverpool in 1801 was 77,653; in 1861 it was 269,742.

Manchester and Salford, though one is now a city and the other only a borough, are in some senses almost inseparable: they both made rapid progress, following the rise of the staple trades, and both received their charters of incorporation as Parliamentary boroughs in 1832; their united population in 1801 was only 112,300, in 1831 it was 270,963, and in 1861 it had risen to 529,245. Manchester has been well described as the centre of the largest and most populous area in the world; it has on all sides large and increasing towns and villages, all of which are engaged in the staple trades of the district. The following figures will illustrate: In Manchester itself there are 2,708,000 spindles, in Oldham 11,500,000, Bolton 4,860,000, Ashton-under-Lyne 2,013,000, Rochdale 1,914,000, Blackburn 1,435,000, and there are some other towns in the neighbourhood each of which has close on a million spindles. Without detailing the marked progress in the other districts, it will perhaps equally well show the fact if we quote the population returns for the whole county.

In 1801 there were 673,486 persons, in 1851 there were 2,026,462, being an increase in fifty years of 1,352,976 persons; this is considered one of the most remarkable features in the official returns of England in 1851. In 1831 the population was 1,336,854, so that in twenty years it was nearly doubled. According to the returns of the last census (1891) Lancashire is the most densely populated county except Middlesex, and to every square mile of its surface there are 1,938 people.

We have now traced the history of the county palatine of Lancaster from the time when it was first inhabited by mortal man, through all its varied and not uneventful course, until we now leave it with, we may hope, a bright future dawning upon it—a future that will still find it, as it for so long has been, an important power in that great kingdom on whose domains the sun never sets.

CHAPTER XIII.

MISCELLANY.

THERE are many traditions relating to the county, some of which are worth preserving; others are only the result of some fertile brain which first invented the tale and then told it as a tradition. Several of Roby's "Traditions of Lancashire" are of this class; others are of considerable antiquity and of historic interest.

Scattered all over Lancashire are the remains or traces of roadside crosses, which at one period must have been very numerous, many of them being of great antiquity. At Burnley, near to the church, is one of these, which is of undoubted Saxon origin; it is known as Godly Cross, and associated with it is a tradition to the effect that long before the church was built religious rites were celebrated on the spot indicated by the cross, and that Paulinus baptized his converts in the waters of the Brun, which flows close by. The legend further asserts that upon an attempt being made to build an oratory on an adjacent site, the stones were nightly removed by supernatural agents, in the form of pigs, to the place where ultimately the church was erected. Similar traditions as to the removal of foundation-stones obtain as to the parish churches of Winwick, Rochdale, and one or two others. Very few parishes in Lancashire are without some trace (if only in a name) of these ancient crosses. The following furnishes a good example of the use to which these relics of a past age were applied as late as 1624. John Stirzaker and others, on July 25 in this year, confessed to the Bishop of Chester that they had been present and assisted in carrying the corpse of Thomas Bell of Garstang to the parish church there, and that they were in the company and consented " to the settinge downe of the said corse att crosses and yielding obeysance to the same superstitious manner as they went alonge, and that they carryed, or agreed thereto, the sayd corps by the church porche, and afterwards it was buryed without the mynister's ayd or any prayers made at the buryall thereof." The Bishop's sentence was that the offending parties should acknowledge their faults " in their accustomed apparel on the Sundaie next, being att Morning Prayer tyme," and also be prepared to receive the Holy Communion before the Feast of St. Michael, or in default they were to be excommunicated.

In this same parish of Garstang there still exists near Cross House the socket of one of these crosses, about which a curious bit of folklore obtains, to the effect that any persons troubled with warts or similar excrescences would get instant relief by washing their hands in the water from time to time collected in the hollow place where the base of the upright shaft once stood.

In the town of Wigan is a portion of a very ancient stone cross, known as Mab's Cross. The origin of the cross itself is unknown, but its name is derived from a family tradition connected with the Bradshaigh family, one of whom, Sir William Bradshaigh, in the time of Edward II., having been absent from home for ten years, on his return found that his wife Mabel (daughter of Hugh Norres of Haghe) had married a Welsh knight, who, on hearing of the first husband's return, took to flight, but was overtaken and slain by Sir William. For her unfaithfulness, Mabel was enjoined by her spiritual adviser to walk barefooted and barelegged once every week to the cross at Wigan, and there to do penance.

The most interesting monument in Wigan Church is the tomb of Sir William and Lady Mabel Bradshaigh.

In a county where there are so many ancient private houses, the successive owners of which led not unadventurous lives, it is no wonder that there are not wanting those old legends which add a charm and an interest to the remaining vestiges of what were once the family mansions of the oldest settlers in the county. Of these traditions a selection only can be taken.[1] At Kersall Hall, near Manchester (see p. 209), Peverill, the last Saxon owner, is said to have been slain whilst defending his ancestral home against the Norman intruder, who forthwith caused his dead body to be cast into the Irwell, and having taken possession, he retired for the night. But before the dawn he was called to account by ghostly visitors, and was found dead next morning on the threshold of the hall, and on his brow was written in blood a warning that all future intruders would meet with a similar fate, which threat the legend records was carried out against a succession of occupiers of the old dwelling-place. Not far from Bolton is a small farmhouse called Timberbottoms, which is also known as the Skull House, in consequence of the tradition that the taking away of two human skulls which had for generations been kept there would bring bad luck to the inhabitants; the tale goes that many times and oft had these relics been buried at Bradshaw Chapel, but they had always found their way back to their old quarters.[2] The dragon often figures as the hero of

---

[1] See Roby's "Traditions of Lancashire"; Harland and Wilkinson, "Legends and Traditions of Lancashire," etc.

[2] A somewhat similar tradition obtains of Wardley Hall, where the skull of Roger Downes, who was slain in London in 1676, was preserved for centuries.

legendary lore, and associated with particular localities. The dragon of Rusworth is the only legend of the kind referring to Lancashire.   At Rusworth is a house at one time owned by the Rusworths, one of whom in the remote past is supposed to have slain the beast which was devastating the district.   In the house are several old oak carvings illustrating the event.   In connection with Townley Hall, near Burnley, the spirit of some former owner, who demands a life every seven years, was supposed to wander about the demesne crying :

> " Lay out, lay out
> Horelaw and Hollinhey Clough."

The late Mr. Harland, in his " Lancashire Legends," quotes this as a singular instance how these old tales frequently have some foundation ; for in 1604 James I. granted by letters patent to Charles, Lord Mountjoy, the Earl of Devon, for services rendered in the time of Queen Elizabeth, *inter alia*, " all that parcel of land called Horelaw Pasture, abutting on Hollinghey, part of the Duchy of Lancaster, and formerly inclosed by John Townley." Here was evidently the source of the legend. Townley had without authority inclosed the land, and on the King reclaiming it, an imaginary grievance was created.

Turton Tower had its ghostly visitant — a lady in white, who passed from room to room in rustling silken dress.   Samlesbury Hall had a similar apparition, which was accounted for by the reputed murder of the lover of one of the daughters of the house.   Osbaldeston Hall (like Holyrood) has in one of its rooms traces of blood which cannot be washed out; the story told is that at a large family feast a quarrel arose, which by the interference of friends was apparently made up, but later in the evening Thomas Osbaldeston met his brother-in-law in this particular room, and at once drew his sword and murdered him in cold blood.   For this he was outlawed, and ever since the place has been haunted by the ghost of the victim, who walks through the silent rooms with uplifted hands and blood-stained clothes. How many of these old superstitions arose cannot ever be explained, but there is scarcely an old hall in the county but has associated with it a "ghost story." In Lancashire still linger many very ancient bits of folklore and superstitious beliefs, but a large proportion of these are not peculiar to the county, but are also common in Yorkshire and other Northern parts of the country. Some are, however, purely local, and are worth a passing note. In Ashton-under-Lyne is an annual festival known as the *Gyst-ale* or *Guisings*, at which is performed the ceremony of "riding the black lad," which is said to have had its origin from a grant made to Rauf and Robyn Assheton in 1422.

The custom is still observed in a modified form. An effigy of a man in armour is fixed on horseback, and led through the streets, after which it is dismounted and made to supply the place of a shooting butt, at which all kinds of firearms are discharged.

Rushbearings have already been referred to (see p. 123). They have now practically become a thing of the past; the people who formerly remained at home to celebrate these old rites now go away by the numerous cheap trips which mark the dates when the fairs were held.

Most of the old grammar schools had several customs, strictly observed by many generations of scholars—*inter alia*, barring out (Burnley Grammar School), which consisted in an assumed right for the boys at the end of each term to exclude the masters from the school, on which occasion a tallow candle was used to illuminate each pane of glass in the windows. Cock-penny was an annual present claimed by the head-master from each boy; this was probably intended as a payment for the game-cocks which in former years were provided. One of the statutes of the Manchester Grammar School, made about 1525, appears to have been especially designed to put a stop to this custom; it runs: "He" (the master) "shall teach freely and indifferently[1] every child and scholar coming to the same school, without any money or other reward taking therefor, as cock-penny, victor-penny, etc." Another clause provides that the scholars shall "use no cock-fights nor other unlawful games, and riding about for victors, etc."

The payment of the cock-penny was continued in some places until a few years ago.

At funerals many old customs not common in other parts of the country were here observed, and, indeed, have not yet quite died out.

The promiscuous giving of the penny manchet (often provided for by will) was almost universal amongst the richer classes; but the gift to each person who was "bidden" to the funeral, of a cake called the "arval cake," was not quite so common.

These cakes were generally given with ale, provided at the nearest public-house. In the neighbourhood of Burnley guests attending a funeral are met at the door by an attendant, who offers spiced ale (or other liquor) from a silver tankard. In some districts, those who went round to invite the guests to the funeral presented each of them with a sprig of rosemary; this inviting was sometimes called "lathing." At Poulton-le-Fylde, at the beginning of this century, the older families always buried their dead at night by torchlight, when every householder in the streets through which the cortège passed placed a lighted candle in his window. In the seventeenth century a singular privilege was given to women dying in childbed, their bodies being allowed interment within the church without the usual fee.[2]

[1] A curious instance of the alteration in the meaning of words. Of course, by "indifferently" is meant *alike to all.*

[2] See "Hist౨y of St. Michael's-on-Wyre," p. 64.

The peculiar rites appertaining to All Hallows' Eve (October 31) are well known ; but in the Fylde district it was celebrated by the lighting of bonfires, and it was locally known as Teanlay, or Teanley, night. Pace-egging in the same district is called "ignagning."

In Rochdale, Good Friday, some fifty years ago, was called "Cracknel Friday," as on this day people regaled themselves with small thin cakes called cracknels. St. Gregory's Day (March 12) in the northern parts of the county is characterized as *the* day on which onion seed must be sown, or no crop will be yielded. Lancashire is rich in this kind of folk-lore.

Bury simnels are now known all over the country; they are a kind of cake, which derives its name from having originally been made from the finest part of flour, which in mediæval times was called " siminellus." They are used on Mid-Lent or Mothering Sunday. This day in other parts of Lancashire is called Bragot or Bragget Sunday, and on it a peculiar drink known as bragot was used ; it consisted of spiced ale, which was always taken hot.

Did space permit, this chapter might well be extended, as the county is rich in old tales, ancient superstitions, "wise saws and modern instances," charms, divinations and omens, many of which, however, are not of local historical interest, as they are more or less common to other parts of the country.

INDEX.

ERRATA.

Page 8, note, *for* " Rev. William Harrison" *read* " Mr. W. Harrison."
,, 53, line 18 from top, *for* " Hollard " *read* " Holland."
,, 58 ,, 7 ,, bottom, *for* " Ellet " *read* " Ellel."
,, 73 ,, 7 ,, top, *for* " Tollington " *read* " Tottington."
,, 200 ,, 4 ,, bottom, *for* " Busset " *read* " Bussel."
,, 270 ,, 12 ,, ,, *for* " Wall " *read* " Watt."

Elliot Stock, 62, Paternoster Row, London, E.C.

In demy 8vo., cloth, 7s. 6d.; Roxburgh, 10s. 6d.; large-paper copies, 21s. net each volume.

THE NEW SERIES OF
COUNTY HISTORIES.

VOLUMES ALREADY PUBLISHED IN THE SERIES:

A HISTORY OF WESTMORLAND.
By RICHARD S. FERGUSON, M.A., LL.M., F.S.A.

A HISTORY OF HAMPSHIRE.
By THOS. W. SHORE, F.G.S.

"A very valuable volume. It presents to the reader, for the first time in a condensed form, a general view of the entire history of Hampshire."—*Hampshire Advertiser.*

A HISTORY OF CUMBERLAND.
By RICHARD S. FERGUSON, M.A., LL.M., F.S.A.

"If Mr. Stock can find a Mr. Ferguson to write the history of each of the other counties of England and Wales, the success of his series of 'Popular County Histories' may be considered as assured."—*The Speaker.*

A HISTORY OF WARWICKSHIRE.
By SAM TIMMINS, F.S.A.

"Mr. Timmins has made many useful discoveries in the history of his county, which are here set forth. But the book appeals quite as much to the general reader as to the Warwickshire man."—*St. James's Gazette.*

A HISTORY OF BERKSHIRE.
By LIEUT.-COL. COOPER KING.

"Colonel King has done his work well, and his sketch of the 'History of Berkshire' is both useful and entertaining."—*Morning Post.*

THE HISTORY OF DERBYSHIRE.
By JOHN PENDLETON,
Author of "Old and New Chesterfield."

"An entertaining and very instructive guide to all that is most interesting in the county."—*Times.*

THE HISTORY OF DEVONSHIRE.
By R. N. WORTH, F.G.S.,
Author of the "West Country Garland," etc.

"Ought to be greatly popular with the residents, and will have general interest for all who have the talent for locality."—*Contemporary Review.*

A HISTORY OF NORFOLK.
By WALTER RYE,
Author of "The Norfolk Antiquarian Miscellany," etc.

"At once the most learned and entertaining county guide that has ever been compiled. It is difficult to describe Mr. Rye's delightful book."—*Athenæum.*

ELLIOT STOCK, 62, PATERNOSTER ROW, LONDON, E.C.

ND - #0055 - 200924 - C0 - 229/152/17 - PB - 9781331237389 - Gloss Lamination